# THE ROTHSCHILDS

## ALSO BY FREDERIC MORTON

### FICTION

*The Hound*

*The Darkness Below*

*Asphalt and Desire*

*The Witching Ship*

*The Schatten Affair*

*Snow Gods*

*An Unknown Woman*

*The Forever Street*

### NONFICTION

*A Nervous Splendor: Vienna 1888 / 1889*

*Crosstown Sabbath: A Street Journey Through History*

*Thunder at Twilight: Vienna 1913 / 1914*

# THE ROTHSCHILDS

*PORTRAIT OF A DYNASTY*

FREDERIC MORTON

KODANSHA INTERNATIONAL
New York • Tokyo • London

Kodansha America, Inc.
114 Fifth Avenue, New York, New York 10011, U.S.A.

Kodansha International Ltd.
17-14 Otowa 1-chome, Bunkyo-ku, Tokyo 112-8652, Japan

Published in 1998 by Kodansha America, Inc.
by arrangement with the author

In different form some of the material in this book appeared in *Holiday*.

The Rothschild family tree that follows the index originally appeared in *Rothschild: The Wealth and Power of a Dynasty*, published in 1988 by Charles Scribner's Sons.

This is a Kodansha Globe book.



Library of Congress Cataloging-in-Publication Data

Morton, Frederic.
The Rothschilds : portrait of a dynasty / Frederic Morton.
p. cm.
Previously published: New York : Collier Books ; Toronto : Maxwell Macmillan Canada ; New York : Maxwell Macmillan International, 1991. With new epilogue and afterword.
Includes bibliographical references and index.
1. Rothschild family. 2. Bankers—Europe—Biography.
I. Title.
HG1552.R8M6 1998
332.1'092'2—dc21 98–14815
ISBN 1–568636–220–X

Manufactured in the United States of America

98 99 00 01 02 10 9 8 7 6 5 4 3 2 1

# *INTRODUCTION TO THE NEW EDITION*

THE Rothschilds entered my life long before I sat down to write their story. At the age of fourteen I was introduced to this glistening subject under the most glowering circumstances. The time: July 1939. The place: the Jewish Affairs Office of the Gestapo in Vienna. With the *Anschluss,* the Office had taken over the great palace of Baron Louis de Rothschild on the Prinz Euger Strasse; and that's where we stood in line—my father, my mother, my younger brother and I, applying for the passports we needed to be saved.

All day we inched and trembled our way up a grand staircase white as ermine. SS men shouted *"Stand straight"* the moment any of us leaned on the exquisitely carved balustrade. They acted like guards in a museum whose splendor awed and enraged them at the same time. In my own mind, horror could not keep out wonder: could human beings ever have lived amid such fairytale marble?

I had no idea, of course, that the human dimension of the Rothschild myth would one day become a professional concern of mine. I do know that all the cowering I did on that imperial staircase proved doubly useful when twenty years later I researched my Rothschild project as an American writer. For one thing, Baron Louis' palace had by then been long demolished, victim of a bombing raid during the war. Courtesy of the Gestapo, I had a dramatic experience inside a historic mansion of which now only photographs survived. But the Gestapo, posthumously, also smoothed my personal contact with members of the dynasty.

In the spring of 1960 I was ushered into the sternly paneled executive suite of Baron Guy de Rothschild, in the Paris headquarters of Rothschild Frères at 21 rue Laffitte. The Baron, head of the French bank, seemed a bit aloof, distracted by a busy schedule. Yet he was observant enough to detect what I was trying to disguise: my nervousness. He asked for its reason. I said that this was my second visit in a Rothschild house and that my agitation might relate, in part, to memories of the first. "Well," asked monsieur le baron, "what about that first time?" I told him about the endless hours spent on his cousin's staircase in Vienna. Instantly the Baron warmed: "You stood in line all day? As a child? Didn't you get hungry?" I confessed that hunger had not been the predominant emotion. "Just the same," the Baron said "it would seem that our family owes you some nourishment." He picked up the telephone and arranged lunch for my wife and me at the great family estate of Ferrières. The meal led to other introductions within the clan.

From these face-to-face encounters I came away with much more than facts. Rothschild family resemblance often stretches beyond generations. The way a twentieth-century Rothschild scratched his ear quickened to life the daguerreotype of his ancestors. My basic calling is that of a novelist; instinctively I dig for character, even in nonfiction. There was much to dig for while interviewing and researching for this book. Now and then I was lucky to strike a mother lode. Perhaps that is one reason why this Rothschild biography, preceded by scores of others on the subject, was the first to become an international bestseller. It led the list in the United States as well as in Britain, and did almost as well in South America and Israel. I must be among the few to profit from all the Rothschilds without doing business with any of them.

Business, of course, is the world in which the Rothschilds have been supreme virtuosos. But my biography appeared near the beginning of the 1960's, a decade not culturally or intellectually obsessed with business. Nevertheless the book received a National Book Award nomination and benefited from major, positive reviews. Naturally the author hopes that the author had something to do with that. At the same time I will admit that other factors came into play as well.

These emerged from letters forwarded to me. For a surprising number of readers the Rothschild image did not suggest the arch-capitalist, lord of that fortress of establishmentarianism, the investment bank. Many of my correspondents were 1960's dissidents for whom the clan's ascent from the depths was a dazzling mutiny. Actually this view had been voiced more than a hundred years earlier by Heinrich Heine, a close friend of Karl Marx's. Heine admired those five Rothschild brothers erupting out of Jew Street because "they usurped the last pretensions of feudalism." Of course my readers saw Heine's vision with Sixties' eyes. And with such eyes I had pictured the empowerment of the five who not only broke out of the ghetto but who, by personal example and political demand, began to break the ghetto itself.

In the 1960's the phrase "ghetto youth" was attaching itself to another desperately disadvantaged minority, and that was just the point. It is still the point: next time you see a young, impatient black coming your way, remember that you might be encountering a Rothschild descendant, metaphorically transmuted by history.

An unexpectedly large percentage of readers engaged this very issue, fastening on the early, insurgent part of the family chronicle. Then, in 1970, rehearsals began for the Broadway musical *The Rothschilds*. Sherman Yellen dramatized my book, with music by Jerry Bock and lyrics by Sheldon Harnick (a team whose previous Broadway show had been *Fiddler on the Roof*.) One of the key songs was a cry—a roar, really—for equality, skillfully distilled from my pages. It could be a motto for black activism today:

It's a curious, dangerous malady
we are all afflicted with:
We want everything, everything
just like other men do!

Another musical sequence carried a more intricately barbed message. We see Papa Rothschild starting out as a coin dealer at the Frankfurt Fair, hawking "genuine fine gold doubloons" that may or may not be genuine fine gold doubloons. Sudden trumpets drown out his spiel. Retinued by a regiment of Hessians, accompanied by a British general, the Prince of Hesse struts into the market place. And this lofty lord in his silk breeches and powdered wig continues the song intoned by the caftaned Jew, using the same tune, the same melodious dance around the truth but for a much baser purpose. Peddling his Hessian soldiers to Britain, the Prince hymns them as genuine fine warriors, an excellent value in mercenaries with whom to keep down the American Revolution. Here is a moral straight from my book: The Jew oversells his coins so that his family can eat. The Prince oversells soldier flesh to fill his coffers. In its fight for survival the underclass mirrors the cunning with which the ruler gilds his castle.

This scene was last played during the musical's out-of-town tryout in Philadelphia. By the time the show reached New York, Papa Rothschild sang quite a different song at the Frankfurt Fair—a charming one, to be sure, about numismatic lore—one that beguiled rather than disturbed.

The contrast between the original number and its blander replacement was the contrast between the 1960's and the two decades that followed. Also reflecting the difference was a new response to my "Rothschilds" book, which still remained in print and found new readers in a new generation. Attention shifted to another aspect of the story: success at its most formidable. Naturally success is at all times a principal fascination of the Rothschilds' saga. But in the 1960's the family's rise was seen mostly as a dashing, inspiring grand adventure of outsiders breaking through to the inside. By the 1970's, on the other hand, and yet more so in the 1980's, many reader letters put a hard, practical, downright pragmatic focus on the Family That Made It Like No Other Ever Did. These readers seemed to believe that I had designed the book as a how-to manual sold on the self-help shelf. Fathers invited me to their sons' forthcoming bar mitzvahs: for a consideration, would I enrich the occasion with instructive anecdotes on the family's genius at getting ahead of the pack? Other letters inquired whether I had ferreted out Rothschild business secrets too hot for public print. Would I, again for a consideration, part with them privately?

Still other letters—and there were dozens of these—laced lucre with sex. They came from people identifying themselves as Rothschild bastards. Most documented their provenance graphically: in what hayloft grandma had rolled with what Rothschild fifty-seven years ago to what solemn promises long unfulfilled. Wouid I include the tidbit in the next edition? And add to the family tree a branch on which a love child could perch with nice visibility until the overdue bequest arrived?

No, I could not satisfy any of these correspondents. But the latest turn the fortunes of my book has taken does satisfy *me*. In 1990 the musical was revived—and directorially revised. The new version, Off-Broadway, uses a smaller stage, fewer actors and simpler props. Yet these Rothschilds are much more mine than their Broadway incarnation. Yes, they overcome kings through their mastery of the market. But it is through strength of principle that they keep their soul. Off-Broadway the emphasis is on their truer triumph: they show how a father, a mother and their children can, by their joint resolve, defeat the prejudice that confines them to a mean margin; and how their victory first redeems them, then works for the reclamation of others.

The family as instrument of cohesion. The family as wellspring of power. The family as organ of conscience. Animating this trinity is a spirit that fascinated me throughout the writing of *The Rothschilds*. Perhaps I longed for just such a spirit in the terrifying ghetto the Gestapo once made out of a grand staircase. At any rate it is a spirit I hope to share with the readers of this new edition.

F.M.

# *PREFACE*

FOR the last 150 years the history of the House of Rothschild has been to an amazing extent the backstage history of Western Europe. How the Rothschilds gained eminence and kept it to this day is a phenomenon that transcends business ability. It is rooted in the virtuoso use of the family as a power unit.

Being a novelist, I have an incurable interest in emotion. A money-changer becomes a great banker, not just because he is good at arithmetic, but because his impulses and reflexes are geared for success. The pages that follow, therefore, focus most closely on the "human" side of the Rothschild epic.

The importance of arithmetic remains. I am neither a trained economic historian nor a trained financial expert. I am aware, furthermore, that a team of scholars might have to spend years in the tremendous archives of the London and Paris banks to produce a detailed technical chronicle of the House. The aim of this book is different. It is to dramatize the personal, flesh-and-blood reality of the myth known to the world as "Rothschild."

Nonetheless, I have tried to provide the story with all necessary economic and historic underpinnings, and here as well as in other phases of the manuscript I have had the advantage of help from others.

I want to thank most members of the present-day Rothschild clan for the toleration and even encouragement of my curiosity in their offices and homes. Specifically, I am grateful to Baroness Hilda de Rothschild for a general introduction to the subject; to Baron Philippe and his wife Pauline for directing my attention to numerous social and esthetic Rothschildiana; and to Baroness Elie for her information on family art collections. Much appreciated was the cooperation of Baron Guy, head of the French house; his sister, Bethsabée, and his mother, Baroness Edouard; Lord Rothschild; Mr. Edmund, senior partner of the English bank, and his wife, Elisabeth; and the dean of the family, Baron Eugene, and his wife Jeanne. Various members of the family have also provided me with portraits of their ancestors.

I am indebted to a number of Rothschild business associates, such as Mr. Leo Spitzer and Mr. Leonard Keesing of New York; Mr. Leo Kelly and Mr. J. F. Goble of London; Major Peter Barber of the Exbury estate; M. Robert Jablon of Paris. In Vienna, Ritter Wilhelm von Gutmann, Frau Clementine von Ruzicic and Herr Richard Karlberger have given me some valuable facts; as has Mr. Cecil Roth of Oxford, and not only through his excellent account of the Victorian family phase in England, *The Magnificent Rothschilds.*

For their advice and comment, I am also grateful to Mr. Cecil Beaton, Mr. James J. Rorimer (Director of the Metropolitan Museum of Art), Mr. Vincent Sheean, Mr. Peter B. Kenan, of Columbia University's economics faculty, and Mr. Gilbert Millstein.

Dr. Wilhelm Schlag, cultural officer of the Austrian Consulate General in New York, has been invaluable in procuring art material.

While everyone mentioned above has contributed to the manuscript, no one except myself is responsible for its inadequacies or mistakes.

This is the place to record my obligation to Ted Patrick

and Harry Sions of *Holiday*, who first presented me with the idea of the project. Sections of this manuscript in an altered form have been printed in their magazine.

And now I must admit the biggest debt of all. My wife, Marcia Colman Morton, has been an indispensable partner in this enterprise, from initial research to final revision. The writing of this book has constantly benefited from her editorial resourcefulness and her mysterious good humor.

*F. M.*

# *CONTENTS*

# ILLUSTRATIONS

# ILLUSTRATIONS

# THE ROTHSCHILDS

# I

# *ARE THEY STILL THERE?*

## 1. *A Procession at Pauillac*

ON Saturday afternoon, March 4, 1961, an expectant crowd shifted its feet on the cobbles of a small village in southwestern France. Windows brimmed with faces, bristled with binoculars. Shortly after two P.M. a crimson-sashed band sent a fanfare across adjoining vineyards. A specially imported battalion of gendarmes took up positions along the curb. And slowly the fairytale came into view.

It was headed by a master of ceremonies with ivory staff, black garb and silk stockings and by two tiny pages in breeches. Behind them glided, at slow ceremonial pace, the presidential fleet of limousines usually reserved by the mayor of nearby Bordeaux for General de Gaulle. A splendor of orchids smothered the first car from figurehead to tail lights. It bore a princess on her wedding day.

She was gowned in white satin (signed by that august overseer of contemporary idylls, Monsieur Balenciaga), crowned with a diadem of white mink and diamond stars. Her hand held a spray of apple blossoms flown in that morning from Turkey. The bridegroom at her side was—with gratifying appositeness—a very handsome, very talented, very poor young man.

The guests riding behind them had been brought from Paris by a private contingent of Pullman cars added to the Sud Express. And since weddings must have picture-takers, this one had Cecil Beaton, on leave from his post at Buckingham Palace as her Majesty's official photographer. Here he attended to his duties in top hat, striped trousers and morning coat.

Still, any occasion can glitter for a hundred thousand dollars. It's not mere shininess that makes a fairytale, but the glow of familiarity; the magic comes not from telling, but from telling once again.

It was being told once again in the village of Pauillac on March 4, 1961. This was a Rothschild wedding. Baron Philippe of Château Mouton Rothschild was giving in marriage his daughter Philippine. Each tint making up the iridescence of the occasion had a tradition handed down by nanny, butler, dowager—by all the archivists with and without livery. Even as the procession still filed down the street, the service entrance of Château Mouton admitted a wedding cake nearly seven feet tall. In pure spun sugar it celebrated the five Rothschild arrows: the family escutcheon conceived a hundred and forty years before, amid Frankfurt pogroms, in the face of cross fire from Austria's College of Heraldry. And when the wedding limousines stopped before the great gates of the château, a troop of estate workers helped the gendarmes form a cordon; they all wore armbands of yellow and blue—the famous colors that had marked Rothschild couriers as they raced through disaster and triumph from Napoleon to World War I.

No modern name breathes a more storied eminence. No nonroyal family has held so much power so consistently, so peculiarly. Today many members of the clan cannot disguise a lordliness which has become exotic, if not downright exasperating, in our age. It would be insufficient to sum up the family as "still very wealthy." The Rothschild fortunes in England and in France are as ineffable as ever.

To the world at large, "Rothschild" means proverbial and rather dead money. But to the very rich, to those who actually know the clan or would like to, "Rothschild" conjures something very alive, something enviably, ridiculously, unattainably exaggerated; something like a gilt coach drawn by twelve white steeds.

In the private railroad cars that whisked the clan to the wedding, the Byzantine implications of the name were confirmed by a Byzantine amenity. Alexandre, the Dior of the world's coiffeurs, admits to his Paris establishment only Tout-Paris (as highest society in France is called) or certified Olympians such as Jacqueline Kennedy and Princess Margaret. Aboard the Pullmans scuttling to Bordeaux, Alexandre and selected stars of his staff waited, combs ready. Their presence was a prewedding favor from the host. Any Rothschild guest could have her tresses perfected by the master himself while white-gloved butlers offered her champagne and caviar. Alexandre well knows the splendor of the family. His own appointment book, a daily Almanach de Gotha, gives a clue. In that book, as in the imagination of the *haut monde*, a designation like "Comtesse Pierre" is meaningless if a surname isn't added. But "Baronne Elie" or "Baronne Philippe" can *only* mean "de Rothschild."

"They are the true successors to the Bourbons in France," an editor of the French *Vogue* sighed early this year. "There are no others where the first name is enough."

In fact, the celebrants at Pauillac and the people over at Buckingham Palace seem to be the only families left with great functioning kingdoms at their disposal. And for generations the people at Buckingham Palace have recognized the kinship: Queen Victoria often dined and slept in Rothschild houses; the Duke of Windsor fled to a Rothschild (an Austrian one) directly after his abdication. Where kings have vanished, presidents must suffice: the only time President Coty of France dined officially at a private residence was with Baron Philippe, the bride's father, at his Parisian duplex in 1952.

Like any child born at such an altitude, the bride inherited, in addition to everything else, history. It has been said that on the day of its birth the average Rothschild baby is 150 million dollars rich and 150 years old. The figures may be imprecise, but the idea is accurate. Over the past century and a half, a Rothschild personality has crystallized itself with such definition that no new bearer of the name can entirely escape it. The young Rothschilds today (there are over a dozen under the age of twenty-one) may discuss Sartre or dig cool jazz, but their lives are still part of an old genealogical design. This is due to inbreeding on a royal scale. It is also due to a formidable sense of the ancestral—a Jewish as well as an aristocratic characteristic.

Even the most shocking aspect of the event at Pauillac rested on family precedent. The village priest had solemnized Philippine's union with a Catholic (delivering a somewhat embarrassed sermon on the Old Testament and the virtues of the Jews). Actually he was only refreshing a venerable Rothschild scandal. From the very first this vehemently Jewish dynasty has permitted its daughters—not its sons—to marry Christians.

Also traditional was the confusion of the guest register at

Château Mouton. Seventy-odd Rothschilds signed it. And many of them, through many generations, have the same given names. By this the house emphasizes its unity and continuity, re-creates its ancestors and infuriates its biographers. There is nothing so confounding as the Rothschild family tree. The English branch, for example, began with Nathan Mayer; proceeded to Lionel and Nathaniel; went on to Lionel Walter, Lionel Nathan, James Nathaniel and Nathaniel Charles. Today it contributes to family reunions the present Lord Rothschild, named Nathaniel Mayer Victor, and a son of his, Nathaniel Charles.

Not content with the repetition of first names, the Rothschilds have evolved a lineage of pseudonyms—a peculiarity relevant to the nuptials at Pauillac. Henri de Rothschild, the bride's grandfather, wrote some successful dramas under the nom de plume of André Pascal. His son Philippe produced plays and motion pictures as Philippe Pascal. And Philippe's daughter Philippine, the bride herself, receives billing as Philippine Pascal at the Comédie Française. The fact that in Jacques Sereys she married a director of the Comédie shows how every Rothschild interest finds dynastic expression.

What would be a trifling inclination elsewhere becomes here a stately family landmark. The clan's sweet tooth has not only given the Rothschild soufflé to the world's menus; not only goaded the master chefs in family employ to push the art of pastry beyond its previous frontiers; not only produced a clause in the 1905 will of Baron Alphonse leaving 25,000 gold francs to his "dear son-in-law Albert . . . so that he may buy himself some chocolates"; but also engendered the delectable dogma that on all intrafamily visits chocolate soufflé be served.

## 2. *Chutzpah and Orchids*

The orchids decking the bridal car manifested another Rothschild habit: impatience with imperfection, however slight. For the Rothschilds, sticking to the best is an obvious imperative, the equivalent of a shoemaker sticking to his last. More than any other group in the world, they have *chutzpah*. This is a Yiddish word related phonetically and philosophically to the Greek *hubris*. The latter term conveys uncompromising and in the end self-destructive pride. Achilles died of *hubris*, but Rothschilds positively prosper on *chutzpah*.

The orchids lighting up Philippine's limousine came from a giant estate in Exbury near Southampton. Here stand thirty hothouses, built of teak and putting nearly four acres under glass. They belong to Edmund de Rothschild, the present senior partner of the family bank in London; and the petals he breeds owe their queenliness to the imperious connoisseurship first instituted by his father, Lionel. During World War II, for example, much of the hothouse personnel was drafted. Lionel realized he could not provide for all his young seedlings. "Many, many hundreds were destroyed," Lionel's orchid man recalls. "Mr. de Rothschild did not feel inclined to sell them, thinking it impossible for another man to give them as much care as their quality required. . . ."

Turn to the rhododendrons, also very much in evidence among the floral garlands at Pauillac. They, too, had been imported from Exbury. Once Lionel de Rothschild's army of two hundred gardeners nourished and manicured his vast flower pavilions there. Today Edmund, his heir, owns a landscape which contains more hundreds of thousands of superb rhododendron plants than any other spot on earth. This is due not only to care, but to a *chutzpah* unmerciful.

"Mr. Lionel," recalls the estate manager, Peter Barber, "developed over twelve hundred rhododendron hybrids. But he was ruthless with his burnings. He might watch a large batch of seedlings for ten years. He'd wait till they had all flowered in order to pick out the very best ones in the lot—and destroy all the rest. This was a strict rule. He wanted not one flower of merely good quality in his gardens."

In unpleasant contexts, too, the family remains addicted to the impeccable. During World War II Chaim Weizmann, the head of World Zionism, lived in London's Dorchester Hotel. The present Lord Rothschild had also moved there, since the drafting of male servants had made the maintenance of more elaborate households impossible. During a German raid Weizmann watched the young lord trying to calm his three tots in the bomb shelter—a vain occupation that lasted through the whole bomb-ridden night. At last Weizmann asked his Lordship why he hadn't sent his children to the United States, like so many other people of means?

"Why?" his Lordship said, squashing the pacifier in his fist. "Why! Because of their blasted last name. If I sent those three miserable little things over, the world would say that seven million Jews are cowards!"

Even in a frivolous milieu like Paris' Saint-Germain-des-Prés quarter, the family's consciousness of a special responsibility will not go to sleep. One evening last year three smart young couples sat on the sidewalk terrace of one of the more bohemian cafés. A hurdy-gurdy player came up with his cap. The three men in the group reached for some coins. "Merci," said the hurdy-gurdy player and was about to leave when in a twinkling the handsome girl called Philippine pressed a note on him. Nobody took much notice, except perhaps those knowing who she was: no longer just a girl on a date, but suddenly a Rothschild confronted by a beggar.

## 3. *A Golden Silence*

And yet a bourgeois practicality has always tempered such royal self-awareness, such imperial wealth. There is, for example, a curious garment of Baron Philippe's which may well have seen use that great day in Pauillac. A very early riser and therefore an early retirer, Philippe likes to be asleep as soon as the postprandial amenities are finished. And so his tailor must design a silken, soft-collared item which serves both as dress shirt under his dinner jacket—and as night shirt. A pleasant ingenuity, it lets him play the impeccable host in his pajamas.

The same spirit invests the dozen or so châteaux and mansions from which Philippine's relatives converged on Pauillac. These huge baroque bowers are studded with more Louis XIV, XV and XVI furniture than the three kings had together. For decades now, in interior decorators' argot the phrase "Rothschild style" has connoted Bourbon *meubles* sprinkled with Renaissance bibelots, an opulence of ormolu and *boiseries*—"the Rothschild grand French manner," Cecil Beaton terms it. But all this expresses delight in luxury, not distraction by it. In the midst of frank splendor sits a wholesome Jewish appreciation of the utilitarian. The great Paris town house of the Baroness Edouard, for example, has a master bathroom orchestrated in marble and silver. Only one element seems dissonant; on closer inspection it turns out to be a small telephone switchboard. With it the Baroness can secure any number or extension quickly, discreetly, privately, without her usual secretarial apparatus.

But the clan keeps more than random switchboards secluded. It is no accident that Philippine's principal wedding banquet took place in the wine cellars of Château Lafite Rothschild, another family chateau near Pauillac. For all its matchless splendor and concentration of wealth, the feast was held underground in a remote corner of France. Rothschilds love to glisten. But to the sorrow of the socially ambitious, Rothschilds glisten only *in camera*, for and among their own kind.

Their penchant for reticence seems to have grown in recent generations. The founder of the house enjoined it a long time ago; but some of his sons, while storming Europe's innermost bastions of power, wrapped their hands around every weapon, including the rawest publicity. Today the family grooms the inaudibility and invisibility of its presence. As a result, some believe that little is left apart from a great legend. And the Rothschilds are quite content to let legend be their public relations.

The two big banks in London and Paris (probably the world's largest private financial institutions) and Baron Edmond's huge business headquarters in the French capital have not so much as a name plate outside. Though they control scores of industrial, commercial, mining and tourist corporations, not one bears the name Rothschild. Being privately held partnerships, the family houses never need to, and never do, publish a single public balance sheet or any other report of their financial condition.

On the social side "Rothschild" means Society with an S superbly, softly, capital. In Europe, where snobbery is measured on a more languid scale than on our side of the Atlantic, a mere four generations of wealth do not inevitably entitle a family to a place at the very heart of fashion. Yet just here the Rothschilds are, barely glimpsed and rarely heard, behind the walls of the St. James Club in London, inside the hedges of the Comtesse de Paris; not so much partaking of the exclusiveness of such sanctums as confirming it by their presence.

The family's giant charities are also carried on quietly. Not too well known is the fact that Guy, the head of the French house, is president of the Fonds Social Juif Unifié (the name of United Jewish Appeal in France); or that a special department of the London bank draws up a monthly list of charities (Jewish and non-Jewish) to be dispensed by the senior partner; or that a very powerful—and very shy—B. de Rothschild Foundation, supervised by Bethsabée, Guy's sister, operates in New York, Paris and Tel Aviv. It sponsors (and houses) the Martha Graham Dance Company, supports French ballet and Israeli artisans, contributes extensively to the education of American Indian tribes, backs research into the arts of classical India—all under an umbrella of silence.

The clan, finally, abstains from press agentry in its maze of cultural and sporting endeavors. True, racing fans may know that the blue-and-yellow silks of Baron Guy, riding winners at Ascot, Longchamps and Deauville, are the same color as the banners over Rothschild castles on both sides of the Channel. Zoologists might be aware of an *ornithoptera Rothschildi* (a gorgeous "birdwing" butterfly in New Guinea) and a *Rhea Rothschildi* (a South American ostrich), both creatures found on Rothschild-financed expeditions. Wine drinkers may worship Mouton Rothschild and Lafite Rothschild as two of the world's supreme clarets. Botanists and garden lovers have benefited from the family fondness for thoroughbred flowers—the Rothschild supreme azalea, the many Rothschild-named rhododendrons and the fantastic orchids developed at Exbury.

These golden footprints of the family are recognized, at least by specialists. But at the Louvre, at the British Museum, at a dozen other institutions, there are this very moment hundreds of researchers and art students bent over a cornucopia of treasures without knowing that once all this glittered in Rothschild libraries and drawing rooms. The Rothschild donations *in toto* make the Medicis' look meager.

In Vienna the House of Rothschild vanished under the heels of the Wehrmacht in 1938. Yet it survives, and not merely in the giant collections left to the Kunsthistorisches and the Kunstgewerbe museums. Its memory is literally fragrant: every spring the city floods its parks and squares with flowers which come from the former Rothschild hothouses in the Hohe Warte suburb.

Every day peasants from all over Austria pilgrimage to the Stefanskirche, the national cathedral. All Austrian provinces provided native materials for its reconstruction after World War II damage. The family, a province unto itself, contributed the stones from their principal *palais*. The residence in the Prinz Eugenstrasse was too monumental to find a new owner in 1956. It was demolished just when the Stefanskirche needed a transfusion of precious marble. And so the stones from the Jewish dwelling were brought directly to the Catholic cathedral.

There is only one crucial Rothschild city which bears few palpable imprints of the clan. Frankfurt does have a Rothschild Park; its municipal archives contain some yellowed clues to the family's beginnings. But the bombed ruins of the original Rothschild house were cleared away four years ago to make way for a new office building. Not many Rothschildiana survive by the Main River.

Yet here, in a cramped ghetto dwelling, the great Pauillac wedding had its roots. Here, with a yellow star pinned to his caftan, Mayer Amschel Rothschild kept a small store two centuries ago, and married Gutele Schnapper, and raised with her those five incredible sons who conquered the world more thoroughly, more cunningly and much more lastingly than all the Caesars before or all the Hitlers after them.

Here their story—and their name—entered history.

# II

# *JEW STREET*

## 1. *Little Orphan Mayer*

IT IS almost impossible to meet a present-day Rothschild without first meeting his forefathers. The hall of his house and the anteroom of his office invariably teem with paintings, busts, reliefs, sometimes even small monuments, of ancestors. All these Valhallas are curiously incomplete: of the dynasty's founder no likeness is known, although Mayer Rothschild could have afforded, toward the end of his life, the finest brush strokes money can buy.

Still, the very absence of a solemn portrait fleshes out the impression contemporaries have handed down. It is a picture quite different from those of the squat, relentless, monstrously practical geniuses he fathered. The patriarch was a tall, gentle person with a scholar's hunch to his narrow shoulders. In his smile there hovered a not very businesslike twinkle.

A strange dream must have stirred inside the man; something prompted him to consistently peculiar choices. The most peculiar of all resulted, one spring day of 1764, in his return to his native Frankfurt on the Main.

Mayer's ancestors had long been small merchants in the town ghetto. But his best prospects lay elsewhere. As the brightest in a brood of children, he had been sent to a Yeshiva near Nürnberg to become the family pride—a rabbi. He studied well, but briefly. Both his parents died, and with them the source of tuition. Luckily some relatives secured for young Mayer an apprenticeship in the Jewish banking house of Oppenheimer at Hannover.

Another lad in his position would have clung to just that city. Germany was still a patchwork of principalities, each with laws unto itself. In contrast to Frankfurt, Hannover tolerated Jews—tolerably. Mayer did well. His path was clear: to stay at Oppenheimer's; to advance; to become chief clerk; and, with God's help, possibly even to die a partner. Instead, Mayer went home. He did the wrong thing and became immortal.

Yet when he re-entered Frankfurt that spring day, not a shred of grandeur greeted him, only petty humiliation. Crossing the river Main, he had to pay Jew toll. From afar he could see, and smell, the quarter where he had been born twenty years earlier. The ghetto brimmed along a single dark alley, just twelve feet broad. It stretched, as Goethe later said, "between the city wall and a trench."

On his way Mayer could not escape the street urchins whose favorite amusement was to shout, "Jew, do your duty!"—whereupon the Jew had to step aside, take off his hat, and bow. Having thus entertained the local children, Mayer reached the heavy chains with which soldiers manacled the Judengasse (Jew Street) every night.

Inside, the ghetto was not very encouraging either. Shops spilled heaps of secondhand clothes and soiled household goods into the alley; this welter reflected an ordinance that barred Frankfurt Jews from farming, from handicrafts, even from dealing in nobler goods such as weapons, silk or fresh fruit.

And the young Jewish girls Mayer encountered—they, too, were subject to the stern hand of the gentile. Another city edict limited the Jews to five hundred families and to no more than twelve marriages a year.

Even when Mayer reached his own block and an old friend hailed him with "Heh, Rothschild!" that very word could only be a reminder that he really had no family name at all. It was a privilege his race did not possess. To invent some sort of identification, Jews often used the house signs which predated numbered addresses. Mayer's ancestors had once lived in a house with a red shield (*Rothschild*) at the more prosperous end of Jew Street. The name still stuck, though the family had declined to a danker, humbler place behind the Sign of the Saucepan.

It was at the Saucepan that Mayer finally turned in. He walked through a gloomy and littered court to the back-yard quarters where his brothers Moses and Kalmann ran a secondhand shop. It was here that he reached the end of his journey and the beginning of an epic.

## 2. *A Dreamer in the Ghetto*

In the damp quarters of the Saucepan, Mayer Amschel proceeded to toil patiently for years. And at this point we must ask: Did he really foresee the advantage of sacrificing a bright and orderly progress in a Hannover counting house for the sake of a dark hole in Frankfurt's Jew Street? Had he understood the opportunity sleeping in his native city? Did he know that the local lord, young Prince William of Hesse-Hanau, was a plutocrat among princes; that at William's court a financial empire was being built which would need financial viceroys? Did the dream really descend through the narrow roof and touch Mayer's thought at night?

But in daylight—what a distance between Mayer and a prince! In the daylight he was one of three brothers in caftans, rooting about among old chests, hip-deep in high-grade junk and low-grade antiques. He couldn't have afforded one horse of the many splashing mud against ghetto walls as they sped to William's castle at Hanau.

As time went on, it appeared that Mayer would not even be able to afford a saddle. He had begun to develop, with more enthusiasm than profit, a new department in the secondhand store: he traded in old coins. The years in the Yeshiva still lived in him. He was a rabbi *manqué* and carried on his bent back old racial longings for poetry and lore. The dinars and thalers he now bought up; the obscure mintages from Russia, from the Palatine and from Bavaria; these he could analyze, annotate, interpret, explain, describe, relate—but not sell.

Or so it seemed at first. In Jew Street there was too great a need for current money to bother with the retired kind. Nor were Christian burghers more receptive to such trinkets. It was necessary to go farther, into the manors and castles around Frankfurt. Mayer ventured forth. After all, he had the shadow of a connection; back in Hannover he had run errands for a General von Estorff, now attached to the court of Prince William at Hanau.

And the General deigned to remember. Mayer found that the General's courtier friends showed a nice interest in his quaint coins and heirlooms. They listened to his surprisingly learned numismatic chatter. They were amused by the ghetto music with which he celebrated his wares.

They fingered the catalogue written with such loving flourishes. And then they bought!

They bought again from time to time. Mayer, emboldened, sent his curlicue-embellished catalogues to princes and princelings all around. One day he was ushered into the presence of William himself. His Highness, legend claims, had just won at chess and therefore regarded the world kindly. Mayer sold him a handful of his rarest medals and coins. It was the first transaction of a Rothschild with a chief of state.

He returned to Jew Street, triumphant but not rich. He had thoughts of marriage, but the upkeep of his family could not depend on random euphoria in high places. So Mayer instituted in the House at the Saucepan a *Wechselstube*—that is, a rudimentary bank where the multifarious currency of the Germanies could be exchanged. The fairs held in Frankfurt brought all sorts of ducats, florins, carolins and what-nots into town. From this diversity Mayer now steadily profited.

He became good son-in-law material. One began to see him quite often over at the home of Gutele Schnapper, a small but energetic seventeen-year-old, whose father kept shop at the good end of Jew Street. The dowry here promised to be fair. Gutele was sweet, her beef stew excellent. Could a nice young Jew ask more?

Mayer did. Those old coins and the high gentlemen who bought them. . . . Again the dream stirred *sotto voce* and further bent his shoulders. Again he rejected the sound bourgeois way to merely sound success. He did not use the exchange profits to enlarge the *Wechselstube*, his primary source of income. The money was invested in the numismatic trade.

Mayer bought out some needy coin collectors. With his newly bolstered line he attracted the Duke Karl August

(Goethe's patron at Weimar) and other spectacular customers paying drab prices. He sold consistently, if sparsely, to his lord, William. And he enjoyed himself.

His brothers—who pursued the solid, stodgy used-goods department of their common business—could never quite fathom that persistent smile in Mayer's beard. They watched him, puzzled. How he hovered over his catalogues! How carefully he had them printed now, in complicated Gothic letters! How he kept revising their elaborate title pages, how he worked on their phrasing which, even for those days, seemed a bit odd and archaic. He was, the brothers thought, like a Talmudist writing a book.

And indeed, Mayer really began to write. They were letters of practical import, petitions to various local princes. Yet their convoluted charm and their painstaking love of formalities, sometimes lapsing into ghetto idiom—all that seemed typical Mayer.

"It has been my particular high and good fortune," he would begin, "to serve your lofty princely Serenity at various times and to your most gracious satisfaction. I stand ready to exert all my energies and my entire fortune to serve your lofty princely Serenity whenever in future it shall please you to command me. An especially powerful incentive to this end would be given me if your lofty princely Serenity were to distinguish me with an appointment as one of your Highness' Court Factors. I am making bold to beg for this with the more confidence in the assurance that by so doing I am not giving any trouble; while for my part such a distinction would lift up my commercial standing and be of help to me in so many other ways that I feel certain thereby to make my way and fortune here in the city of Frankfurt."

And sure enough, one day, on September 21, 1769, passers-by in the poor end of Jew Street had something new to look at. A stooped young man with a black beard was nailing a sign onto the Saucepan house. It bore the arms of Hesse-Hanau, and underneath proclaimed in gilt characters: M. A. ROTHSCHILD, BY APPOINTMENT COURT FACTOR TO HIS SERENE HIGHNESS, PRINCE WILLIAM OF HANAU.

Now, a factorship was a commonplace honor. The appointment only confirmed publicly that the appointee had done business with the court. It carried no obligations on the part of the prince, gave no magic fillip to Mayer's career.

Yet it created a certain excitement in the neighborhood. The Saucepan landlord was impressed and agreed to sell a quarter-share of the house to the three brothers—something Mayer had long wanted. Gutele's father, hitherto reluctant, let her become the new dignitary's wife. The title also exempted its owner from a few of the disadvantages from which Jews suffered; a kind of passport, it made traveling a little easier.

Whenever Mayer passed the front of the Saucepan, he lingered for a moment and played his odd smile over the plaque. Gutele began to bear him children, and he even held his babies up to the sign, explaining the escutcheon and the lettering. His brothers smirked. His wife was busy cooking and washing. But the tots in his arms stared at the plaque with serious eyes. They seemed to recognize it as the first fragment of an enormous fulfillment.

## 3. *Mayer's Serenity*

The young prince who conferred the distinction—a supporting player in the Rothschild drama—was an interesting man. Despite the relatively small size of his domain, William had blood as blue as any monarch in Europe. A grandson of George II of England, a cousin of George III, he was also a nephew of the King of Denmark and brother-in-law of the King of Sweden. Obviously his relatives were doing well. What made them even more important to William—and what gave him a signal part in Mayer Rothschild's story—was the fact that just about the entire collection of majesties owed money to little Hanau.

When it came to money, this nabob, whose crest had been famous in Germany since the Middle Ages, was sharper than next year's parvenu. He was the first great royal burgher. Like his father, Landgrave Frederick of Hesse-Cassel, William trafficked in valor. But the son squeezed out of this commodity a good deal more than had papa. William conscripted his male subjects and processed them for the auction block. He refined and perfected his troops; he shined and sharpened them on the parade grounds; he made sure of the officers' pigtails and the enlisted men's muskets. And when a batch was ripe and enticingly packaged, he sold the lot to England, which used "the Hessians" to keep peace in the Colonies.

William's merchandising of the peacekeepers brought him enormous wealth. Every time a Hessian was killed, the prince received extra compensation to soothe him for the victim's trouble. The casualties mounted, and therefore his cash. This he loaned out, with shrewd lack of prejudice, to just the right people—candlestick makers with impeccable credit ratings or kings who paid interest in the form of favors. Between the influx of royal dispensations and bourgeois thalers, he became the richest ruler in Europe. Quite probably he amassed the greatest personal fortune between the Fuggers and—the Rothschilds.

In a life so austerely filled with business, William knew

only one avocation: adultery. Even to that enterprise he applied himself with, one might say, touching conscientiousness. In addition to the three children by his official wife, the Princess Royal of Denmark, he sired at least twenty-three illegitimate offspring by other consorts. They were all very *soigné* bastards, with patents of nobility purchased by William from his august debtor, Emperor Francis of Austria.

An indirect consequence of one of Serenity's liaisons helped strengthen the so-far tenuous bond between him and Mayer Rothschild. The eight children of Frau von Ritter-Lindental, one of his fertile mistresses, had a tutor named Buderus; and Buderus' son Carl attached himself to the court as a treasury official. Young Carl, whom we will encounter again, soon endeared himself to the prince's thriftiness. According to a chronicler, he conceived a plan "for increasing the milk profits from one of the prince's dairies by the simple expedient of forbidding the practice . . . of omitting fractions of a heller [penny] in the accounts. Young Buderus showed that this would increase the revenue by 120 thalers. This discovery appealed so strongly to the prince . . . that he entrusted Buderus with the accounts of his private purse in addition to his normal duties."

It was Buderus who helped invent the Hanau salt tax, out of which Serenity's multitudinous progeny was supported. And it was Buderus who began to be quite interested in Mayer Amschel, appearing at Hanau every so often with quaint wares. Buderus liked the Jew. He liked, as well, the rare coins he got as holiday presents. There were many holidays in the year. Through Buderus, Mayer's *Wechselstube* was given a few of Serenity's London drafts for discount—that is, for cashing. Rothschild had at last broken into state banking.

But in a tiny and insignificant way. Prince William was

not at all aware of Jew Mayer. He just liked to scatter his foreign bills of exchange among as many discounters as possible; a concentrated dumping might depress the exchange rate. Buderus could help Mayer to a few further footling transactions; then the flow seemed to stop altogether. An event occurred which made even greater the gulf between low little Mayer and the high prince.

William's father died. In 1785 his Serenity succeeded to the immense possessions, to the palace, and to the title of Landgrave of Hesse-Cassel. William's retinue—complete with wife, mistress, scions, bastards, courtiers, and all—left Hanau and thus the vicinity of Frankfurt. The whole splendid court settled into the great palace of Wilhelmshöhe at Cassel.

That same year Mayer and his wife Gutele pushed their pots and barrels to a somewhat larger ghetto house, this one with a green shield: an obscure, cluttered, piddling migration within Jew Street, worlds below the princely progress from Hanau to Wilhelmshöhe. Yet it was Mayer's, not William's, journey that ended in a landmark meaningful to our day.

## 4. *A Dynasty Aborning*

In his old age Mayer looked back on his life and confessed that the 1780's were his favorite years. He was in his own forties then, and the decade had a kind of homey, cheerful cast. On the one hand, the fury which was to raise the Rothschilds to *The Rothschilds* still bided its time. On the other hand, they had shaken off the ghetto's more soiled and naked exigencies.

The ugly back yard at the Saucepan lay behind them.

The Green Shield was a much finer house. It fronted the street, rose three stories high and expressed Mayer's standing as an established merchant. True, here as everywhere in the ghetto space was scarce. The Green Shield, though tall, was narrow, its rooms small and dark. Two bedrooms must serve the parents and their constantly growing brood (twenty children were born, ten survived). Cupboards had to be wedged under the steep, creaking staircases, and a few were built into the wall.

It was not a quiet existence, either. Outside, Jew Street surged and screamed. Inside, staircases and flooring, both venerable, groaned. Every time the front door opened, an ancient bell clanged. It had, during its lifetime, warned not only of customers but also of pogroms and police.

The bell sent Mayer scuttling a hundred times a day. He was busier than ever. To maintain the house, to support the family, he had added a dry-goods counter to his regular business—the coins, the *Wechselstube*, and the secondhand trade. No one shared the burden, for brother Kalmann had died in 1782, while brother Moses had withdrawn. Mayer sweated through all these struggling departments and smiled his odd smile.

Indeed, he found increasing cause for contentment here. The store, with its more spacious quarters, invited more attractive customers. Schönche, the eldest child, who sat behind the cashier's desk, was given a new dress. Mayer soon rid his place of the disorder of the used-goods trade. Eventually he dealt not only in cotton but also in wine and tobacco, and the dignity as well as the aroma of these wares pervaded the whole building.

Also on the ground floor was the kitchen, a mere twelve by five feet large and with a hearth just big enough for a single pot. Next to it stood—extraordinary luxury!—a pump. The Rothschilds were among the blessed few in

Jew Street who needn't leave their four walls to get drinking water.

The kitchen, of course, constituted Gutele's province as mistress of the house. So did the carefully kept living room upstairs. (Many years later it was to be called "The Green Room" because of the color of its faded upholstery and because Gutele stubbornly persisted in living and sitting in state there while her sons reigned over Europe from their palaces.)

On Saturday evenings, when prayer was done at the synagogue, Mayer liked to inveigle the rabbi into his house. They would bend toward one another on the green upholstery, sipping slowly at a glass of wine, and argue about first and last things deep into the night. Even on work days, when Mayer had finished with his coins and cottons and drafts, he was apt to take down the big book of the Talmud and recite from it in happy Hebrew singsong while the entire family must sit stock-still and listen.

But Mayer was not just bookish. The Green Shield had a kind of terrace looking out on the back yard. Since Jews were not allowed to set foot in public gardens, this served as the family recreation ground. Here Mayer played with the children while Gutele, like the good Jewish wife she was, sat quietly in the background, knitting, sewing, crocheting, mending. On the terrace Mayer showed his daughters how to tend some grass and flowers and talked in fanciful tropes about the various plants—almost as though they were old coins. Here, too, he celebrated the Feast of Tabernacles (which must not be held under a roof) beneath pine twigs through which the ghetto stars were shining.

The building had another feature to which he resorted just as often but much more circumspectly. On the other side of the small yard lay the counting house—the first, primitive Rothschild bank, covering all of nine square feet.

It contained a large iron chest with a mechanism so contrived that it could not be opened on the side with the padlock but only by lifting the lid from the back. Yet the chest served largely as decoy. The walls were riddled with secret shelves, and a trap door led down into a hidden cellar which was quite separate from the "official" house cellar. Equally separate was the purpose of this second cavern. In it were stored documents, contracts, deeds and, after a while, strange papers relating to his Highness, Landgrave William of Hesse-Cassel—seemingly so distant.

Invisible bonds began to connect an underground hole behind the Green Shield with the great towers of Wilhelmshöhe. Few knew of the tie while it was being forged. And no one suspected that the tycoon prince would be eclipsed by the ghetto peddler; or that the Jew Street family would, within Serenity's own lifetime, surpass by far his own fabulous wealth; would drown the fame of his ancient name with their own; would, in fact, reduce him to a thoroughbred steppingstone.

# III

# *FIVE FLYING CARPETS*

## 1. *The Boys Erupt*

NO TRUMPETS announced the Rothschild accession to world power. At the end of the 1780's Mayer Rothschild meant little or nothing to Prince William in his high castle at Wilhelmshöhe. Mayer's name remained entirely inconspicuous in the Frankfurt ghetto itself.

The premise of the family's conquest lay in the very unobtrusiveness of their crouch and the silence of their leap. Their aim was so high; compared with it, their position so low; their first foothold so precarious, their resources so feeble; any alerted rival could have destroyed them with a single stroke.

Yet the three puissant devices by which Mayer's house was to overwhelm a continent were already doing their work in miniature.

1. The Rothschild clientele consisted, to a calculated degree, not of other bourgeoisie but of some of the noblest personages in Germany—and never mind if their high posi-

tions exacted low profits.

2. Rothschild courted the Landgrave with low prices (thus faithfully imitating William's own tactics with the imperial palace in Vienna). This earned Mayer the increasingly crucial cooperation of Buderus who, as the prince's financial lieutenant, exerted influence over the greatest money hoard in Europe.

3. Mayer had sons.

Here was, and is, the simplest, most important power instrument of all: to have sons. In essence the dream poem in Mayer's soul was dynastic. All the connectionmaking, the storytelling and charming, the bit-by-bit selling he did at local courts was dynastic investment. Had he not been a father, it would have been vain gesticulation; he would have died unknown, a species of feckless Semitic troubadour. But since he had sons, he became a mover of mountains. All his travail turned out to be the perfect seed for his children to grow and pluck; and all their tireless harvesting toil would be but new sowing for *their* children and their children's children.

Perhaps the early Romans were the most successful nation we have known; perhaps Napoleon the most formidable individual. It is quite possible that the people still bustling obscurely at the Green Shield were the family par excellence in modern history. As long as Mayer lived alone with his wife, he was just another Jew—or, if you will, a Caesar without centurions. But soon those boys marched out of Gutele's womb like so many dauntless legions.

First came Amschel, future treasurer of the German Confederation. Then Salomon, who in the end achieved exactly the exalted station in imperial Vienna that remained Landgrave William's perpetual daydream. Then Nathan, who rose to more power than any other man in England. Then Kalmann, who wound the Italian peninsula around his hand. Then Jacob, who was to lord it in France during Republic and Empire.

In the beginning, of course, those five, together with their five sisters, were just an eager litter of ghetto apprentices, taking the load off Mayer's stooped shoulders. They ran errands, manned counters, added figures.

But swiftly their characters became plain. They were quite different from old Rothschild. When Mayer talked Jewish history (would one of them perhaps go to the Yeshiva?) or spun yarns about his coins, their eyes, while obedient, turned blank. They became alive at the market place. They vibrated at the *Wechselstube*. They were fiendish calculators. They came running into the house with something—often cotton cloth—they had snatched up for a song and which they sold dearly, with an astounding pressure and speed, a few hours later.

Success itched in their bones. Yet their gentler father was needed to release it. A precedent established itself to pattern the future: in the House of Rothschild, brilliance may be individual but accomplishment is joint. Brothers and cousins complement each other, and so do generations.

The harsh, tremendous new energies in the House of the Green Shield might have foundered if not for Mayer Amschel. He softened them. He supplied graciousness, the one thing the brothers would always lack. He put forward a pleasant face at a time when the skill of pleasing was still more useful than the ability to negotiate. In other self-made success stories the more polished sons build from the spadework done by the father. Here the father put the subtle touches on the sledgehammer schemes of his boys.

The first scheme consisted of a complex and ingenious putting together of two and two. On the one hand, there was the Rothschild cotton-cloth line, paid for with money going *to* England—that is, to textile jobbers in Manchester.

On the other hand, his soldier-vending Serenity, the Landgrave, got money *from* England in the form of drafts. On the third hand (Rothschild reasoning is usually octopus-armed), those English cotton jobbers could be paid directly with the Landgrave's London drafts—and the discount fees pocketed both ways—if only William would give Mayer such discount business again and in more generous quantities. On the fourth hand, why couldn't Mayer show up at William's new court in Cassel right now, with some good stories and a do-me-a-favor-priced collection of fine old coins?

"Right now" meant 1787, two years before the French Revolution. Mayer packed his velvet case of numismatic treasures. Shortly afterwards the Landgrave acquired very cheaply a score of rare items, together with a petition from M. A. Rothschild recalling Mayer's Court Factorship and some of the minor discounting he had done in years past.

The court took its time. At last, in 1789, drafts worth 800 pounds sterling arrived at the *Wechselstube*. It was a first trickle that became steady and strong and hugely profitable.

But this new income did not nearly satisfy the dynamic new impatience at the Green Shield. What was draft-discounting—which was really just check-cashing—compared to the handling of bonds in which the Landgrave invested much of his gigantic income? And who did the handling? Wasn't it those big Frankfurt bankers, Bethmann Brothers and Rueppell & Harnier? Weren't there spats between court and counting house?

Suddenly the Rothschild boys stood, hat in hand, before the big bankers. "Please," they said in their funny Jew Street German, "let us be go-betweens between you, the dignified financiers, and him, the difficult William."

The bankers looked amused at these eager, uncouth apparitions. Yes, in them there wasn't an iota of dignity to be hurt, and maybe they had just the raw vitality to satisfy Serenity's "mach' schnell" needlings. Established Frankfurt agreed. It paid those young ghetto louts a small commission for being its messengers and William's butts.

Established Frankfurt was served well. William liked the way the youths snapped to. And his treasurer, Buderus, became a secret partner in the *Wechselstube* now turned regular bank.

Soon Salomon was an almost daily fixture at Cassel, incorporating Rothschild into the financial apparatus of the court. Soon Amschel was arranging—and participating in—some of the Landgrave's mortgage business. Soon Nathan, who had quarreled with an English textile salesman over prices, found himself in Manchester; soon he sent directly discounted cotton right through the French Revolution to the Rothschild store, just as prices started rocketing. Almost by accident the family had taken its first step toward forming an international network.

Soon the Green Shield team fanned out in all directions. In every stagecoach a young round-faced Rothschild sat, portfolio wedged under one arm, eyes avid but impenetrable. And Mayer himself followed, soothing where there had been too much sharpness, conciliating and smiling as consummately as his sons had argued and promoted.

Soon the Jewish community at Frankfurt took a surprised look at the phenomenon in their midst. For over twenty years Mayer Amschel's tax assessment had been the same, a moderate figure of 2,000 gulden. Abruptly in 1795 the amount was doubled. The next year his official worth reached 15,000 gulden, the highest possible fiscal category in the ghetto.

This change did not constitute a world-shaking event, like some others about to take place. Napoleon was inventing imperial France. Corsican thunder rolled down the shores of Europe. But in Frankfurt another brand-new power reached beyond national borders. It marched on tiptoe, and not with hobnailed boots. Mayer Rothschild executed in total secrecy his first important loan operation involving a foreign state.

## 2. *Something Rotten in Denmark*

Someone once said that the wealth of Rothschild consists of the bankruptcy of nations. There is more to it than that, of course. But certainly the family's initial international coup took place in 1804, when the entire treasury of Denmark consisted of a deficit.

Mayer, kept *au courant* by Buderus, knew the fact well. He knew furthermore that Landgrave William suffered from an almost unbearable surplus. Highness, therefore, was beyond doubt willing to help out Denmark—particularly since a kingdom makes pretty good collateral. Only, the Danish monarch was Highness' uncle. It's always bad business to show poor relations how rich you are: loans within the family can easily degenerate into gifts.

The thing to do was to make the loan incognito. Not through Bethmann Brothers, of course, or through Rueppell & Harnier, or any of the other big banks identified with his Highness. Why not use an obscure but efficient outfit; an outfit which would turn the trick for a smaller commission, yet with guaranteed anonymity; an outfit—well, let's see now . . . an outfit, say, like Rothschild's?

Mayer just dropped his intricately wrought hint to Buderus. Buderus redropped it into Highness' ear. Highness smiled. From Frankfurt to Copenhagen the stagecoaches began to swarm with Mayer's boys.

Bethmann Brothers and Rueppell & Harnier, the big Frankfurt bankers, did not notice anything at first. After a while, though, they could not help wondering. The Rothschild outfit seemed so awfully preoccupied each time they asked it to do some menial brokerage chores. Furthermore, quite some time had passed since the Landgrave had last asked them to arrange foreign loans.

Inquiries directed to his Highness' treasurer, the Honorable Herr Buderus, received polite impassive answers. Questions put to Copenhagen met with a most curious statement: all Danish loans, replied the finance minister, had been handled by people acting for some nameless but terribly nice millionaire.

"What people?" exclaimed Bethmann Brothers.

". . . schild something." These people moved so fast it was hard to catch their names.

". . . schild?" Rothschild? *Rothschild!* Bethmann Brothers were in an uproar of investigation. And the cat was out of the bag. Those ghetto hawkers! Daring to undercut the most powerful and long-established bankers in Germany!

Furious appeals went out from Bethmann and Rueppell & Harnier to the Danish government, to the Landgrave, even to Buderus—flaming statements about Mosaic presumption and Christian loyalty. Patrician Frankfurt was up in arms. Broadside after broadside crashed against the Jew Street schemers, who were still, after all, chained in at night.

The court at Cassel hemmed and hawed. In the end the shouting did no more than make the shouters hoarse. That family was simply too useful to his Highness. Buderus said so, and the prince knew it for the truth. Their energy, their funny accents, their ubiquity had become indispensable.

The last quality was decisive. They were everywhere. One father and five sons had become a preternatural force that devoured distance, precedents, limits and frontiers.

Old Mayer now gave this new force formal status. In 1800 he entered into a partnership with his two eldest sons. He established rules which became pillars of a dynastic constitution. All key posts in the firm were manned by members of the family—luckily a large one—not by hired hands. (To this day, only Rothschilds are partners or owners of the great Rothschild banks.) When Schönche, the eldest daughter, married, her husband was not employed in the business; but when Amschel wed a year later, his wife promptly received a position. (To this day the female line is as rigidly kept out of Rothschild affairs as the male line is included.) Mayer also began a system of secret bookkeeping in addition to the official one. (Today Rothschild business is "secret" to the extent that it consists, despite its immense size, of private partnerships which need publish no balance sheets or other information.)

Family and business were welded into one formidable machine. Daily the Rothschilds exerted smoother and greater power. They still lived in Jew Street, but their commercial quarters expanded to offices and a stockroom outside the ghetto. In the subterranean passages under the Green Shield counting house the gold mounted, together with packets of securities.

Above all, the Rothschilds' position with the Landgrave was supremely entrenched. Mayer had been appointed Oberhofagent (Superior Court Agent); the two eldest sons could now call themselves Hessian Pay Office agents. Daily their influence over the Hessian court, and over its income of a million thalers per year, was widening. They loaned money to the Landgrave's son, in loyal imitation of the Landgrave, who loaned to the royal dukes of England. They were on the point of becoming chief bankers to William, one of the world's richest monarchs.

And then, in the year 1806, when Mayer's dream almost became substance, Napoleon seemed to sweep it away. He was sweeping away everything else. Prince William, like the cautious billionaire he was, tried to straddle the fence between Bonaparte and the Austro-British alliance. But the French Emperor had small patience with vacillators. When the Grande Armée came down on Prussia in October, 1806, it came down on Hesse as well.

It appeared to be all over. Frankfurt suffered occupation. The lines of international commerce were shattered. Nathan, the Rothschilds' foreign bastion, looked marooned in England. And in the wee hours of the morning of November 1 Prince William himself panted into his carriage and had the horses goaded northward to Schleswig.

The next day French troops flooded into his castle, Wilhelmshöhe. "My object," read Napoleon's order, "is to remove the house of Hesse-Cassel from rulership and to strike it out of the list of powers."

Thus Europe's mightiest man decreed erasure of the rock on which the new Rothschild firm had been built. Yet, curiously, the bustle didn't diminish at the House of the Green Shield. The clouds which the great Emperor had blown so grandiosely across Europe were joined by smaller but no less portentous counterparts. Dust whirled behind the carriages in which those round-faced young Rothschilds still sat, avid and impenetrable, portfolios wedged between body and arm.

They saw neither peace nor war, neither slogans nor manifestoes nor orders of the day, neither death nor glory. They saw none of the things that blinded the world. They saw only steppingstones. Prince William had been one. Napoleon would be the next.

# IV

# *ROTHSCHILD VERSUS NAPOLEON*

## 1. *Round One: Contraband*

IN THE predawn blackness of November 1, 1806, there was a glow of muffled lanterns in the secret back-yard cellar of the Green Shield. Mayer Rothschild buried as quickly as he could a cartful of documents—minutes of Prince William's Privy Council. Those weren't the only things William wanted hidden from Napoleon's troops; that same hour some trusted footmen shoveled a hoard of jewels beneath the staircases of the prince's various castles.

Unlike the dossier entrusted to Mayer, the jewels were found. Thereupon Carl Buderus, now William's undercover representative in occupied Hesse, called for his carriage. He had tea with the French governor-general, La Grange. Subsequently, about a million francs dropped into La Grange's palm. This brilliant interpretation of the law of gravity had brilliant results. The greater part of William's bright treasure was permitted to move out of the staircases, beyond musket reach of the French, into the hands of the evicted prince.

Still, jewelry made up only the merest fraction of the prince's wealth. As Europe's most blue- and cold-blooded loan shark, William had huge debts maturing in his favor all over the continent. In addition, there were his British investments that paid him dividends of nearly 2,000 pounds * (18,000 dollars) a month. And now he sat in Denmark, exiled, cut off from the administration of such affairs. For the stewardship of much of William's vast and complicated riches Carl Buderus chose Mayer Rothschild.

Of course, corporatively speaking, Buderus himself had become a quasi-Rothschild. A secret contract signed in 1809 confirmed the old verbal agreement that gave the prince's treasurer a certain share in the Green Shield business. But was this vested interest enough cause to hand a ghetto merchant such enormous responsibility? Wasn't Buderus pressing his luck too far? Who were the Rothschilds, after all? Without great financial or noble antecedents; as Jews, without civic status; without protection now that Serenity had been cast beyond the frontier—they seemed no different from the mass that thrashed about helpless on the tidal wave of Napoleon.

Yet they *were* different, as Buderus knew. Theirs was a wonderfully lopsided knack. A heroic energy drove them. But since they lacked the heroic imagination to go with it, they were never driven too far. This gained them a thing rarer than triumph then: survival.

In those seething teens of the nineteenth century, millions of men were undone by the history which a few

* This translation into today's dollars—like all others in this book—is necessarily a rough calculation; the establishment of exact dollar equivalents is in most cases impossible.

grandly made. The victims were pushed into disaster. The victimizers strutted into it in regal uniform. Rothschild & Sons juggled ledgers quietly, unrelentingly, through ruin and havoc. Their limitations were as miraculously appropriate as their talents. It was an unconquerable combination —the steady-eyed sobriety of the burgher, powered by a demonic drive.

Napoleon's finance ministry could not cope with the family. The ministry was declared by the Emperor the legal successor to William's exchequer. It thoroughly canvassed all princes and potentates who owed William money. It tried every device, from threats to rebates and easier terms, to direct all due sums into the Emperor's purse. It toiled in vain. Mayer's boys skimmed through Europe in their coaches and scooped up the debts as they flew by. During their years in Highness' employ they had acquired connections, knowledge, persuasiveness and momentum—all irresistible.

They were impossible to stop or to get hold of. But their father at Frankfurt was a more stationary target. Yet when the French police swooped down on the House of the Green Shield, all they found was a careworn old Jewish couple trying to run a store, with most of their grown sons gone—ach! scattered by the brutal war. Their books appeared to be in order. Pro-Serenity or un-Napoleonic activities? Hardly a trace of them.

The moment the boots died away, old Mayer descended into his back-yard cellar to resume work with his real books and his real correspondence.

Before long this correspondence was conveyed in the private Rothschild coach. The coach had a false bottom, and the letters a secret language consisting of a jumble of Hebrew, Yiddish and German and a code system of pseudonyms. English investments were called "stockfish." Old

Rothschild turned into "Arnoldi," as if he were the hero of an Italian romance; whereas His Serene Highness, Prince William, was Judaized into "Herr Goldstein."

The care and feeding of Herr Goldstein became Mayer's province. Not an easy job, because Herr Goldstein kept throwing fits over a certain embarrassing circumstance: the Rothschild boys were collecting whole fortunes of Hessian moneys, but only a trickle reached Herr Goldstein, and no precise accounting whatsoever.

Old Mayer, a genius when it came to cajolery, explained, appeased, pacified. Buderus helped as well as he could. But sometimes old Rothschild had to do his tranquilizing in person and undertake the seven-days journey over rough roads to William's exile near the Danish border. He reported how closely the awful French were breathing down his neck and his boys'; how often he had been searched and questioned, harassed and fined; how it became daily more arduous and dangerous to play games with Napoleon. Was it any wonder, then, that the swift transmission of debt collections or accounts thereof had grown impossible these days? Downright suicidal for his boys and himself? Let it please his Highness to content his Serene Self in patience. Nothing was surer than the fact that his Highness would get his money.

Mayer was right: his Highness did get every last penny —eventually. Meanwhile . . .

Meanwhile it just so happened that Nathan in London found himself in possession of very considerable funds. He happened to buy not only cotton—his original line—but foodstuffs, colonial wares and every other kind of goods which Napoleon's blockade had declared contraband on the Continent.

Nathan's bales and boxes then happened to vanish, to reappear shortly on Hamburg docks. Here Amschel and Salomon happened to hover. And then fresh wares happened to materialize on starved store shelves everywhere: in Germany, in Scandinavia, in the Lowlands, in France itself. Cotton goods, yarn, tobacco, coffee, sugar, indigo—there it was at last, at famine prices gladly paid. Who cared if somebody made a famine fortune?

Napoleon's one-track-minded police cared. After a while the constabulary became downright obsessed with the quaint idea that there was a connection between such widely separated things as contraband, Prince William's debts, and old Mayer of Jew Street.

On October 30, 1810, two French infantry regiments combed Frankfurt's warehouses, especially the Green Shield establishment in the ghetto. There they found nothing, for a better reason than usual. The Rothschilds' hands were really clean. Toward the end of 1810 they had gotten just about all they could out of smuggling.

On September 27 of that year a printed letter had gone out to all business friends of the family. Mayer (said the announcement) was changing the name of his enterprise to "Mayer Amschel Rothschild und Söhne." The firm's shares were now held not only by himself, but also by Amschel, Salomon, Kalmann and even Jacob, at that time seventeen years old. Of Nathan the announcement did not say one word. Nor did the official new partnership contract allot him a single share. Yet, as usual, the officially omitted was really the most important. Nathan, who lived in England and therefore in enemy country, did more crucial work than ever in Mayer's business. It was he who had organized the smuggling. And it was he who conceived the family's next strike, beside which contraband would look like an outdated trifle. It had been just the beginning.

## 2. *Round Two: A Million-Pound Idea*

In 1804 Nathan Mayer had moved from Manchester, the textile center, to London, the hub of the world. Here the cotton merchant turned merchant-banker, a designation under which N. M. Rothschild & Sons are listed in the London telephone book even today.

All the early English merchant-bankers began as traders with wares and credits everywhere; eased naturally into trading-*cum*-financing; and wound up as the first great international financiers of modern times. Among these *condottieri* Nathan ranks first. Through him the Rothschilds stopped buying and selling goods, even profitable contraband. Through him they switched to the ultimate commodity. From 1810 on, and to this very hour, the family would buy and sell money only.

Nathan sized up the opening provided by Napoleon, that unruly but on the whole useful market factor. And Nathan's secret letter put it to the Green Shield in Frankfurt: Bonaparte had now swallowed up nearly all the countries in which Prince William had once put his idle millions out to pasture—right? Only England was left to loan to—right? England, that rock against Napoleon. And consols (English state bonds), the Gibraltar among European papers. His Highness had invested in them in times past—right? Wasn't it time his Highness invested in them again, thoroughly, and through the good offices of Nathan Rothschild, who was so chockful of connections, willingness and go?

Mayer and Buderus laid the suggestion at Prince William's feet. Highness, however, felt a reluctance. There had been all those debt-collecting troubles with the family. On the other hand, the collected moneys *were* coming in by and by, adding to an already vast hoard.

Those countless thalers itched. Father Mayer charmed and blandished under a fine new wig and three-cornered hat. The old man's accent remained unchanged, as did his synagogue-going. Yet he had bloomed from a hustling tradesman to a full-fledged courtier. He now not only sold old coins to the Landgrave, he also bought them from him for his own private collection. He put his coach (with those secret compartments) at the disposal of the Landgrave's mails. He helped arrange Serenity's sundry exiles in Schleswig, Denmark and Bohemia.

If his Highness trusted him that far, why not entrust to his son Nathan the purchase of consols? Particularly since the dear boy was willing to waive commission and only asked the teeny brokerage fee of one eighth of one per cent?

At last William agreed. Why not, indeed? Between February, 1809, and December, 1810, Nathan received 550,000 pounds sterling with which to buy consols for the prince. It was, and is, a breathtaking sum, the equivalent of some five million current dollars. It dwarfed all the Landgrave's loans and dividends which had so far passed through Rothschild hands.

The moment it touched Nathan every farthing became a shilling, every shilling a guinea. The dear boy struck with such bull's-eye intuition, so powerfully, so fast, and at the same time so discreetly that no lucid records have survived. We do know that the agreement with William called for a purchase of consols at an average price of 72. Nathan did not buy at 72. He invested the money for his own account, took a rapid profit, and then took a second profit when he bought the prince's consols. These had meanwhile dropped to 62, just as he had foreseen. The saving in price, of course, went into his own pocket.

At the same time he harnessed his infallibility to another chance. With stunning spunk, precision, speed, he speculated on the rise of gold bullion. Daily he leaped in and out of the market with tens of thousands of princely pounds, never missing a beat, never too early or too late.

After a while, of course, William began to fidget. So little news was forwarded to him from London, and not a single bond certificate. Mayer went to work, conjuring all the difficulties of communication Napoleon interposed between Dear Boy's London and Serenity's Prague. Serenity subsided. He even released further substantial funds.

Then, in 1811, young Kalmann Rothschild smuggled himself in and out of England to present the prince with his first consol certificates for 189,500 pounds sterling. William was relieved. But he had had enough of nervous exertions. "I am getting sick of my investments," he wrote to Buderus. "I really prefer to have my money lying idle."

In 1811 this decision no longer bothered the Rothschilds much. Another, a last, milestone had been turned.

Nathan, the milestone specialist, was the first to round it. Seven years before, he had come to London as a raw-tongued foreigner. Now, barely thirty-four, he enjoyed a preternatural reputation. All purchases he had made on behalf of the Landgrave had been registered in the name of Rothschild. Few suspected that the torrents of capital coursing through Nathan's office weren't necessarily his own. His actual wealth, though, had mushroomed as explosively as his credit. It waxed so huge that even William, the richest prince on the Continent, became too puny to be the chief account in Rothschild's book. He was just the beginning. Something still bigger had to be found.

## 3. *Round Three: The Giant Gold Smuggle*

"The East India Company," Nathan would reminisce at a dinner party near the end of his life, "the East India Company had 800,000 pounds' worth of gold to sell. I went to the sale and bought it all. [Nearly eight million dollars!] I knew the Duke of Wellington must have it. The government sent for me and said they must have the gold. I sold the gold to them, but they did not know how to get it to the Duke in Portugal. I undertook all that and sent it through France. It was the best business I have ever done."

This sums up rather gruffly an enormous, incredibly cunning operation. Basic to it is the fact that Napoleon played handmaiden to the family one more time.

In 1807 he had produced for them an ideal goods shortage; in 1810, just the perfect kind of poor investment situation. Now he obliged with an exquisitely placed front line. The Emperor's marshals were fighting Wellington behind the Pyrenees, far away from English supply lines. To feed his army, the Duke had to issue drafts on the English treasury. A whole mob of Sicilian and Maltese financiers cashed these at outrageous discounts and pushed them along laborious paths to London for redemption. Sporadically the Rothschilds had participated in the traffic. But until 1811 this had been a sideline.

Now 800,000 pounds' worth of gold waited for Nathan in a vault. What scores of bankers had done by way of IOU's and notes seeping toward London, he and his brothers wanted to accomplish alone by hard money seeping to Spain. By profitable commission from His Majesty's Government, Nathan became, in effect, chief broker and paymaster general to England's most important army.

There was only one way to route the cash: through the

very France England's army was fighting. Of course, the Rothschild blockade-running machine already had superb cogs whirring all over Germany, Scandinavia and England, even in Spain and southern France. But a very foxy new wheel was needed in Napoleon's capital itself.

Enter Jacob—henceforth called James—the youngest of Mayer's sons. On March 24, 1811, he registered with the French police on his arrival in Paris, his domicile being 5, rue Napoleon. Undoubtedly he was helped by Grand Duke von Dalberg, a high Napoleonic dignitary who had just been given a most advantageous loan by old Mayer. Probably James knew Paris a little from some previous visits. But he was only nineteen. He had lived in the ghetto most of his life; he spoke only German and Yiddish. Yet he moved through the sleek, treacherous ground of French high finance with a blinding speed and a sure-footed virtuosity that matched any exploit of Nathan's.

Two days after his official arrival, Mayer's youngest was already the hero of a report by the French finance minister to Napoleon. "A Frankfurter named Rothschild," wrote the minister, "is now staying in Paris and is principally occupied in bringing British ready money from the English coast to Dunkirk. He is in touch with bankers of the highest standing in Paris. . . . He states that he has just received letters from London . . . according to which the English intend to check this export of gold. . . ."

In fine, the minister had been fed some very carefully edited gossip, which gave away the existence of a gold stream but kept him in strict innocence of its destination. He had swallowed James's "letters" and other custom-tailored evidence showing—the exact opposite of the truth—that Britain feared being weakened by the outflow of money.

James calculated well. What the British enemy seemed

to fear, Monsieur le Ministre automatically desired. In the space of a few hundred hours Mayer's youngest had not only gotten the English gold rolling through France, but conjured a fiscal mirage that took in Napoleon himself. A teen-age Rothschild tricked the imperial government into sanctioning the very process that helped to ruin it. What had happened to Bethmann Brothers would now happen to an empire.

The family machine began to hum. Nathan sent big shipments of British guineas, Portuguese gold ounces, French napoleons d'or (often freshly minted in London) across the Channel. From the coast James saw them to Paris and secretly transmuted the metal into bills on certain Spanish bankers. South of the capital Kalmann materialized, took over the bills, blurred into a thousand shadowed canyons along the Pyrenees—and reappeared, Wellington's receipts in hand. Salomon was everywhere, trouble-shooting, making sure the transit points were diffuse and obscure enough not to disturb either the French delusion or the British guinea rate. Amschel stayed in Frankfurt and helped father Mayer to staff headquarters.

The French did catch a few whiffs of the truth. Sometimes the suspicious could be prosperously purged of their suspicion. The police chief of Calais, for example, suddenly was able to live in such distracting luxury that he found it difficult to patrol the shoreline thoroughly. On the other hand, the commissioner of the Paris police proposed more than once that young James be arrested. But the protection of the finance ministry proved stronger.

While Napoleon struggled his might away in the Russian winter, there passed through France itself a gold vein to the army staving in the Empire's back door.

Soon the Rothschilds became England's lifeline not only to Wellington but also to her allies. During the final years of the Napoleonic war, Britain appropriated immense subsidies for Austria, Prussia and Russia. Yet she had no convenient means with which to effect payment. The shipping of bullion involved a prohibitive risk. Issuing single huge drafts on the British treasury would ruin the sterling rate. John Herries, the Exchequer officer in charge of foreign financing, knew one sure answer: let Nathan do it.

Nathan and his brothers did it by operating simultaneously from their variously shifting bases. Between them, Mayer and boys established the first great international clearinghouse. They expedited most of the fifteen million pounds Britain advanced to her friends. With so light a touch were these stupendous transactions juggled, with such soundless grace, that the sterling rate never suffered a dent. The only perceptible commotion was the abacuses clicking in the counting houses. To this day the Rothschild commissions are unknown and incalculable.

But even all that was just the beginning.

## 4. *Round Four: The Scoop of Scoops*

The Battle of Waterloo established England as the foremost European power. To the Rothschilds, her chief financial agents, Waterloo brought a multimillion-dollar scoop. The fame of that scoop has endowed it, in later years, with carrier pigeons and other legendary appurtenances. But like most family feats, it was based on very hard work and very cold cunning.

The hard work had started a long time before. As soon as the boys had fanned out from Frankfurt, they had started sending each other industriously, endlessly, items of commercial or general interest. Soon a private news service developed. (At the London house it survived down to World War II in the form of a dozen blue-clad couriers ready to fly off at a moment's notice to Rio, Melbourne or Nairobi.)

Rothschild coaches careered down highways; Rothschild boats set sail across the Channel; Rothschild messengers were swift shadows along the streets. They carried cash, securities, letters and news. Above all, news—latest, exclusive news to be vigorously processed at stock market and commodity bourse.

And there was no news more precious than the outcome of Waterloo. For days the London 'Change had strained its ears. If Napoleon won, English consols were bound to drop. If he lost, the enemy empire would shatter and consols rise.

For thirty hours the fate of Europe hung veiled in cannon smoke. On June 19, 1815, late in the afternoon a Rothschild agent named Rothworth jumped into a boat at Ostend. In his hand he held a Dutch gazette still damp from the printer. By the dawn light of June 20 Nathan Rothschild stood at Folkstone harbor and let his eye fly over the lead paragraphs. A moment later he was on his way to London (beating Wellington's envoy by many hours) to tell the government that Napoleon had been crushed. Then he proceeded to the stock exchange.

Another man in his position would have sunk his worth into consols. But this was Nathan Rothschild. He leaned against "his" pillar. He did not invest. He sold. He dumped consols.

His name was already such that a single substantial move on his part sufficed to bear or bull an issue. Consols fell. Nathan leaned and leaned, and sold and sold. Consols dropped still more. "Rothschild knows," the whisper rippled through the 'Change. "Waterloo is lost."

Nathan kept on selling, his round face motionless and

stern, his pudgy fingers depressing the market by tens of thousands of pounds with each sell signal. Consols dived, consols plummeted—until, a split second before it was too late, Nathan suddenly bought a giant parcel for a song. Moments afterwards the great news broke, to send consols soaring.

We cannot guess the number of hopes and savings wiped out by this engineered panic. We cannot estimate how many liveried servants, how many Watteaus and Rembrandts, how many thoroughbreds in his descendants' stables, the man by the pillar won that single day.

## 5. *Round Five: Conquering the Victors*

The climax of Waterloo was followed by peace—and a bleak surprise. During the war the Rothschilds had been irresistible. Now a snag developed, perhaps because someone indispensable had passed from the scene.

On September 16, 1812, on the Day of Atonement, old Mayer prayed and fasted the entire day in the Frankfurt synagogue. The next morning an old wound from an operation broke open. He had barely enough strength to dictate a new will, which placed his business exclusively in his sons' hands.

> . . . my daughters, sons-in-law and their heirs having no part whatsoever in the existing firm M. A. Rothschild und Söhne . . . nor the right to examine the said business, its books, papers, inventory etc. . . . I shall never forgive my children if they should against my paternal will take it upon themselves to disturb my sons in the peaceful possession of their business.

Any violator of family harmoniousness was to be limited to the legal-minimum share of a total estate probated at far below its real value.

Then, the last dynastic chore completed, initialed, notarized, at 8:15 P.M. on September 19, 1812, he died in Gutele's arms, the last truly Biblical patriarch of our time.

What he could not bequeath to his sons was his personality. They had no pliant dignity, no easy graciousness, no *savoir-vivre* with which to beguile a prince or flirt in a salon. Their fortune was the product of elemental vigor and precision-timed craft. These had served them well during the urgencies of war. But now older values resumed their accustomed place. One didn't smuggle at the Congress of Vienna. One danced. The Rothschild boys were not dancers; *ergo*, they would not do as bankers.

The economics of post-Napoleonic Europe centered largely on the efforts of various countries to tap financial resources from within; that is, to float national loans. Here the Rothschilds, with all their immense new capital, found themselves treading air.

Only little Prussia let them handle a loan. Austria, the big plum, preferred more genteel company. Its ancient court lived on precedent and punctilio. Already back in 1800 there had been a brush with those pushy Frankfurters. They had signed a letter "k.k. Hofagenten" (Imperial-Royal Court Agents) when actually entitled to merely one "k." (Imperial only). Now in 1816 the brothers were multimillionaires. Yet only after the strongest pressure from John Herries, their particular supporter in the English treasury, would Vienna accept an English subsidy managed by these grabbers of the extra "k."

The boys, trying hard for a good impression, acquitted themselves with special subsidiary brilliance. By devising ways of waiving commissions and interest charges, they saved the Austrian treasury several millions. As a result, in 1817 Vienna threw them the little "von," much as one throws a dog a bone.

But the Rothschilds were not the kind to be fobbed off with a distinction by no means singular even for Jews. Nathan asked for the honorary Austrian consulship in London. He was answered by evasions. The five brothers together worked out far-reaching and favorable propositions. There was no real reply at all.

In France the situation seemed even worse. Here Louis XVIII had literally borrowed the splendor of the Bourbon restoration from Nathan and James Rothschild. They had advanced him British drafts to finance his magnificent entry into Paris. But that had been in 1814, with cannonades still a palpable memory. Now, three years later, the old patrician bankers were back, calling the tune from their drawing rooms. Compared to their manners, any move from the Rothschilds sounded like a hopelessly rude noise.

The new French government prepared a great loan of 350 million francs and entrusted it to Ouvrard, a distinguished French financial name, and to Baring Brothers, fashionable English bankers. To these, Mayer's sons were "simple coin changers." The loan, sans Rothschild, became a huge success.

In 1818 negotiations began for an additional issue of some 270 million francs. Again Ouvrard and Baring were front runners; the Rothschilds, futile haunters of the finance ministry. This loan, though, was to liquidate the French war indemnity. Its ultimate disposition would take place at a conference with the victorious powers at Aix-la-Chapelle.

In terms of family history, the forgotten congress at Aix is a much more important landmark than the still notorious scoop of Waterloo. Aix marked the first social confrontation between the great world and the newly great Rothschilds. It began as a round of banquets and soirees à la Congress of Vienna, with the Rothschilds fascinated and frozen out like children before a Christmas window. It climaxed with a furious thunderclap. And when the roar subsided, the children were in possession of the store.

Nobody foresaw this development during the first week, possibly not even Salomon and Kalmann, who attended as family representatives. To begin with, England had sent Lord Castlereagh instead of John Herries, their old friend. Salomon and Kalmann must have felt at sea in a world so charged with antique protocol, with such finely beveled compliments. Their natural habitat was the stock exchange, not the ballroom.

Still, the most expensive tailors had fitted them vests and cravats of the finest material. Their coaches glittered. Their horses shone. What if their grammar was a little primitive? Furthermore Kalmann had just married Adelheid Herz, of the most *soigné* Jewish family in Germany. The bride was to spearhead the family's bon ton.

Yet it was all no use. Whenever the brothers wanted to see Prince Metternich, he was just being feted by the Duke de Richelieu. Lord and Lady Castlereagh could not be found, since they kept driving about with Prince Hardenberg. The Rothschilds were left out of all these cordialities. Baring and Ouvrard, their rivals, seemed included everywhere.

Only secretaries were available, and the secretaries smiled coolly: Yes, negotiations with Baring and Ouvrard were proceeding toward a conclusion. Why change partners in midwaltz? Hadn't Baring and Ouvrard succeeded with the 1817 loan? Weren't the bonds of the 1817 loan rising on the Paris bourse that very moment?

The Rothschilds decided to try once more. They completed their purchase of Friedrich von Gentz, a brilliant publicist, friend to Metternich, and man-about-congress. They took a big option on David Parish, a stylish young banker sporting good connections with Baring. They bought every buyable social grace in sight. They checked and rechecked the impeccability of their trousers and frocks, of the servants' livery. Everything was in order.

Nothing worked. In the salons, one was amused by the puzzlement in Kalmann's face, by the Levantine frowns of Salomon. Unnoted in the general merriment went another circumstance: the couriers who entered and left the brothers' residence with growing frequency.

Through October, 1818, Aix bowed, gamboled, promenaded and ignored those Rothschild clods. On November 5 something strange happened. The French government bonds, the famous loan of 1817, began to fall after a year's steady rise. Day after day they dropped more steeply. And not only that—other securities wavered. Tempests came down out of a blue sky. A crash loomed, not just in Paris, but in bourses all over Europe.

The music stopped at Aix. The noble gentlemen stood about dazed in the suddenly suspended splendor. After all, one had made one's little investments.

It was the princes who frowned now while, curiously, Kalmann and Salomon smiled. A rumor shivered through the drawing rooms. Could those Rothschilds have . . .

Those Rothschilds had. With their boundless reserves they had bought the rival-issued bonds for weeks and weeks, bulling the paper while secretly cornering it. And then, in one relentless swoop, the boys had dumped the whole appalling load. Across the entire Continent the underpinnings of finance groaned. The great world knew now what it meant to cut a Rothschild.

Metternich, the Duke de Richelieu, Prince Hardenberg did what must be done. A stern interview ensued between them and Ouvrard and Baring, in whose (as yet unborn) new loan they had already reserved parcels on their own account. One talked; one parted; the loan-to-be dissolved into nothing.

Then Salomon and Kalmann were bowed into the presence, and lo! their clothes were now the very eye of fashion, their money the darling of the best borrowers.

And as the music began again, and two princesses obediently took the arms of two stout, round-faced men, everyone knew that it had happened at last. Europe had become richer by a great name. The boys had become *The Rothschilds*.

# V

# THE MISHPOCHE MAGNIFICENT

## 1. *By No Other Name as Great*

ON THE last day of May, 1838, a weird battle took place in Bossenden Wood near the village of Dunkirk in England. The Forty-fifth Regiment came down on a band of insurrectionary mystics and in a bayonet charge killed their leader, John Nicols Toms. Half visionary, half charlatan, Toms had whipped up the countryside with his messianic tirades. Until the army made an end of him, he was receiving veneration as King of Jerusalem, Prince of Arabia, King of the Gipsies—and Count Moses S. Rothschild.

His last claim seems the most remarkable. The name Rothschild had been prominent for barely two decades. The five brothers wearing it were the sons of a curio dealer in Frankfurt's Jew Street, their origin branded unmistakably on their manners and their speech. What moved the popular imagination to invest "Rothschild" with a lure as shimmering as "Prince of Arabia"?

Money is part of the answer. Of money the brothers now had unimaginable amounts; or rather, amounts rendered imaginable only by comparison. Lytton Strachey, considering Queen Victoria "exceedingly wealthy" even among great reigning monarchs, put the maximum value of her fortune at five million pounds. Poor Victoria. A shopping spree involving almost her Majesty's entire worth could be managed by one family branch effortlessly, at a moment's notice. This the Suez Canal purchase was to prove.

The total wealth encompassed by the clan during most of the nineteenth century has been estimated at well over 400 million pounds (6,000 million dollars). No one else, from the Fuggers to the Rockefellers, has come even close to that hair-raising figure.

But it takes more than a vast fortune to create the myth that celebrated Rothschild. It takes, above all, a compelling air on the part of the celebrity itself. After Aix the five brothers walked in the sober and unshakable belief that the divine right of kings had been overthrown by the divine right of money and that Amschel, Nathan, Salomon, Kalmann and James *were* money. The doubts and hesitations to which other *nouveaux riches* are heir did not trouble the five brothers much. A story goes that Nathan was once asked by his small son how many different nations there were in the world. "There are only two you need bother about," Nathan is reported to have answered. "There is the *mishpoche* [Yiddish for family] and there are the others."

No matter how apocryphal this conversation, it reflects a real attitude, which has survived to this day. It still puts subtle, superb capitals on two common words the Rothschilds use when speaking of their clan. They say: "The Family"—which is quite different from the family of other people. The birth of those capitals can be read plainly on the Family tree.

Starting at the topmost branch, we find that of old Mayer's five sons, the two oldest married solid, simple German-Jewish girls. The next wedding took place in 1806, when "Rothschild" already signified a comer to insiders. Nathan brought home Hannah Cohen, daughter of Barnett Cohen, the richest Jew in England. Next it was Kalmann's turn in 1818. By then it was natural that any Family member could option the very pick of brides. Kalmann chose Adelheid Herz, the Herzes being the cream of cultured Jewish society in Germany.

Finally James, the youngest, took a wife. The Austrian Emperor had already created him and his brothers barons, and they themselves the world's wealthiest family. At the previous celebration they had been very important. Now they knew themselves unique. July 11, 1824, expressed that uniqueness forcibly. James walked under the *chupah* (the Jewish wedding canopy) with Betty, his own niece, child of his brother Salomon.

It quickly became a dynastic dogma that, as in the case of the Habsburgs, the most brilliant possible match for one member of The Family was another. Of the twelve marriages consummated by the sons of the original five brothers, no less than nine were with their uncles' daughters. Of fifty-eight weddings contracted by the descendants of old Mayer, exactly half took place between first cousins.

What caused so many intramural infatuations? For one thing, there was the fact that only a Rothschild father could afford a dowry worthy of a Rothschild son-in-law. There was also a desire to consolidate, not dissipate, fortunes; and, perhaps most important, not to squander the name on strangers.

The name was the thing. The growth of the myth consisted largely of the nurture, breeding and thoroughbreeding of the name. In 1836 an incident made plain just what those two magic syllables signified to the men who bore them. At that time one other family meant still more to Jewry. The Montefiores, of ancient, most aristocratic Jewish stock, had long been the standard-bearers and great philanthropists of their faith in England. Sir Moses Montefiore had been knighted long before a grandson of Nathan was. Now a young Montefiore, himself extremely wealthy and closely allied to The Family by marriage, approached his aunt, Nathan's wife, about the possibility of a partnership in the Rothschild bank.

A long, shocked silence ensued at the Rothschild offices in New Court, St. Swithin's Lane. At last the answer came forth: ordinarily, New Court would never entertain the admission of an outsider (as a matter of fact, no Family house ever did again, to this day). However, they might be willing to create young Montefiore a junior partner, in view of his close relationship and the exceptional patrician luster of his name—provided, of course, he change that name to Rothschild.

## 2. *The Escutcheon*

Montefiore (who decided to remain Montefiore) would have been less surprised at this pronouncement had he looked into the records of the Heralds' College of the Austrian Empire. This office, charged with the correct preparation of patents of nobility, was the first to feel the almost engagingly naïve hauteur with which the brothers imposed their favorite ten letters, Rothschild, upon the world.

Early in 1817 the College's collective patience was tried

by a communication from The Family. The boys had just performed their standard miracles in the transfer of British subsidies to Vienna, had whisked more money sooner and cheaper than other bankers, and had promptly insinuated that they were ripe for an honor or two. Privy Councillor von Lederer, who sat at the Austrian distinction-conferring desk, felt that a gold snuffbox, bearing his Majesty's monogram in diamonds, would be in order.

The finance minister, Count Stadion, like finance ministers everywhere, was more sensitive to Rothschild expectations. He thought the privy councillor's proposal painfully inadequate. After all, the five wizards in question had the same relation to diamonds, however arranged, as Newcastle had to coal.

At last a compromise was achieved between his urgings and the privy councillor's frosty mention of "the special consideration that the brothers Rothschild are Israelites." Austria raised the brothers to the bottom level of minor nobility, with the right to carry the simple prefix "von." The Rothschilds were requested to devise a coat of arms consistent with their rank.

This is where the letter to the Heralds' College came in. Enthusiastically it set forth the boys' idea of their escutcheon:

> First quarter . . . an eagle sable surcharged in dexter by a field gules * (having reference to the Imperial and Royal Austrian Coat-of-Arms); second quarter . . . a leopard passant proper (a reference to the English Royal Coat-of-Arms); third quarter, a lion rampant (with reference to the Hessian Electoral Coat); fourth quarter, azure, an arm bearing five arrows (a symbol of the unity of the five brothers) . . .

* *Gules* is the heraldic word for red.

The heraldry office choked. People who were barely "vons" thinking they could get away with a positively ducal inventory of honor symbols!

And still their impertinence continued:

> In the center of the coat a shield gules. Right-hand supporter, a greyhound, a symbol of loyalty; left supporter, a stork, a symbol of piety and content [*content!*]. The crest is a coronet surmounted by the Lion of Hesse.

This from persons who even with their "von" would, strictly speaking, not even be truly noble, but merely members of the gentry! The College drew a deep breath and composed a report to the court.

> They ask for a coronet, a center shield, supporters, the Leopard of England, and the Lion of Hesse. . . . Their suggestion is entirely inadmissible . . . the gentry are entitled only to a helmet . . . otherwise there would be nothing to distinguish the higher ranks, as coronets, supporters and center shields are proper only to nobility. Moreover, no government will grant the emblems of other governments, as nobility is conferred for services to one's prince and one's country, but not for services to other countries. The lion is a symbol of courage only, which does not apply to these petitioners.

The College then got out its knives and cut presumption down to its proper size. It slashed away until the seven-pointed coronet—consonant with a baronial dignity at least—became a poor little helmet. Almost the entire honorary fauna was slaughtered, pious storks, loyal greyhounds, sundry lions and all.

Only a fraction of one bird survived: half the Austrian

eagle. The arm holding the arrows was also spared; but even here the College wrenched away one in the bunch, so that only four arrows remained (the fifth brother, Nathan, was not officially involved in the money transfer). This sadly plucked crest became the Rothschild escutcheon on March 25, 1817.

Not for long. For then came the Congress of Aix; and after Aix, a personal loan of 900,000 gulden obtained from the House of Rothschild by Prince Metternich, his Majesty's almighty chancellor. It was, on the one hand, a perfectly straightforward transaction, fully repaid seven years before its due date. On the other hand, it was contracted on September 23, 1822. And six days later an imperial decree raised all five brothers and all their legitimate descendants of either sex to the rank of baron.

At the Heralds' College the teeth that daren't bite now gnashed. The Rothschilds' armorial headgear bloomed into the very seven-pointed coronet the brothers had first proposed, attended now by three plumed and truly splendid helmets. The center shield was restored, the illustrious beasts resurrected in a form even more magnificent and allusive than the erstwhile version had intended. In place of the loyal greyhound reared the brave Hessian lion, while the pious stork had been transfigured into nothing less than a prancing unicorn. The half-eagle now shone whole, and a second royal bird raised its wings among the helmets. *Concordia*, *Integritas*, *Industria*, proclaimed the scroll upon which the entire splendor was pedestaled.

But most gratifying seemed the lower left and upper right panels of the escutcheon. Each contained the full, unstinted, intrinsic symbol of The Family. In each, a hand grasped not four but *five* arrows.

If you hold up against the light the present-day stationery of N. M. Rothschild & Sons, London, you will see, under the contemporary typeface imprinted by the latest electric typewriters, this same old escutcheon. Amid all the heraldic opulence, those five arrows glow the brightest, representing the five demon brothers who, having conquered, now began to reign in five different capitals as five great unofficial kings.

## 3. *The Five Dynasts*

### (a) *Mr. Nathan*

It seems a paradox that Nathan Rothschild, for whose sake The Family had sneaked that extra arrow into the escutcheon, never displayed that escutcheon; never used the baronial title or let himself be thus styled; and never wore any of the various medals bestowed on him in the course of his life.

Actually, his behavior conformed exactly to the clan's dynastic logic. Every brother settled in the country most fitted to his temperament, or else he fitted his temperament to the country. Nathan sensed that liberal England would take poorly to a baron manufactured by absolutist Vienna. As a naturalized British citizen, he was wary of foreign honors. More importantly, he disdained fanfare, flounce and flourish. His forte was not manner but power. Like the English, the master race of shopkeepers, he pocketed continents while grunting dryly about the weather.

Of course, he grunted with a ghetto accent. But that did not keep him from becoming the greatest and most phlegmatic of Whig tycoons. He knew even before Heinrich Heine phrased it that "the main army of Rothschild enemies is made up of have-nots: they all say to themselves, 'What

I have not, Rothschild has.' "

Nathan sensed that the kind of envy his kind of wealth excited could not be smiled or bowed or entertained away. And so he dealt with it through the loaded pistol that always lay under his pillow. He dealt with it through gruffness and bluntness. The Austrian Empire appointed him consul general in London for his enormous influence, not for his diplomatic tact.

Almoners, particularly those acting on behalf of the poor Jews of London, reported that they got thousands, even hundreds of thousands, of pounds out of Mr. Rothschild, but hardly a word and never a courtesy. Other rich men could enjoy their charity. It is, after all, an honor to give much. But not for Nathan Rothschild. He was so renownedly rich that all he could ever give was not enough.

In his own fashion he liked to revenge himself on paupers for giving him such trouble. "Sometimes," he said to his good friend Sir Thomas Buxton, the antislavery leader, "sometimes to amuse myself I give a beggar a guinea. He thinks I have made a mistake, and for fear that I should find him out, off he runs as hard as he can. I advise you to give a beggar a guinea sometimes; it is very amusing."

But he did not shed gold coins on those who knew who he was. A predatory light gleamed in the eyes of porters and footmen as soon as they recognized the stocky, thick-lipped Rothschild silhouette, and this always irritated him. To a bootblack who asked why his tip consisted of a penny when his son always dispensed a shilling, he answered, "The boy has a millionaire father. I don't." The Rothschild penny was the ancestor of the Rockefeller dime.

Art dealers, thriving on millionaires with one tenth of his fortune, had little luck at Mr. Rothschild's house. "Can't throw away money on paintings," he said. And when Nathan said something, no argument, snobbish or esthetic, could unsay it. The world of beauty was irrelevant to him. And snobbery—a fine imitation of self-esteem for those who can't afford the real thing—meant nothing to a man who let a baronage lie fallow. Once an art dealer, equipped with a letter from the Chief Rabbi of England, did make something of a dent. "All right," Nathan said, "give me a thirty-pound picture. I don't care which one. Good-bye."

To the top echelons of society he was not much more suave. "Yesterday," wrote Wilhelm Humboldt to his famous naturalist brother, Alexander, "Rothschild dined with me. He is quite crude and uneducated, but he has a great deal of natural intelligence. He scored off beautifully Major Martins who was being fatuously sentimental about the horrors of war and the large number who had been killed. 'Well,' said Rothschild, 'if they had not all died, Major, you would presumably still be a lieutenant!' "

The Duke of Wellington made a habit of the Rothschild house, and though his Grace could be a magnificent boor himself, he brought along some of the most exquisite gentlemen, and ladies, of the realm. None could ameliorate Nathan's manners. Talleyrand, France's ambassador to the Court of St. James, often visited Rothschild, delighting Nathan's wife with his *ancien régime* courtliness, enchanting the children with the miniature statuary he could fashion from bread lumps. Nothing rubbed off on Nathan.

At a ball given by the Duke of Wellington, the Duke of Montmorency appeared to talk rather pointedly of his long line of ancestors. "So you are the first Christian baron," Nathan rasped before the whole assembly. "I'm the first Jewish baron. That's more interesting, but I make less fuss about it." The ladies blanched. The orchestra quickly struck up a minuet. The Iron Duke smiled.

When Nathan did make a fuss, the Bank of England trembled. He once presented for payment there a draft he had received from his brother Amschel. The bank returned it on the ground that it cashed only its own notes, not those of private individuals.

"Rothschilds are not private individuals!" the banker thundered. His revenge is legendary. He appeared in Threadneedle Street next morning and asked that a ten-pound note be exchanged for gold. An astonished teller complied. Nathan repeated the request all morning, all day long; and so did nine clerks of his, with nine other equally swollen purses at nine other windows. In one day he reduced the bank's gold reserves by almost 100,000 pounds.

At the opening hour of the next day the stout, relentless man was back again with his note-laden clerks. A bank executive appeared and asked, with a nervous laugh, how long this jest was to be kept up?

"Rothschild will continue to doubt the Bank of England's notes," said Nathan, "as long as the Bank of England doubts Rothschild notes."

At Threadneedle Street a directors' meeting was hastily convoked. It declared that henceforth the bank would be pleased to cash any check of the five brothers.

By that time Nathan had already moved his family from New Court, St. Swithin's Lane (now completely absorbed by his offices) to the great mansion at 107 Piccadilly. Informed that his younger daughter, Hannah, possessed musical gifts, he gave her a harp of pure gold, and Rossini and Mendelssohn taught her to pluck sweet sounds from the instrument. His wife filled the halls with treasures, gathered great people around the table. They all came to see this phenomenon which had soared out of the Frankfurt ghetto to the summit of the British Empire. They admired the queer marvel. Some fawned, and more than one became a sincere friend.

Inevitably, sniggers hid beneath certain smiles. It was

then that the ambiguity of his eminence stirred in Nathan. On one such occasion a great violin virtuoso had finished a private recital at 107 Piccadilly. It was the host's duty to pronounce a few words of thanks. "You made beautiful music," said the man with the Jew Street accent. There seemed to be an imperfectly suppressed laugh. Nathan stopped. He jingled some change in his pocket. "That's my music," he then went on. "People listen to it just as carefully. But somehow they don't respect it as much."

In one very practical way (the way he preferred) Nathan was wrong. The most practical form of respect is memory. Today we remember the virtuoso only as background to a Rothschild bon mot. As for Nathan, not only his words but his works endure into our time. The English state loans he issued, to the tune of twelve million pounds, tied his house to His Majesty's Government for generations to come, so that even today the bank at New Court is still gold broker for the Bank of England. He founded the Alliance Insurance Corporation, a giant that still flourishes mightily and is still headed by the London Rothschilds. And the three-million-pound loan with which he saved Brazil's finances still has its repercussions. New Court, in 1962, clips more South American coupons than any other private bank.

A cold self-confidence, a lightning-quick astuteness marked each of his ventures. "I'm an offhand man," he once said to Buxton. "I never lost any time. I came prepared for everything and closed bargains on the spot. . . . I always said to myself, what another man can do, I can do too."

The fact was, of course, that other men could not do what he did. The stock exchange has never known his like before or (with all due respect to Bernard Baruch) since. His darts and feints and intricate ferocities there are about as hard to trace as tracks in a jungle. But we do know that he practiced upon his rivals the gambit of Waterloo with an invincible variety of wiles.

Say, for example, that his brothers' couriers brought him news likely to produce an eventual rise in stock X. By some unostentatious purchases he would accumulate a moderate quantity of the stock. At the same time word would go out from him to each of a number of secretly commissioned agents: buy a bit of X. Then Nathan would suddenly sell his holdings. The mass of speculators, always on the lookout for a bellwether, would begin to watch X worriedly. Whereupon, at a predetermined signal, all Rothschild agents would rid themselves of every X share they had. The speculators would panic. The sudden rush knocked even professionals off their skeptic stance: Nathan's infallibility was once more proved. *Everybody* dumped his X shares. Meanwhile another set of Rothschild agents bought up all the X available at a very depressed price—just prior to the general release of the news that raised the stock higher than ever.

The next time the competition prepared itself for that kind of Nathan trick—only to fall into a trap constructed of opposite elements. You couldn't stop or even comprehend Rothschild, nor even the reason why he, having so much, wanted to conquer more. How many yellow stars imposed on how many ancestral caftans, how many flinchings and humiliations on Frankfurt sidewalks would this man avenge today after driving from New Court to the bourse?

Napoleon on the battlefield was clad in no more dread mystery than Nathan Rothschild on the Royal 'Change. Like Napoleon, he always materialized in the same pose: he leaned against the "Rothschild pillar" (the first on the right as one entered from the Cornhill entrance), hung his heavy hands into his pockets, and began to release silent, motionless, implacable cunning. An anonymous contemporary has described it well:

> Eyes are usually called the windows of the soul. But in Rothschild's case you would conclude that the windows are false ones, or that there was no soul to look out of them. There comes not one pencil of light from the interior, neither is there one gleam of that which comes from without reflected in any direction. The whole puts you in mind of an empty skin, and you wonder why it stands upright without at least something in it. By and by another figure comes up to it. It then steps two paces aside, and the most inquisitive glance that you ever saw, and a glance more inquisitive than you would ever have thought of, is drawn out of the fixed and leaden eye, as if one were drawing a sword from a scabbard. The visiting figure, which has the appearance of coming by accident and not by design, stops just a second or two, in the course of which looks are exchanged which, though you cannot translate, you feel must be of most important meaning. After these the eyes are sheathed up again, and the figure resumes its stony posture.
>
> During the morning numbers of visitors come, all of whom meet with a similar reception and vanish in a similar manner. Last of all the figure itself vanishes, leaving you utterly at a loss. . . .

This sovereign calm never left Nathan. It was his armor against the high world over which he was a ruler without ever having been its equal. The story goes that one day there swept through Nathan's offices in London an august ducal personage. He wore a visage of such fury that no clerk dared stay him. He broke into Nathan's private chamber and shouted his grievance. Nathan, not lifting an eye from his ledger, said, "Take a chair."

The personage, purpling, roared his ancient lineage at the Jew, his illustrious connections, and slapped down a crested card before the banker's nose. Nathan glanced at the card for a fraction of a second.

"Take *two* chairs," he said and continued writing his accounts.

### (b) *Beau James*

If the classic English backdrop of the nineteenth century is the counting house, the classic French one is the drawing room. If Nathan Rothschild became Britain's most formidable business myth, his small red-haired brother, James, cast the longest shadow through the best French salons.

This youngest of Mayer's boys had come to Paris early enough to speak quite well the language in which he loaned. Soon he joked, laughed, and almost scintillated in it. Before long he became an odd but triumphant combination of beau and octopus. His red hair was always carefully curled in the latest dandies' fashion. In 1817, when he was less than twenty-six and had hardly washed the gold dust of the Wellington smuggle off his hands, he already knew how to throw a dinner that included the Austrian ambassador and Paul von Wurttemberg, one of the gayer princes of the blood. Four years later, at the age of twenty-nine, he was considered for the general consulship of the Austrian Empire in Paris—an honor coveted by some pedigreed grand seigneurs.

A confidential report to the Austrian Emperor was decisive:

> It is true that in the decision regarding the appointment of the London Rothschild as Consul . . . your

> Majesty expressly laid down that it would have to continue to be the rule that no Israelite be appointed Consul. Yet if the exception made by your Majesty in favor of the London Rothschild has proved in the highest degree beneficial, it is likely to be no less so in the case of the Paris Rothschild. . . . He is a young man of parts, who is intimately acquainted with several members of the Polytechnical Institute in Paris and of the Conservatoire des Arts et Métiers, as well as with many of the most cultured French manufacturers and businessmen. . . . I cannot suggest a more suitable person for his Majesty. . . .

On August 11, 1821, our young man of parts received the appointment. To house his dignity in style, he bought the magnificent Palais Fouché in rue Laffitte. Formerly occupied by Napoleon's police commissioner (the very one who had once tried to arrest James), it now opened its portals to the finest and most expensive paintings, sculptures, *meubles*—and guests. The youthful Baron could even afford what George IV of England kept trying, vainly, to lure away from him: the ineffable, the historic, the by-ordinary-millionaires-quite-unattainable chef Carême.

But James did not truly begin to reign until he had found a consort. Betty Rothschild, his niece, became not only his bride but his foremost social engine. She was a dark beauty in the grand manner. Ingres painted her in a famous portrait. She excited gallantries in breasts as different as Heinrich Heine's—who immortalized her in a poem called "The Angel"—and General Changarnier, commander-in-chief of the National Guard, whose *sentiment de coeur* for the Baroness furnished some luscious Paris gossip.

At rue Laffitte, Belle Betty and Beau James held a continuous glittering levee. Heine and the general were not the only attendant luminaries. Rossini came almost daily and composed little musicales for Rothschild receptions. Meyerbeer was a close friend. Honoré de Balzac quaffed James's coffee by the liter. The writer had noticed Rothschild at Aix-les-Bains, and made his acquaintance and borrowed his money at almost the same time. The debt was repaid with an amusing story about the creditor, "Roueries d'un Créancier," dedicated to James. Another tale, "L'Enfant Maudit," Balzac inscribed to Betty. At the great novelist's funeral Baron James was among those walking immediately behind the coffin.

Relations between James and George Sand were somewhat more acidulous. At a charity bazaar he kept avoiding the perfume booth manned by the author in her renowned trousers. Finally she left her station to waylay the rich man: Baron James simply must buy a bottle for 5,000 francs.

"What would I do with perfume?" James grinned. "Give me your autograph. I'll sell it and we'll split the proceeds."

Sand wrote a few words on a sheet and handed it to James. It read, "Receipt for ten thousand francs for the benefit of the poor oppressed Poles. George Sand."

Heine, who was watching the baronial face that moment, put his arm around his friend's shoulder and said with mock emotion, "For a great sorrow it is always difficult to find words."

James did not really grieve. His social standing gained if he lost interesting amounts in interesting ways to interesting people. It was his policy to figure in chic anecdotes connected with the *beaux arts*. When Eugène Delacroix wanted to paint him as a beggar, he agreed instantly. The following morning a pauper in rags rang the bell of Delacroix's studio. A disciple answered, looked at the pitiful creature, and sent it away with a franc piece. He thought no more of the incident until twenty-four hours later a liveried servant handed him the following letter: "Dear Sir, You will find enclosed the capital which you gave me at the door to M. Delacroix's studio, with the interest and compound interest on it—a sum of ten thousand francs. You can cash the check at my bank whenever you like. James de Rothschild."

The story enriched his pleasant notoriety. So did the fact that he bought the great Lafite vineyards (for four million francs, or 1,540,000 dollars) merely because their name resembled his Paris address.

For all his Bohemian dalliance, James never forgot to be the richest man in France. His bank, de Rothschild Frères, outpaced every rival. His wealth was estimated at over 600 million francs, or about 150 million francs more than all other French financiers put together. He loaned the King of Portugal twenty-five million francs. He increased the five million francs the King of Belgium had left in his safekeeping to twenty million. He became one of the principal creditors of the French treasury.

Heine wrote:

> I like best to visit the Baron in his office at the bank, where, as a philosopher, I can observe how people . . . bow and scrape before him. It is a contortion of the spine which the finest acrobat would find difficult to imitate. I saw men double up as if they had touched a Voltaic battery when they approached the Baron. Many are overcome with awe at the door of his office, as Moses once was on Mount Horeb, when he discovered that he was on holy ground. Moses took off his shoes, and I am quite certain that a lot of these financial agents would do the same if they did not fear that the smell of their feet would be unpleasant

> to him. This private cabinet of his is a very remarkable spot, inspiring one with lofty ideas, as the sight of the sea or the starry heavens does. Here we see how little man is and how great God!

The passage suggests Heine's ambivalent thoughts about his friend. This German Byron realized he was just another exotic item in the great Rothschild collection. Once, when James threw a great feast for a select company of bankers, the poet was invited to brighten the dessert with intellectual display. Dessert arrived, but not Heine. A footman, sent to his lodgings, brought back Heine's regrets to James: "M. le Baron, I usually take my coffee where I have had my dinner."

In the same mood he would write: ". . . I went to see M. de Rothschild, and saw a gold-laced lackey bringing the baronial chamber pot along the corridor. Some speculator from the bourse, who was passing, reverently lifted his hat to the impressive vessel. . . . I have committed the name of the man to memory. I am quite sure that he will become a millionaire in the course of time."

There were commentaries still sharper than that. Ludwig Börne was, like Heine, a prominent German writer resident in Paris; like James, he had been brought up on Frankfurt's Jew Street. He bore down sardonically on those other local boys made good:

> Would it not be a great blessing for the world if all the kings were dismissed and the Rothschild family put on their thrones? Think of the advantages. The new dynasty would never contract a loan, as it would know better than anybody how dear such things are, and on this account alone the burden on their subjects would be alleviated by several millions a year. The bribing, both active and passive, of minis-

ters would have to cease; why should they be bribed any longer, or what would there be to bribe them with? All that sort of thing would be ancient history, and morality would be greatly promoted.

In point of fact, all French kings after Napoleon (except Louis XVIII, who died in office) *were* dismissed. James participated crucially in every reign. But as each ruler toppled, the Baron emerged more powerful than ever. He and Betty ran a salon so lavishly balanced that it always rode the crest, no matter what the wave.

On July 31, 1830, for example, the rule of Charles X suddenly collapsed. It seemed only logical that Baron James would harmoniously collapse with it. In many ways he had been the monetary arm of the regime. The Bourbon had entrusted to him the conversion of a series of 5 per cent state loans into 3 per cent—a gigantic deal. He had financed the Bourbon side of the Spanish civil war of the 1820's. The badge he wore of the Legion of Honor was pinned on him by a Bourbon. To all intents and purposes, he was an integral part of the Bourbon plague.

At any rate Rothschild appeared quite unprepared for the change that threatened in July, 1830. His rivals took obvious precautions, but Beau James gave balls attended by the Duke of Chartres and the Duke of Brunswick. He seemed to sleep through the summer dawn while barricades mushroomed in the streets, the old king fled and the people cheered into power Louis Philippe, son of the famous Philippe Egalité of the Revolution and himself a supposedly zealous proponent of liberal ideas. Conservative Rothschild seemed in for a brute awakening.

Then—surprise!—a month after the overturn a deputation called on the "Citizen King" to congratulate him on ascending the throne. And who should be among them but Baron Rothschild? Who was signaled to remain behind after the ceremony was over, who was given the honor of a long, intimate chat? James, that Bourbon conspirator, turned out to be a long-time friend, dinner companion and financial advisor to the newest Majesty.

Louis Philippe was even more *nouveau* to the purple than James to multimillionairedom. Out of this fact Rothschild welded a powerful camaraderie between two self-made men. Under his flatteries the new king's reign turned into a paradise for the *haut bourgeoisie*. The Baron's star shone high. De Rothschild Frères was given a virtual monopoly on all state loans; it handled Louis Philippe's private investment accounts. James became a shaper of French foreign policy. The royal presence often graced Betty's parties. Her husband now received the Grand Cross of the Legion of Honor.

Eighteen years later the barricades were up again. Again James, apparently unconcerned, seemed to dance into the very muzzles of the revolution. On February 23, 1848, he attended a ball at the Austrian ambassador's. On February 24 the Citizen King fled. Mobs began to loot the Palais Royal, to destroy the royal castle at Neuilly and to burn capitalist pleasances like the Rothschild villa at Suresnes.

James sent his wife and daughter to the safety of London. He also paid 250,000 francs to M. Ledry-Rollin, Interior Minister of the Revolution, "for patriotic purposes." Furthermore he wrote and publicized a letter to the provisional government which today hangs in the office of Baron Guy de Rothschild. In it James offers to give 50,000 francs to those wounded in the street fighting. The letter is dated February 25—the very first day of the post-Louis Philippe era. He was still the old magician. He had lost nothing in speed, calm and efficiency since the days of the Wellington gold smuggle. And he still came out on top. After a few weeks, even fanatical republicans considered him indispensable.

The editor of the radical *Tocsin de Travailleurs* wrote:

> You are a wonder, sir. Louis Philippe has fallen, the constitutional monarchy and parliamentary methods have gone by the board. . . . But you have survived. The banking princes are going in liquidation and their offices are closed. The great captains of industry and the railway companies totter. Shareholders, merchants, manufacturers and bankers are ruined en masse; big men and little men are alike overwhelmed; you alone among all these ruins remain unaffected. . . . Wealth fades away, glory is humbled and dominion is broken, but . . . the monarch of our time has held his throne; but that is not all. You might have fled this country where, in the language of your Bible, the mountains skip about like rams. You remain, announcing that your power is independent of ancient dynasties, and courageously extend your hand. . . . Undismayed you adhere to France. . . . You are more than a statesman, you are a symbol of credit. Is it not time that the bank, that powerful instrument of the middle classes, should assist in the fulfillment of the people's destiny? . . . After gaining the crown of money, you would achieve the apotheosis. Does that not appeal to you?

It did not—once more for shrewd reasons. The ministers whose ranks James had been invited to join were replaced in turn. Louis Napoleon swept them away when he was elected President of France in December, 1848. Four years later he proclaimed himself Napoleon III, by the grace of God and the will of the people, Emperor of the French.

But now James really seemed stranded. He had no positive connection with *this* new power. Quite the contrary.

Everyone knew how he and his brothers had made their first great fortunes at the expense of Napoleon I, the present Bonaparte's uncle. And as if that were not sufficient, Louis Napoleon's favorite financiers were James's worst rivals.

The Baron, however, was his usual unfazed self. "Ah," he is reported to have said with a smile when the news broke that Achille Fould, his archenemy, had been appointed the new Napoleon's finance minister. "I think I smell a new Waterloo."

It was a premature remark. The battle into which he launched now was so long and so intricately vehement that a separate chapter must accommodate it. And yet the long run proved Beau James right. The history of Rothschild is the history of other people's Waterloos.

## (c) *King Salomon*

Quite early in the nineteenth century his Highness, Prince Metternich, Chancellor of Austria, had some public thoughts about bankers who interfered in matters of state. "The House of Rothschild," he said, "plays a much bigger role in France than any foreign government. . . . There are, of course, reasons for it which seem to me neither good nor gratifying: money is the great motive force in France, and corruption is quite openly reckoned with. . . . Among us [in Austria] this commodity finds but few friends."

For the *mishpoche* those were hardly hospitable words. Austria still maintained an anti-Semitic hauteur. In contrast to England and France, the Jews were not permitted to own land anywhere in the Habsburg domains. They could not serve in the government or the courts of justice.

The practice of law was closed to them, as was the teaching profession or any kind of political function. Jewish marriages, restricted in number, required special permission. A Jew must pay poll tax and report regularly to the "Jewish Office." If he was of foreign nationality, he was given a residence permit good for a short period only. In fact, the Austrian police bore down so conscientiously on aliens of the wrong religion that the clan did not risk sending a representative to the Congress of Vienna. Waterloo came and went, and no Rothschild had got within earshot of an Austrian minister.

But after the explosion at Aix, the Danube became ripe for The Family. It acted with its usual dynastic prudence. The precisely most suitable brother assumed charge of the Habsburg department. He was not an ill-humored daredevil like Nathan; not a luxuriant dandy à la James. Those two would not have done nearly so well in the lofty shadows of the Hofburg. No, it was Salomon who went forth. Among all Mayer's sons, he most favored the father. A courtier by temperament, his specialty was ingratiation. He could talk to Austria's hallowed nobility as though they all sat perched in a splendid forest of family trees. Last, not least, he was a diplomat.

No foreign minister could have planned his first move toward Vienna better. Casually he hinted to an Austrian official that the entire House of Rothschild might shift the center of its worldwide operations from Frankfurt to a more congenial place elsewhere. This inspired a confidential report which shortly afterwards reached some exalted desks. On September 26, 1819, the minister of the interior of the Empire, asked to comment on the matter by the finance minister, replied:

> Your Excellency must be aware that foreign Israelites may reside here only on obtaining the special

> "toleration" permit . . . special exceptions can be made only with the personal approval of the Emperor. Meanwhile your Excellency may rest assured that we are far too well aware of the advantages that would in many respects accrue to the Imperial State of Austria through the settlement of such an eminent firm within its borders not to advise his Majesty most emphatically to give his consent as soon as a formal application in this matter is received.

The house *in toto* did not move, of course. Salomon journeyed alone to Vienna, where he received a residence permit in expectation that the entire business of all the brothers was to follow. And though he only opened a firm of his own, disappointment never had a chance to set in. Salomon had a way with negative sentiments. Before the government could catch its breath, he floated an Austrian state loan of some fifty-five million gulden as an Austrian loan had never been floated before.

It took the form of a lottery, an unusual and attractive feature. But that was just the beginning of Salomon's wisdom. He released only a fraction of the issue. Not a word was said about there being much more to come. The thing was to appetize, not to gorge, the Viennese investing public. And he made the hors d'œuvre even more palatable by anticipating the mouth-watering arts of Madison Avenue. A public-relations campaign began. Articles in newspapers praised thrift, advised the investor, broadcast the meaning and the rewards of high finance. The issue rose mightily. When Salomon announced another thirty-five-millions worth of bonds, there was surprise, anger—and finally a rush to buy.

Everyone who got hold of the issue gained; most of all, Salomon. The operation, he was to confess later, had netted him six million gulden. Such profits, of course, were apt to produce a little indignation. But it was not easy to stay indignant at the man. He bore himself so simply and modestly. Since he could not own a house, he rented a single room at the Römischer Kaiser, one of the city's better hotels.

True, he soon rented another room, and then another, and then an entire floor, until—by accident, as it were—he had hired all of the hotel. The parties he gave here were terribly pleasant and *sympatisch* to a select roster of guests that soon included Metternich himself.

In an unpretentious way Salomon's inn radiated amusement, advice, even practical help. The Rothschilds' early Frankfurt rival, Moritz Bethmann, visited Vienna in the early 1820's and came away amazed. "Salomon has won the people's affection here," he said, "partly through his general modesty and partly through his readiness to be obliging. Nobody leaves him without being comforted."

The persons Salomon comforted became steadily more important and profitable. In 1825 he was called upon to finance Europe's most delicate *affaire d'amour*. It involved no less than the Archduchess Marie Louise, daughter of the Austrian Emperor and wife of the exiled Napoleon. The Congress of Vienna had considered her victimized by an errant deportee of a husband; as compensation, she got the dukedoms of Parma, Piacenza and Guastalla. For additional relief Metternich provided a manly young majordomo named General Adam Albert von Neipperg. The General wore a black eye-patch (the result of a sword thrust during the war), had considerable social gifts and diverted the Archduchess so well that on May 1, 1817, and again on August 8, 1819, two events took place, both blessed.

Both were also clandestine, because Napoleon, far

away on St. Helena while being fruitfully cuckolded, did not die until May, 1821. The children of so august a womb had to wait many months before they came into anything like an official life. Their births were not registered. Their nannies nursed them in closed-off castle halls. Until Marie Louise's secret morganatic marriage to the General in September, 1821, she pretended even to her imperial father that little Albertine and little William Albert simply did not exist.

The tots were the bastard offspring of an adulterous union, but they were also the grandchildren of the Emperor of Austria. His Majesty created them the Counts von Montenuovo, this name being the Italian equivalent of Neipperg (Neu-berg, or "new mountain"). Besides a name, they also needed a fitting inheritance. Their mother's dukedom—a kind of hardship grant—was not hereditary. Something had to be done, in a soundproof way.

Something was. Salomon Rothschild tiptoed into the picture. It became his assignment to conjure a safe, no-risk patrimony for the Montenuovos without selling any of their mother's lands; without an unpopular increase in Parma's public debts; without raising an undue commotion.

At the Römischer Kaiser the hotel tenant got busy with his army of clerks. As usual, he found an ingeniously comfortable solution. Marie Louise was to declare that she had spent much of her private revenue on an itemized list of public buildings in Parma; that as reimbursement she took some ten million francs of state funds for herself, a sum to be instantly converted into bonds by Rothschild and sold on Marie Louise's behalf to a great number of different people in different countries. Some four of the ten million would be reapplied for public purposes, so that, as Salomon stated, "any bad impression . . . would be counteracted by the argument . . . that the proceeds went to projects bene-

Baron Philippe de Rothschild and his daughter Philippine entering the church at Pauillac on her wedding day, 1961.

Baron Elie de Rothschild (left) with the late Aly Khan at the Chantilly races, 1951.

The Rothschild family's original house in the ghetto of Frankfurt on Main.

Gutele Rothschild
in old age.

Nathan Rothschild,
founder of the London branch.

Salomon Rothschild,
founder of the Vienna branch.

James (Jacob) Rothschild,
founder of the Paris branch.

Amschel Rothschild,
of the Frankfurt branch.

Carl (Kalmann) Rothschild,
founder of the Naples branch.

Early 19th-century caricature of Nathan at his "Rothschild pillar" on the London Exchange.

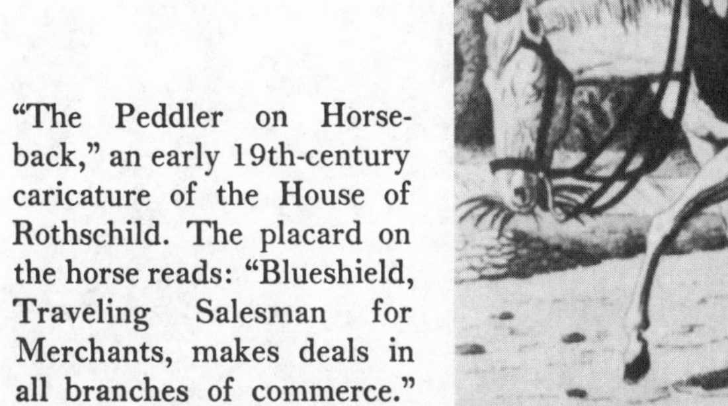

"The Peddler on Horseback," an early 19th-century caricature of the House of Rothschild. The placard on the horse reads: "Blueshield, Traveling Salesman for Merchants, makes deals in all branches of commerce."

"A Rothschild Wedding," an 1826 water color by Richard Dighton, depicting Nathan of London (bald man), his son Lionel (extreme right), his daughters Hannah and Louise, and (seated) the bridal couple: Anselm of Vienna and Nathan's eldest daughter, Charlotte; at left, two unidentified wedding guests.

Carl Rothschild's wife and child in an early 19th-century Italian portrait.

An experimental ride on Salomon von Rothschild's Austrian railway, 1839.

Salomon with a rail map of the project.

"Full Cry," an 1855 painting by Sir Francis Grant, showing Baron Lionel (on white horse) and his three brothers hunting with the Rothschild Staghounds in the Vale of Aylesbury.

Baron Lionel de Rothschild (top hat) takes his seat in the House of Commons, 1858. (From a contemporary magazine drawing.)

Contemporary Austrian caricature showing Napoleon III (right) and Baron James de Rothschild on the occasion of the Emperor's state visit to Ferrières in 1862. The word "Anlehen" on the money bags means "loans."

The Ingres portrait of Betty de Rothschild, (daughter of Salomon of Vienna) who married James of Paris in 1824. (From the collection of Baron Guy de Rothschild.)

Nathaniel,
the first Lord Rothschild
("Lord Natty").

Leopold de Rothschild.

Max Beerbohm caricature of Alfred de Rothschild, 1907. Sir Max's caption reads: "A Quiet Morning in the Tate Gallery. The Curator trying to expound to one of the Trustees the spiritual fineness of Mr. William Rothenstein's 'Jews Mourning in a Synagogue.'"

Alfred de Rothschild.

Waddesdon Manor.

Baron Alphonse de Rothschild of Ferrières,
at the turn of the century.

Baron Louis de Rothschild,
last head of the Austrian house.

James Armand ("Jimmy")
de Rothschild,
mounted for the Whaddon Chase
point-to-point race, 1939.

Baron Edmond de Rothschild, from a picture postcard sold in Palestine in the 1920's.

Baron Henri de Rothschild on his 1,000-ton yacht, the *Eros*, in 1934.

Baron Maurice de Rothschild with Dolores del Rio at Santa Barbara, California, in the early 1930's.

Baron Eugene de Rothschild, dean of the family today, with his wife, the former Jeanne Stuart, at their home in Long Island after their wedding in 1952.

Baroness Philippe de Rothschild,
the former Pauline Potter,
at Chateau Mouton, 1961.

Baroness Louis de Rothschild,
the former Countess Hilda
von Auersperg, 1961.

Above a label designed by Georges Braque for Baron Philippe's Mouton Rothschild wine, and below the Lafite-Rothschild label showing the chateau.

Christopher Fry (left) with his French translator, Baron Philippe de Rothschild, 1960.

Two Rothschild arrivals in New York: Below, Baron Edouard, head of the French house, reaches America in 1940 after a flight from Lisbon with his wife, Germaine, and his daughter, Bethsabée, all refugees from Occupied France. Right, Baron Edouard's son, Guy, lands at Idlewild Airport in 1957. He is the present head of de Rothschild Frères, once more the paramount private bank in France.

ficial to the community. . . ." The rest of the moneys would be the little Montenuovos' legacy, secure from anybody who might question their right to it or their ticklish genealogy.

"It is quite important," wrote Salomon to Metternich, ". . . that the claims of the Archduchess' legal heirs cannot be disputed. The preparation of bearer bonds (issued by an eminent firm like Rothschild's), the holders of which will be constantly changing, seems to me to meet any possible eventuality." A weapon more modern and more powerful than a great army's ten thousand muskets would prevent seizure of such bonds or of the money received for them —the Rothschilds' hell weapon: loss of international credit standing.

"All governments," Salomon continued, "who have an interest in maintaining an inviolate credit system would use their influence to prevent such a thing from being done. . . . I am pleased to say that I am confident of arranging this matter to the full satisfaction of her Majesty the Archduchess and of his Majesty the Emperor and King."

When it came to investing the sum thus produced, Metternich extended to the Archduchess "the guarantee that your Majesty cannot do better than act in accordance with Rothschild's suggestion."

Was this the same lofty prince who had once sniffed at a Rothschild's interference in France?

Now the first minister of the continent's first empire went to great lengths to avoid crossing the Jew Street boy. The year of the Marie Louise affair, Salomon intimated that he would like to have a decoration conferred on his coreligionist and executive employee, von Wertheimstein. A *démarche* from a great kingdom could not have aroused more wary diplomacy from Metternich.

To Marie Louise's husband he wrote:

> Herr von Rothschild wants a little St. George (of the order of Constantine) for his managing clerk. . . . I feel that it is not in the best of taste . . . that such an order be conferred upon a clerk, and I suggest that you reply that the order of Constantine constitutes a genuine religious brotherhood, and is not simply a distinction, and, as the Jewish religion forbids its adherents to take the statutory oath of the order, the chancellor of the order would not be able to confer the cross. Temper your refusal with appropriate expressions of your extreme regret, and the matter will be disposed of. Write to Herr Salomon on these lines, but do not mention me, as nobody can take offense at a statutory provision, while a single personal remark can do untold mischief, and I myself have committed the great offense of making it impossible for the Rothschild family to obtain an Austrian decoration. If he thought I was implicated he would regard me as a positive cannibal.

The Metternich-Rothschild alliance endured. In 1835 a deathbed intrigue in the Imperial palace welded it still closer. During the early March days of that year, old Emperor Francis was bled three times, and still his fever increased and his lung inflammation grew worse. Not only the life of a man but the future of the Empire trembled in the dark halls of the Vienna Hofburg.

Chancellor Metternich was the dying Francis' strong man. Ferdinand, his heir, had somewhat less-than-normal brains and seemed likely to be influenced by his uncles, Archdukes Joseph, Carl and John—all Highnesses of a not necessarily pro-Metternich bent. Count Kolowrat, the chancellor's opponent, began to loom large in the hushed proceedings by the Emperor's bed. On the bourse the sudden uncertainty produced a panic that rattled the economic foundations of Metternich's government.

Chancellor and banker bestirred themselves. Metternich summoned Bishop Wagner, the Emperor's confessor, to his office. Here a will was drafted containing the provision: "I hereby name ——— as the man whom I most emphatically commend to my son as a loyal counselor worthy of his fullest confidence." The Bishop took the paper to Francis' chamber, and the failing Emperor inserted with his own hand the right name in the right space just before he died at midnight on March 2, 1835.

Not only that: speaking about advice within the family, the imperial will took the extra precaution of passing over the Archdukes Joseph, Carl and John; and instead enjoined Emperor Ferdinand to resort to his youngest uncle, Archduke Ludwig—who was almost as weak and malleable as Ferdinand, the ultramalleable, himself.

While Metternich put things in order at the palace, Salomon (who was kept *au courant* on the latest developments) sped to the bourse. He announced that he had the greatest confidence in the continuity and prosperity of the government. He went further and lined up James in Paris. Both brothers made a radical offer. If anyone wanted to sell any Austrian securities, they would buy them instantly, at the top price of the day. The market listened. The market calmed. The pro-Metternich investors carried the day.

"I must admit," reported Metternich's ambassador from Paris, "that the enormous influence exercised by the House of Rothschild succeeded in immediately curing the panic which had begun to affect nervous spirits."

Some spirits did remain a trifle fidgety. "It is quite well known," a high government officer wrote in his diary, "that the new Emperor's illness has made him feeble-minded. He is prepared to sign anything that is put before him. We now have an absolute monarchy without a monarch."

There was an absolute chancellor, however, in the form of Prince Metternich. And there was Rothschild, his absolute banker. Nothing withstood Salomon. David Parish, that most fashionable of Central European bankers, with whom The Family had been thrilled to conclude an alliance a few years earlier at Aix—David Parish went bankrupt and jumped into the Danube. Other great Viennese banks, like that of Geymueller, crashed. Salomon survived at their expense and waxed.

Through a complicated series of transactions he obtained the lease of Austria's huge mercury mines in Idria. The only other known mercury deposit was in Spain, with whose government Nathan happened to be negotiating at the moment. Couriers careered between the brothers' offices, and soon the House of Rothschild exercised a world monopoly in a key metal, whose price they fixed at will.

Salomon was also the chief banker behind Lloyd, Austria's big steamship line. He financed the first important Central European railways, a quaint and important event of which more in a separate chapter. He became as dazzling a myth as James or Nathan. His first two initials, S. M., happened to be the same as the Austrian abbreviation for his Majesty ("Seine Majestät"), and a popular saying spoke of two local suzerains, Emperor Ferdinand and King Salomon. It was more than a joke. Among the people besieging Salomon's office were those who begged a royal "laying on of hands." King Salomon only had to touch his palm to some bond or stock, and its owner went away certain of its rise.

And yet he knew no rest. After all this he was still a Jew in a very gentile Austria. He was still a hotel guest, although a most glorified one. His brothers luxuriated in castles, and he, who was as infinitely rich as they—was he to leave behind a dynasty living on room service?

By immense charities (from the erection of whole hospitals to subsidizing the municipal water supply) and by immense pressures, he forced Vienna to make him the legal equal of his valet. He became a full-fledged citizen. Now he could *buy* the Hotel Römischer Kaiser. But he was a Rothschild. His retinue would not fit into a single building. He could easily afford a domain on a par with those of the greatest princes in the Empire. By way of the next step he first coleased and, once more by special permission, subsequently bought outright the immense coal and iron works of Vitkovitz in Silesia. Under Hitler and even in our day this purchase was to produce dramatic repercussions. In the second quarter of the nineteenth century Vitkovitz meant to Salomon the possession of industrial real estate—which was almost, but not quite, as good as being a regular landed magnate.

Yet no less than a regular landed magnate Salomon burned to be. Soon a brief was brought before the Emperor for the acquisition of a Rothschild demesne in Moravia. Instantly the nobles of the province were up in arms. Their privilege to be shared, and thus defiled, by a Jew!

Salomon sighed. It would have to be the old room-by-room technique of the Römischer Kaiser all over again. He smoothed the jeers off noble lips by putting something pleasant into noble hands. From Prince Esterhazy on down, practically every other aristocrat began to enjoy his loans. He made himself more serviceable than ever to his old friend Metternich. In the vivacious Countess Melanie Zichy-Ferraris, the Chancellor married his third wife and a Rothschild debtor. There was now a great deal of just plain social entertaining back and forth between the Metternichs' Schloss Johannisberg and Salomon's house in Vienna; "our Salomon" Melanie did not hesitate to call him even before the Emperor. Baroness James de Rothschild of Paris got Melanie frocks; Baroness Kalmann in Naples sent Melanie picturesque scarves; from London came Rothschild gifts in the form of exquisite plant cuttings. There were all these pleasant things. There were Salomon's incomparable philanthropies (the governor of Silesia reported that the institutions set up by Salomon in Vitkovitz were "a blessing and model for the whole country"). And there were unobtrusive but unflagging hints.

In 1843 it came to pass. The last bulwark of prerogative opened. Salomon received permission to purchase inheritable agricultural real estate. He bought, almost at once, four huge and splendid demesnes in Moravia, Prussia and Silesia, all complete with castles, moats, waterfalls, lakes, swans, peacocks, cattle, grottoes, kennels, stables, stud farms and game preserves. Abruptly he had become one of the largest landed proprietors of the realm.

He became more. During the sudden drop on the Vienna bourse in October, 1845, he happened to be attending a Family conference in Frankfurt. An express message conveyed through the Austrian minister begged him to return. The Chancellor cried that it was essential for the state's finances that either Salomon or a deputy in the form of another Rothschild be in constant residence in Vienna. Salomon's bodily presence had grown indispensable to Austria.

That is, to Metternich's Austria. But what if the time of the absolute chancellor were drawing to an end? What would then become of the absolute banker?

In February, 1848, Louis Philippe fell off the throne of France, to the temporary discomfiture of his friend James de Rothschild. Salomon was not pleased, either. The clangor from the Paris barricades rose with such sudden democratic fury that it was heard in Vienna's innermost drawing rooms. His Majesty's first minister was now in his seventy-sixth year, but his ear remained acute. "If the devil fetches me," Metternich said to old Salomon, "he will fetch you too."

At eight o'clock in the evening of March 13, his Highness was fetched. All day long the citizenry marched through the streets, burning the Chancellor in effigy. Metternich resigned. Twenty hours later the bearer of Europe's most formidable name fled to Frankfurt with a thousand ducats' cash loan from Salomon plus a Rothschild letter of credit.

The financier's turn came in a few months. On October 6 another insurrectionary mob broke into the Römischer Kaiser to besiege the nearby Arsenal. S. M. took flight to Germany and never came back, even after order was restored.

Yet the devil could fetch him only as a person, not as a Rothschild. First and last Salomon incarnated the clan, which continued the Vienna house in the resplendent incarnation of Anselm, his son. Great families are not nearly so perishable as great men. The absolute chancellor, too, had descendants. Each year the present Prince Metternich sends a case of his Schloss Johannisberg wine, the Rhineland's greatest vintage, to Baron Elie de Rothschild of Paris. Each year Elie reciprocates with a choice shipment of his Château Lafite, one of the great Bordeaux labels. Each year the two families visit each other's palaces.

So far, at least, the nobs have outlasted the mobs.

### (d) *Carl, the* Mezzuzah *Baron*

"Rothschild has just kissed the Pope's hand," wrote a nasty pen in 1832, "and at his departure expressed his satisfaction with the successor of St. Peter in the most gracious terms. . . . Others must bend down to the Holy Father's toe, but Rothschild is given the finger."

The most interesting feature of the event in question was not the fact that Rothschild kissed something better and more expensive than common mortals could, but that the Rothschild so honored was called Carl—a name hitherto not prominent among the stars of The Family.

Carl (known as Kalmann in the early phases of his career) was slow to develop the worldly fluency, the incisiveness and dispatch of Nathan, James or Salomon. Quiet in manner, almost awkward in speech, paunchier even than the Rothschild norm, he clung most strictly to Jewish observance. Before the ceremonial kiss at the Vatican, Carl's Family nickname was "*mezzuzah* boy"—*mezzuzahs* being the miniature Torah scrolls affixed to doorways. The faithful Jew kisses them at the start of a journey, and Carl's early life consisted of traveling. He acted as the clan's chief courier. Until March, 1821, he remained without portfolio. Then, when The Family had too many satrapies and not enough satraps, the brothers resorted to him.

It all began with the Congress of Laibach, a political festival characteristic of the period, attended by Europe's greatest sovereigns. At Laibach it was decided to restore the absolutist, therefore "legitimate," Bourbon kingdom in Naples. The assembled monarchs authorized the intervention of an Austrian army for that purpose. Naturally the Rothschilds were asked to handle the military subsidies.

But which Rothschild? Nathan of London showed little gusto for an antiliberal venture; besides, he was deeply involved in negotiating several million-pound issues. James of Paris happened to be busy propping up the French Bourbons with mountains of francs. Amschel of Frankfurt could not get away from financing postwar reconstruction in German lands. As for Salomon of Vienna, he was up to his neck in his lottery loans, which gave him as much work and publicity as he could handle.

"I feel it my duty to avoid anything which could attract attention," he begged off to Metternich. "A journey to Laibach at this time would arouse such attention."

Only one brother was left, about whom nobody much knew or cared. *Un petit frère Rothschild*, the Austrian finance minister called him, though he was actually four years older than James. Did The Family, on delegating him, realize that it was creating the financial overlord of the Italian peninsula? For that is precisely what he became. As soon as the *mezzuzah* boy was given a challenge of Rothschild proportions, he unleashed a Rothschild performance. At Laibach he quickly worked out the main features of the subsidy: Vienna was to advance a loan to Naples, which would defray with it the costs of the Austrian occupation.

Rothschild, in brief, went about its usual task of converting crises into bonds. But this time Carl was to man the controls. He began to lay the groundwork and did a neat extra chore on the side. Before their parting, the King of Naples borrowed a few thousand gulden from the Emperor of Austria. Carl expedited the fancy transaction. No less than his brothers, he was now a banker to monarchs.

No less astonishing than his brothers' was his agility. Right after Laibach, a semi-Jacobite uprising broke out in a northern Italian state. Carl flew to his Neapolitan Majesty, who was jittering in Florence. Carl had always been fast for a man of his heavy contours, but now the heat of the job was rapidly thawing a heretofore dull tongue. All eloquence, he predicted that Austrian dragoons would soon trample this sedition underfoot. They did.

All firmness, he pushed his uncertain Bourbon southward.

He was all strength when he reached Naples. He had to be. An Italian money syndicate claimed it could bring off the military-loan operation at a smaller expense to the kingdom. Carl had prompt recourse to the commanding Austrian general—and emerged as sole floater of the loan.

By 1827 Carl's new-founded bank had become a Neapolitan institution that paid the troops that kept the king in power. Carl spoke with a powerful voice to, and for, the local court. Earlier, he had been Austria's monetary arm in Naples. Now he turned into Naples' most important advocate with Vienna. After the royal position had been fortified, it was Carl's argument which moved Metternich to evacuate the kingdom.

Inevitably, Carl's counting house became the greatest in the land. He affixed his *mezzuzahs* to the finest palace on the Vesuvian shore. The native aristocracy repaired here for his lavish entertainments. The Duke of Lucca, Leopold of Saxe-Coburg (afterward the first king of Belgium), and every visiting grand seigneur drank and feasted with the newest Rothschild: the Italian one. His money flowed through the treasuries of most Italian states. It helped the Grand Duke of Tuscany drain the Tuscan marshlands. It went to the Kingdom of Sardinia in a series of thirteen state loans amounting to over twenty-two million pounds. And it fertilized the Pope's domains.

To be sure, Carl insisted on the official promise that the Vatican's anti-Jewish attitude would be reformed. And even in some contractual documents he could bring himself to speak of the Holy See only as "the Roman State." Nonetheless, his unbaptized ducats were not disdained. On January 10, 1832, the event came to pass with which his story started here. Pope Gregory XVI received Carl von Rothschild, gave him his hand rather than the customary toe to kiss, and pinned the order of St. George on the lapel of the Kosher Baron.

### (e) *Amschel of the Flowers*

The four brothers discussed so far shared certain characteristics: a steaming commercial libido; a leaping, grasping vibrancy. Until their death they possessed—or rather, were possessed by—relentless youthfulness. Amschel was different, and not only because he was a thin man. His image comes down to us redolent with the musky air of an old high priest's chamber.

When patriarch Mayer died, Amschel, as his eldest son, inherited the bank in Frankfurt, the position as head of the family and his father's curious ways. To each of these legacies he did justice.

He remained in the native city though it was soon overshadowed by his brothers' great capitals, though "Hepp! Hepp!"—immemorial cry of the German pogrom—kept crashing through the streets. With a snap of his finger Amschel could have raised palaces in more genteel lands. But he stayed and patiently picked up the stones which shattered his windowpanes.

Once an anti-Semitic mob gathered before his great house, now far from Jew Street. Amschel appeared on a balcony to face them. "My dear friends," he said, "you want money from the rich Jew. There are forty million Germans. I have about as many florins. As a start, I'll drop a florin to each of you." The mob cupped hands, caught and went.

In some ways, Amschel spent the rest of his life telling the mob to go home. He became the grand almoner and grand protector to the German Jews; he helped sweep away the chains of Jew Street; he pressed, in the end successfully, for the Jews' enfranchisement as free citizens of Frankfurt.

Amschel was the first of the Rothschilds. It was his chore to apply for honors and consulships on his brothers' behalf; to condole or congratulate emperors and kings; to be spokesman for the Great Five. There is a poetic fitness in the fact that the formal head of the family should be the most ancestral of them all. In Amschel (he would not tolerate the compromise which changed Jacob to James and Kalmann to Carl) the medieval vein of the ghetto ran strongest.

Long after he had under his command a whole battery of literate clerks, he insisted on composing letters laced with archaic figures and Yiddish misspellings. His habit of addressing the British Commissary General as "the most High Herr Comishair" amused his brothers and the Comishair as well. It was, underneath all courtesies, his way of being himself. Later, as Rothschild communications reached the imperial level, he had to filter this self of his through scribes and calligraphers. Nevertheless, congratulating Chancellor Metternich on the recovery of Emperor Francis from illness, he ended, ". . . and may it ever be my fortune in deepest reverence to call myself your Highness' most humble and obedient servant . . ." —which recalls his father's flourishes and also, perhaps, old Mayer's secret grin.

Amschel continued still another tradition of Mayer's: the bond with the House of Hesse. Once the connection had consisted of the fortune entrusted by Landgrave William to Mayer. Now the money streamed the other way. Mayer's son financed William's son. Often Amschel would walk the streets in his ghetto dress—his favorite form of exercise—and suddenly drop in at his Serenity's palace for lunch. His Highness and family were always prepared, with special kosher dishes. "They would," an astonished city chronicler states, "take their midday meal quite *en famille* with their business friend."

Other German princes also held out their hands to Amschel, palm upward. He became treasurer of the German Confederation meeting in Frankfurt, and thus in a sense the first finance minister of the Prussian Empire ultimately born of the Confederation. As the giant among German bankers, he had his finger in every investment pie east of the Rhine and north of the Danube. Hundreds of German factories, railways, highways began with a ledger calculation in his offices at Frankfurt's Fahrgasse.

He lived, as it behooved him, on a princely scale. He had a number of titles and decorations, though as a rule he wore only the ribbon of the Court of Hesse and liked to be addressed simply as "Herr Baron." All foreign visitors to Frankfurt, including the diplomats accredited there, treated him with great distinction. They flocked to the great dinners he gave, honored him at banquets in return. But Amschel ate only kosher food, and he had no flair for social enjoyment.

"A strange man," said one of his acquaintances, "a person of thoroughly Oriental physiognomy, with old Hebrew manners and habits. His hat is usually pushed back onto his neck, his coat is open and falls negligently over his shoulders. . . . Like a chief dervish he sits on a raised platform among his clerks, his secretaries at his feet, and his agents bustling about him. . . . No one is ever allowed to speak privately to him about business; everything is discussed openly in the office, as in the old Rhine courts."

Amschel's business hours were as long as his clerks', his leisure time less. Even when he went to the theater, he was often called away to hear the report of a courier freshly arrived in Frankfurt. At night he would be wakened in his bed to read and answer dispatches from Vienna, Paris, London, Naples; he had a bedside desk for the purpose. Being a business genius of the first rank, he could decide instantly on any offer, oral or written, giving his opinion in a few words. When once he had uttered his brief decision, nothing ever induced him to say another word on the matter.

Unlike his brothers, Amschel wore his wealth and power in a crotchety, joyless, somehow monkish way. "I have never seen any man so distressed," commented a contemporary, "beat his breast so much and implore the mercy of heaven, as Baron Rothschild on the long day [Day of Atonement] in the synagogue. He often faints from the strain of interminable prayer, and strong-smelling plants from his gardens are then brought and put under his nose to bring him around. In earlier years he inflicted severe mortification on himself in order to prevail upon heaven to grant him a child, but it turned out to be in vain."

There was the rub; there throbbed the pain. A love-parched, child-parched marriage weighed Amschel down. Of the five Rothschild branches, the central house in Frankfurt would not continue in the direct line.

Amschel beat his head against his sonlessness. He tried prayer, he tried endless good works. His official charities—over 20,000 gulden yearly—amounted to nine times the total annual income of Goethe's very well-to-do family. The Jewish Hospital in Frankfurt lived on his contributions, and so did most of the poorer families in Jew Street.

But apart from his regular largesse, he gave away unnumbered small sums at all hours of the day, particularly when walking or riding through the city. His benefactions continued even while he ate. More than one guest reported how a begging letter would sail in through the window and land on the table; how the Baron would, almost automatically, wrap a gold piece in it and throw it back with a practiced curve; and how a footman had to report whether the missive had reached its recipient.

None of these good deeds kindled his wife's womb. To distract himself, Amschel tried to learn the foreign languages his brothers spoke. But all that would stick in his mind were prayers and figures. He even tackled horse-back-riding. People, though, always seemed to hold their hands to their mouths when they saw the Baron astride a thoroughbred in his caftan. He gave that up, too. Only the synagogue remained—and the gardens. Those gardens were his greatest worldly joy. He filled them with the rarest, finest blooms and with graceful animals. Here, at least, he could make young things grow. And here he received a young Prussian who was to become the legendary Iron Chancellor of Germany—Otto von Bismarck.

In 1851 Prussia appointed Bismarck its representative at the German Confederation meeting in Frankfurt. Old Amschel, with his sharp eyes, was not long in picking out a comer. The young man seemed about the same age as his phantom son might be, and soon Prussia's new delegate received a card asking him to Rothschild's house. As usual, the Baron had a very crowded schedule, and so the invitation was for a considerable time later. Bismarck replied that he would come if he were still alive. A letter to his wife shows, inadvertently, how pleased he was with the famous Jew's reaction.

"My answer," he wrote, "affected Baron Rothschild so strongly that he has told everybody about it, and goes about saying, 'Why shouldn't he be alive? Why should he die? The man is young and strong!' . . . I like the Baron, though, because he's a real old Jew peddler and does not pretend to be anything else; he is strictly orthodox and refuses to touch anything but kosher food at his dinners. 'Take thome bread for the deer,' he said to his servant as he went out to show me his garden, in which he keeps tame deer. 'Thith plant,' he said to me, 'cotht me two thouthand gulden—on my honor it cotht me two thouthand gulden cash. You can have it for a thouthand; or if you like it ath a prethent, the thervant will bring it to your houthe. God knowth I like you, you're a fine handthome fellow.' He is such a short little thin person . . . childless, a poor man in his palace."

Yet Bismarck was proud of his friendship with the piteous Jewish oddity. In the same letter he enclosed two leaves from Baron Rothschild's garden and instructed his wife to save them with care.

There were other youths to whom Amschel paid even greater attention. He cast an envious but loving eye on the offspring of his brothers. The young Rothschilds interested him most at the crucial point of the dynastic process—their marriages. He supervised The Family's mating policy: boys must choose other Rothschilds, or at least other Jews, for their brides; the girls were sometimes allowed Christian aristocrats. (Nathan's daughter Hannah accepted, against some rather temporary family resistance, a son of the Baron Southampton, the Hon. Henry Fitzroy. Of Hannah's nieces, her namesake, Hannah Rothschild, wed the Earl of Rosebery, later prime minister of the Empire; Annie Rothschild became daughter-in-law to Lord Hardwicke; Constance Rothschild, the wife of Lord Battersea. On the Continent, one of Carl's grandchildren became the Duchess de Gramont, while her sister married the Prince de Wagram.)

To the end of his eighty-one years Amschel insisted that all nuptials be celebrated at Frankfurt. He did not always succeed, but he did compel all new Rothschild spouses—including the gentile bluebloods—to submit to a peculiar ritual. Even if the wedding were not held in Frankfurt, they must immediately proceed there in full retinue. They stopped briefly at Amschel's mansion. In his best caftan he emerged and headed the stately procession moving toward the ghetto. It reached a street too narrow for the splendid carriages. One had to disembark and make one's way across cobbles to a cramped, weathered house. The ladies, in their grand toilettes, could barely squeeze through the small doorway.

In this ghetto cavern Gutele Rothschild, the dowager empress of world finance, lived on—forever, it seemed.* No newcomer, no matter how noble, received full admission to The Family before being introduced, appraised and approved at Gutele's. Here, at the Green Shield, one did her homage.

Here, as a young coin merchant's wife, she had once boiled beef, scrubbed walls, washed shirts, while her husband and five sons attained legend. From here she would not move. And since there was hardly a palace west of the Urals that would not gladly claim her as guest, the palaces came to her. Here, in medieval dusk, the duchesses curtsied. Here the mighty, peacocked with decorations, bent over the rough old hand. They admired obediently Gutele's bridal wreath, which had been withering under glass for much more than half a century.

The ancient woman, covered in stiff lace, moved little. Her face under the *sheitel* (the wig worn by an orthodox Jewish wife) hardly smiled. But her tongue was hu-

* She died, at the age of ninety-six, when Amschel was seventy-five.

morous, sharp, alive. When a grandee observed that Frau Rothschild would probably outlive all her guests, she answered, in arch imitation of her sons' stock-market language, "Why should God take me at a hundred when he can have me at ninety-four?" When another Highness offered her his personal physician, a wizard guaranteed to make his patients twenty years younger, Frau Rothschild said, "People always think I want to grow younger. I don't. I want to grow older."

At Amschel's signal, the state visit departed. Later Frau Rothschild's words would be retold in the best drawing rooms. But her most famous phrase was spoken just after one of those splendiferous assemblies had vanished into its equipages. A ghetto neighbor ran into the house, worried about her sons who had just come of military age. She asked Frau Rothschild if there had been any news from the great personages? Would there be peace or war?

"War?" Gutele said simply. "Nonsense. My boys won't let them."

As usual she was right. "My boys won't let them" summed up much of the invisible politics of the nineteenth century.

# VI

# *RUNNING EUROPE*

## 1. *The Peacemongers*

GUTELE'S sons had soared during Napoleon's wars. But now that they had so superbly ridden a tiger, they proscribed tigers. Upheavals are exhilarating for ambitious youths, not for established men. Rothschild was now banker to empires and continents—to all the principal European countries, to Eurasian Russia, to the Americas, to the Indies. It has been estimated that the London house alone placed 6,500 million dollars' worth of foreign loans during the first ninety years of its existence. In Paris, in Vienna, in Frankfurt and Naples, the titanic brother branches were just as busy. Upon Rothschild vaults converged the credit of the Western World.

Quite naturally, the investments of Gutele's boys depended on the stability of nations. "We have a holding of 900,000 *rentes* [18 million francs nominal]," wrote James to Salomon in 1830. "If peace is preserved they will be worth 75 per cent, while in case of war they will drop to 45. . . ."

Thus the brothers became the most militant pacifists ever. Of course, it takes a great deal more power, ingenuity and statesmanship to promote peace than to preach war. The Family needed all the strength it had. While the ladies glittered in manse and park, while their sons rode to hounds with the finest lordlings in the land, the men worked as hard as ever, intercepting lightning bolts from the chancelleries.

They were helped by their astounding, unshakable solidarity. The Yiddish-German code they had used as five striplings working under father Mayer was the code that now flitted back and forth between the five great national institutions. (Just as Landgrave William of Hesse had once been called "Herr Goldstein," so the Chancellor, Prince Metternich, was now termed "Uncle.") The common-courier system carrying their messages had grown into a mighty continental network operating by land, sea and air. Waterloo was not the last, but the first, of the system's big scoops.

On February 13, 1820, the Duke de Berry, heir presumptive to Louis XVIII, was assassinated outside the Paris opera. Instantly James triggered messengers to London, Vienna, Frankfurt. Long before their governments or their stock-exchange rivals got wind of it, the Houses Rothschild knew that the Bourbon hope was dead. In 1830 James's carrier pigeons outraced any other newsbearers of the July Revolution. And Nathan appears to have been the first man in London to know of King Louis Philippe's ascent to power.

If the breeze didn't carry Rothschild pigeons, it pushed Rothschild sails. "The English ministry," wrote Talleyrand to Louis Philippe's sister, "is always informed of everything by Rothschild ten to twelve hours before the dispatches of the British ambassador arrive. This is necessarily so because the vessels used by the Rothschild couriers belong to that house; they take no passengers and sail in all weathers."

The Family developed a dispatch organization even more reliable than that of other great powers. Various countries began to use its international postmen. A rather piquant situation developed. In the nineteenth century, as in our own, the mails were not only an instrument for carrying letters but also for inspecting them. The Austrian postal service showed a special inquisitiveness. A detective postmaster wrote to Vienna: "I have often noticed that the Rothschild couriers who travel from Naples to Paris . . . take with them all the dispatches of the French, English and Spanish ministers accredited in Naples, Rome and Florence. In addition, they also deal with the communications passing between the courts of Naples and Rome and their legations throughout Europe. . . . These Rothschild couriers travel via Piacenza. As we have an Austrian garrison there . . . it might be possible to *induce* one or another of these clerks to hand over their dispatches for our perusal. . . ."

The matter was deemed important enough to be brought to the Chancellor's attention. A most delicate dilemma confronted Metternich. On the one hand, it would be delicious to read not only foreign diplomatic mail, but, particularly, the confidential exchanges of his dear, inscrutable friends the Rothschilds. On the other hand, the Chancellor himself often used The Family's blue-and-yellow-capped supermessengers. His own high secrets might be revealed to a subordinate postal official.

Metternich was not for nothing Europe's most intricate diplomat. He issued the following order:

> "The couriers of the House of Rothschild passing through Lombardy between Naples and Paris are to

> be regarded and treated as official Austrian couriers when carrying dispatches with the [Austrian] Imperial and Royal seal. . . . If, however, they should be found carrying letters which have nothing to indicate that they are of an official [Austrian] nature, such letters shall be subject to the usual regulations in force."

But The Family outfoxed the fox. It knew that some of its mail was being tapped. It also realized that Metternich would believe some otherwise unconvincing statements if he thought he was not meant to read them. The brothers, of course, had a vested interest in peace, especially between Austria and France. And so there would travel from Paris to the Vienna house an intrafamily letter of supposedly "strictest secrecy" which went on and on about the flattering remarks the French King had made about the Austrian Chancellor: The Family had certain messengers who were excellent at being intercepted.

The Family also had a marvelously changeable shape. Its couriers bound it tightly together; but when it received an awkward request—say, for armament funds—it could sprawl on the instant into five widely separated and quite disorganized brothers. "Your Excellency," the reply of spokesman Amschel would read, ". . . your Excellency will be graciously aware that I can act in this matter only in consultation with my absent brothers . . . and will therefore attempt to inform them of your request." Unfortunately, it would develop that Salomon was deep in the toils of a health cure; that communications to Carl had been cut off by an Italian mutiny; that James was traveling, and Nathan bedded by the grippe.

The five could play infinite tricks with their fivefoldedness. Bismarck discovered that his gardening friend

Amschel had the nerve to support Austria financially against Prussia. He protested. Amschel became unwell—that is, inaccessible. Bismarck remonstrated with the other Rothschilds, and the other Rothschilds declared themselves ever so astonished, perplexed, puzzled by misguided, senile old Amschel.

Then there was the case of Nathan, who backed the liberal, and therefore anti-Metternich, party in the Spanish civil war. Metternich fumed. Thereupon James complained to Salomon, in a neatly intercepted letter, that Nathan had been led astray by his radical wife and father-in-law, and how such transgressions must be prevented in future. Metternich forgave.

No maneuver was too devious for The Family to force the peace. During the tension between quasi-liberal France and ultraconservative Austria, it hatched pacifist plots in most of the government palaces in Europe. Its pipelines reached everywhere. Nathan in London was very close to the Duke of Wellington and to the innermost British circles. Salomon had the eye, ear and purse of Metternich. James saw the French King every few days. Carl kept check on the masters of Italy, from Naples to Sardinia. Quite often it happened that the chief executive of an important power wanted to convey some crucial thoughts to his counterparts elsewhere without committing himself officially. The five brothers were perfect vehicles—if such transmission suited their purpose. After talking to friends in Downing Street, Nathan would send off certain observations, which James produced at St. Cloud, Salomon cited in Vienna's Hofburg. . . . Ostensibly, these were scribblings from Rothschild to Rothschild. Actually, they had the force of privy communications between governments.

At one point Nathan opined that "if France takes action

against the Austrian side, we in England shall join the Austrians. If the Austrians take action, we shall join France." That little Family chat made an enormous impression by the Seine and by the Danube. It helped leash the two empires for the time being.

The brothers knew that sometimes it was not diplomacy they must wield, but unvarnished power. In 1831 Louis Philippe, the semirevolutionary King of France, persisted in abetting the semirevolutionary new Italian states against the Habsburg Empire. Austria talked about defending legitimacy to the last drop of blood. France swore to die for freedom. James in Paris seized on the one chance for peace: Casimir Périer, a prudent financier like himself, must be premier. "I informed his Majesty," James wrote to Salomon, "that if he took Périer into his ministry, his credit would rise."

Périer received his appointment. Austrian troops, however, marched into Bologna. The French government, under strong popular pressure, was about to express itself in perilous language. The credit of France now intervened directly. "Yesterday," James wrote Salomon, "the note was drafted which France is about to send. It contained the phrase: 'évacuez immédiatement Bologne.' . . . I shall see that this is left out."

It was. France made do with Platonic indignation, and war was staved off.

On other occasions the brothers Rothschild waxed blunter still. In 1839 King Leopold of new-born Belgium wanted to wrest by force the provinces of Luxembourg and Limburg from the Netherlands. Gutele's boys would not let him.

"The Belgian government," Salomon declared openly, "will not get a half-penny from us, although they have been begging for money for months. Difficult though I found it to keep refusing, I shall feel compensated if Belgium yields and peace is restored."

Belgium yielded. Rothschild loaned.

"It is in the nature of things," Bismarck advised an aide who was trying to get Prussian armaments financed, "that the House should do everything possible to prevent war from breaking out. This fact shows how delicate one must be in dealing with Rothschild."

## 2. *Short-Term and Long*

Bismarck, not ordinarily a delicate type, did at last get some wars in against Austria and France. But in the end, as another chapter will show, the Rothschilds gave him their own brand of comeuppance.

Just the same, Bismarck had his way. The Family's international veto power waned in the second half of the nineteenth century. In part this must be ascribed to The Family's own success. It had helped to stimulate the economy of the various countries so briskly that they were now beyond dependence on any one group of financiers, however powerful.

The boys' ultimate historical performance proved what any stock-exchange connoisseur knows: short-term consequences of a Rothschild move are usually the very opposite of its long-term effect. The immediate impact of those five brothers was neither sweet nor happy, nor anything but ruinous to competitors. The quintet was not the kind to bother about the social good. They were called Jews of the Bourbons, Coffers of the Reaction, Usurers of Metternich. Some of those epithets seemed hard to refute. And yet all that unprecedented ruthlessness and craft had an eventual positive result.

The efficiency which powered Mayer's sons brought on enormous economic spring cleaning; a sweeping away of fiscal dead wood; a renovation of old credit structures and an invention of new ones; a formation—implicit in the sheer existence of five different Rothschild banks in five different countries—of fresh money channels via clearing-houses; a method of replacing the old unwieldy shipping of gold bullion by a worldwide system of debits and credits.

One of the greatest contributions was Nathan's new technique for floating international loans. Before, the English investor had been hesitant about foreign projects. He didn't much care to receive dividends in all sorts of strange and cumbersome currencies. Now Nathan attracted him—the most powerful investment source of the nineteenth century—by making foreign bonds payable in pounds sterling.

Altogether, the Rothschild work and the Rothschild name (with Napoleon's, the greatest self-made image) served to supplant the era of title and pedigree with the era of money and ability. In one of his more dined-and-wined moments at rue Laffitte, Heine would think of the five brothers as great revolutionaries: Hadn't they usurped the last pretensions of feudalism? Hadn't they abolished the stiff, stagnant pre-eminence of land ownership? Hadn't they created instead the investor's domain of money, capital and state bonds which anyone could possess at any time? Weren't these the most flexible, equitable, productive ruling instruments yet invented? And weren't the Rothschilds the archdemons of progress?

We needn't be so carried away as Heine to concede a fact: Mayer's boys helped abolish the very absolutism which had at first used them for its tool. However unwittingly, the Rothschilds supplied more soil for the flowering of bourgeois democracy than any other five individuals in Europe.

Railroads were a case in point. The Family, more than any other group, brought the locomotive to Europe. As usual, what they saw was the income promised by those shining rails. At the same time, the iron tracks were to become the lifeline of commerce. Hitherto travel had been the privilege of aristocrats and soldiers; now worker and peasant gained a mobility they had not known before.

Yet the Rothschilds practically had to force railroads on a suspicious continent. It was to be the most hotly contested venture in Family history.

## 3. *The Railway Madness*

### (a) *Austria*

The railways were born in England, as George Stephenson's "steam-coaches," right under Nathan's nose. But by the time he began to smell the lucre in their soot, they were no longer buyable. Other bankers had gotten there first. Nathan, of course, would not touch what he could not own or control. He contented himself with alerting his brothers on the Continent.

In Vienna, Salomon picked up the idea. It was a brave move. Austria, the most dashingly backward empire of its time, thought that horseless carriages were almost as weird as socialism. To prepare a more hospitable climate, Salomon dispatched a fact-finding committee to England; it was composed of von Wertheimstein, his general manager, and Professor Franz Riepel of the Vienna Polytechnic Institute, an early advocate of the horseless madness.

The two returned a report full of technical and financial enthusiasm. Nevertheless, they could not very well overlook the resistance to the chimneyed freaks even in liberal Britain. In some English counties a postillion had to ride fifty yards ahead of the locomotives to warn local inhabitants, with cries and trumpet blasts, of the approaching abomination. The gentry, who were fond of their horses, thought it was all a horrid bore. One of Nathan's best friends, the Duke of Wellington, remarked that "railroads will only encourage the lower classes to move about needlessly."

Salomon read the report and paused. In 1830 the July Revolution in Paris produced business vagaries which needed all his attention. But in his mind the conviction grew that enormous profits could be made with a North Austrian railway transporting Galician salt and Silesian coal to Vienna.

Business settled down in 1832. Salomon struck formidably and quietly, as was his wont. For a closer introduction to the transport business he bought the horse-tramway network (operated by Emile Zola's father, of all people) in the Austrian provinces. He also hired a battalion of expert engineers who surveyed, foot by foot, the whole route of the projected line.

Soon afterward (in April, 1835) a great poetic and public-minded document reached the desk of Ferdinand II of Austria. It began with "Most Excellent and Most Puissant Emperor! Most Gracious Emperor and Lord!" and sang ardently the "benefits to the state and to the public weal" a railroad between Vienna and Galicia would bring, begged his Majesty's most gracious sanction and ended, "your Majesty's most true and humble servant, S. M. v. Rothschild."

Prince Metternich favored the application. And since his Most Puissant Majesty was a signature-writing device operated by the Chancellor, the application received All-Highest approval. On November 11, 1835, Rothschild pocketed the concession to build the European Continent's first sizable railway—sixty miles of track from Vienna to Bochnia in Galicia. (The Imperial Postal Service exacted a clause from Baron Rothschild insuring reimbursement if his iron beasts ate up too much mail business.)

The project was estimated at twelve million gulden, and Salomon immediately proceeded to provide it. He issued 12,000 shares at 1,000 gulden each—retaining 8,000 for himself, offering 4,000 on a first-come, first-served basis. Attracted by the confluence of two myths, *Rothschild* and *railroad*, the investing public came in droves.

But a general public existed, too. If the railways caused resistance in top-hatted England, they provoked revulsion in shako'd Austria. Salomon was broadly damned for foisting twentieth-century fiendishness on a peaceful eighteenth-century state. The Vienna press began to seethe with terrors and prophecies. Experts proved the madness of Rothschild's scheme. The human respiratory system, they said, could not stand a speed exceeding fifteen miles an hour. The lungs were likely to collapse, and the organs of circulation jolted out of place. Blood would spurt from the travelers' noses, eyes, ears and mouths. Any tunnel more than sixty yards long would suffocate all the riders in all the carriages; the train would rush out at the other end, a driverless berserk hearse. Certainly no passenger should take a steamcoach trip without being attended by his personal doctor who could intercede with the engineer at the throttle.

And all sorts of doctors did come to the fore—of the front page, that is. So-called neurological experts sounded the alarm. According to their articles, the human psyche, already overburdened by newfangled stimuli, would completely run amok once subjected to the stress of railroad travel. The speed of the machine might drive men to suicide, women might lapse into sexual orgies. There were reports from England that innocent passers-by had been driven jabberingly insane by the mere sight of one of these zooming, smoking serpents. And Rothschild was now given license to finance such savagery in gay Vienna?

There were other reports from England, financial ones, issued by the early railway companies. These were not at all gruesome. Salomon's rivals, particularly the banking house Sina, found them positively mouth-watering. Sina let Rothschild bear the brunt as disturber of North Austria's peace. Meanwhile it unobtrusively applied for, and finally got, a license to build a southern track from Vienna to the Adriatic Sea.

Thus Salomon saw himself attacked on two fronts. Usually he could count on some very well-greased connections with the Vienna press, but his journalist friends were impotent at the height of the outcry. Through Chancellor Metternich he enjoyed the loftiest possible support within the government, but Sina was a power, too, and there was no way of invalidating a rival license once the administrative machinery had ground it out. In fact, when he proposed a concession for a northeastern branch line to his own railway, he was reduced to a competitive basis on a par with Sina.

A Rothschild, however, has not only more money but also more ideas than the next fellow. To handle the impasse, Salomon arranged for another patriotic prose poem to float onto Kaiser Ferdinand's desk. It was a preliminary but resounding progress report on "the great national work, namely the Vienna-Bochnia railway." It culminated in a masterful paragraph:

> The most obedient and loyal servant of your Majesty feels that he may venture in all humility most respectfully to request your Majesty that you may be graciously pleased to permit that the Vienna-Bochnia railway shall be allowed to bear the auspicious name of "Kaiser Ferdinand Nordbahn."

Simultaneously, Prince Metternich received a letter which proposed that his Excellency the Finance Minister and his Excellency the Lord President of the Council "place themselves at the head of this national undertaking" by becoming its patrons, to be so handed down to posterity on all the railway's plaques, scrolls and documents. His Princely Highness, Chancellor Metternich himself, was asked to accept the office of the railway's official High Protector.

As always, Metternich came through. He and his several Excellencies agreed to endorse the Rothschild railway with their names. Indeed, the finance minister advised the Emperor in the warmest terms to do the same.

"This undertaking is on a colossal scale," he wrote, "such as has never been contemplated in Europe before . . . and will remain as an everlasting monument to your Majesty's reign."

On April 9, 1836, an imperial decree promulgated his Majesty's gracious decision to let Rothschild's track be known henceforward as the "Kaiser Ferdinand Nordbahn" (Emperor Ferdinand Northern Railway). With one stone, Salomon had killed two great birds: the Austrian government had identified itself with the fate and prosperity of *his* project, not Sina's; and the renown of the House of

Habsburg now sanctified the railway madness. In the face of such overwhelming auspices, the protests died away. Apparently it was all over but the building.

To that task Salomon now applied himself. Two weeks after the Emperor's grant of the name, he called the first of a series of shareholders' meetings. He transferred his building concession, hitherto held personally, to the company. He saw to the appointment of a provisional board of directors, submitted estimates, blueprints, proposals—and was told he was a cheat and a fake.

Suddenly, within the company and without, a different kind of opposition flared. Secretly sponsored by Sina, a memorandum went from hand to hand. The railroad idea as such was not attacked (after all, Sina had one on the fire), but the arrant misuse of august names was implied. All planners of the Nordbahn stood accused of the grossest scientific blunders. The memorandum set forth its charges in impressive scientific language. It went on about gradients and the relationship of rail curvatures to steam traction, and about the scandalous inability of the Rothschild people to meet any such problems. Last, not least, figures were cited that made the financial future of a *northern* railroad look disastrous.

The memorandum caused so much talk that the court began to prick up its ears. The Emperor forsook his usual existence as a signing machine. "Dear Prince Metternich," he fretted. ". . . Numerous unfavorable rumors are abroad about the railroad which I have permitted to be associated with my name. . . . You will report to me whether difficulties have arisen in the further progress of the work on this railway, and, in that case, what these difficulties are."

Salomon was still Salomon. Again his parry hit home better than the enemy's thrust. He instantly commissioned the authoritative Professor Riepel of the Polytechnic to compose a polemic which met "this insult with the contempt it deserves" and demolished the technical details of the opposition memorandum point by point. Then he summoned the shareholders to a dramatic showdown forecasting the proxy battles of our day. He offered to repurchase all certificates not held by himself, and thus to repossess the building franchise he had transferred to the company. He would proceed as the project's sole owner and director if the shareholders did not give him their full confidence as well as authority to commence construction forthwith.

He got their authorization. He received their full confidence. A landslide vote removed his enemies from the board. Not content with that, Salomon turned the Emperor's note to Metternich from a liability into an asset. He publicly interpreted it as a sign of warm solicitude. In an official letter the House of Rothschild expressed appreciation of this "further proof of his Majesty's gracious concern for the prosperity of the Kaiser Ferdinand Nordbahn."

Thus S. M. reversed public opinion into the Nordbahn's favor. The greatest engineers in the state service were given leave to work on the construction, which started at last. Salomon even managed to borrow the Crown surveyor. The track grew with comparative speed, even though the original cost estimate proved, as original cost estimates will, too low. On July 7, 1839, Austria scooped the rest of the European mainland by opening the first section of the first major railway line. And on the following day it became the first Continental nation to have anything as modern as a train collision, happily a trifling one.

The passengers did not run amok—but the shares, after some initial vagaries, rose madly.

### (b) *France*

The Austrian Rothschild had made a great contribution to the general progress and to his own wealth. The French one did not want to lag behind. James Rothschild opened his Paris–St. Germain railroad in 1837 and the Paris-Versailles line in 1839. After these two successful experiments, he began to create the Chemin de Fer du Nord—for those days, a gigantic project, which connected the capital with the industrial regions of the north.

But his first tracks, too, were not exactly strewn with roses. France also had transport experts who produced headlines dripping with doom. They saw forests and crops set afire by sparks from the trains; inhabitants driven from the countryside by the shrieks and the clangors; cattle stampeding; grass, flowers, bushes withered by soot. France would be streaked with deserts.

In Austria the government had stood up against such rantings. Not here. In 1835 the French Parliament had been presented with the idea of a state-owned steamcoach system and had thrown out the idea as utopian and ridiculous. Now Rothschild's pressure for a private license became irresistible. Thiers, the King's first minister, yielded. But he was no Metternich. "We must give the Parisians this as a toy," he said. "But it will never carry a passenger or a parcel."

There were less highly placed but equally dangerous forces to contend with—a certain Jules Mires, for example, a man of peculiar brilliance. He had begun his career in Bordeaux, where he had published a boulevard paper featuring an exhaustive list of obituaries. With each death he printed the name of the doctor who had failed to save the deceased. The physicians of Bordeaux saw reason. Mires stopped publication, and went to Paris a rich man.

Here he started another paper along similar lines, but focusing on a different subject. The *Journal des Chemins de Fer* vividly pictured rail mishaps, rail frauds, rail atrocities. Its voice grew louder and louder, and Mires grew richer and richer, selling his selected silences.

Over all these stings and yawps Beau James rode in customary grandeur. He floated his Chemin de Fer du Nord with a stock issue worth 150 million francs. Fully seven and a half millions' worth of shares were distributed free of charge (or of noise) to ministers, deputies and journalists. Suddenly the guardians of the public weal began to see the benefits of the Rothschild railroad. Construction proceeded apace. On June 15, 1846, representatives of the Crown, of Parliament and of the press joined to hail Baron James on the opening of *his* northern railway.

He was not yet out of the woods. Locomotive engineers, in the infancy of their profession, had much to learn about curves. Three weeks after the opening, a train rounded a bend too quickly and killed thirty-seven people. The accident stunned France. A virulent anti-Semitic storm broke out against the president of the line. It vented itself primarily in the form of pamphlets, of which "The History of Rothschild I, King of the Jews" became most famous. Afterwards there appeared a counterpamphlet, "Reply by Rothschild the First, King of the Jews, to Satan the Last, King of the Slanderers."

The interesting point about the latter publication is that it was written on speculation. James had not commissioned it, and when he was approached, he did not pay the author. To get a thing done he would bribe, befitting his status, on a munificent scale. Petty graft disgusted him. Besides, the track was completed. The kinks were being worked out. The Northern Railway could stand and succeed on its own merits.

It did. Le Chemin de Fer du Nord became as great a national asset as the Kaiser Ferdinand Nordbahn. No less than the Austrian Rothschild, the French one had captured for himself a great new source of income and given the industrial revolution a big push forward.

A fly—or rather, a vulture—remained in the ointment. After all, non-northern rail lines were possible, too. There were three other directions, and several other men who thought their brains and mercilessness a match for The Family's. Out of the railway competition arose a rival syndicate which overflowed all national borders and challenged almost every department of every Family bank. This enemy severely tested the Rothschilds' invincibility. Another, moving still faster, had already proved them mortal: when the international onslaught was unleashed, the biggest brother was no longer there to meet it.

## 4. *Il est Mort*

In the middle of June, 1836, the city of Frankfurt witnessed an unparalleled assembly. Its greatest family was celebrating its greatest wedding. Lionel Rothschild, Nathan's eldest son, espoused Charlotte Rothschild, Carl's eldest daughter.

From London and from Naples, carriage after carriage thundered into the town, bringing not only parents but also dowries and gifts. From Paris, James arrived in almost imperial pomp, with Rossini among others in his retinue. From Vienna came Salomon in a castlelike coach. Amschel presided, and Gutele, the eighty-five-year-old matriarch (and far from the end of her tether), left her ghetto house to crown the occasion with her presence. It is doubtful that any emperor or chancellor could have matched the total power congregating here.

Yet even The Family must in turn bow to a superior force. Right into the middle of the celebration it reached, and it plucked the most formidable Rothschild of them all.

It began with a carbuncle on Nathan's skin. On the very day of the wedding the inflammation grew oppressive. Nathan refused all entreaties and insisted on standing beside his son while the rabbi pronounced the nuptial blessing. At the feast the bridegroom saw his father shiver with high fever. He was taken to bed. The next day he became delirious. German doctors were consulted; couriers sped to England for Nathan's personal physician, the famous Benjamin Travers. Travers arrived at last—too late. The poison had spread through Nathan's system.

Towards the end his mind cleared. He called his children around him and dealt with death in all his usual shrewd, powerful confidence. Salomon reported to Metternich:

> He told his sons that the world would now try to make money out of us, so that it behooved them to be all the more careful. And he remarked that whether any son had 50,000 pounds more or less was not important to him. All that mattered was that they should all hold together in unity. . . . As he received the last consolations of our religion he said, "It is not necessary that I should pray so much, for believe me, according to my convictions I have not sinned." To my daughter Betty, as she took leave of him, he said in the truly British manner, "Good night forever."

On the afternoon of July 28, 1836, Nathan Rothschild died, not quite sixty years old. At midnight pigeons were released that flew to Rothschild offices and agents all over

Europe. They carried a brief message:

*Il est mort.*

Those three words stirred the world. The London *Times* gathered itself up for one of its rare superlatives. "The death of Nathan Mayer Rothschild," an editorial said, "is one of the most important events for the city and perhaps for Europe in a long time. . . . No operations, comparable to his, have existed in Europe to this time. . . . Mr. Rothschild, like the rest of his brothers, held a patent of nobility with the title of Baron, but he never assumed it and was more justly proud of that name under which he had acquired a distinction which no title could convey. . . ."

London produced a funeral worthy of a royal dying. The body was brought up the Thames by special steamboat. Then it was conveyed, not to his house but—significantly—to his business palace at New Court, where it lay in state. The procession from the Orthodox synagogue to the East End Cemetery blackened the streets. Never had such numbers and such dignities followed a private individual. A group of Jewish orphans whose institution the dead man had subsidized led the cortege, chanting psalms. Behind the coffin walked his sons and brothers (strict Jewish ritual bade the women remain behind in the darkened house), the top echelons of the City, the Lord Mayor of London and sheriffs, a large contingent of the nobility, and the ambassadors of Austria, Prussia, Russia, Naples and virtually every other accredited power.

And yet his tombstone says nothing of his wealth, his honors or his titles. It reads: "Nathan Mayer Rothschild: born at Frankfurt on the Main 7th September 5537 [the Jewish year for A.D. 1777] third son of Mayer Amschel Rothschild, a man known and venerated throughout Europe, whose virtuous example he followed."

In life as in death, this greatest single Rothschild was only a fragment of The Family. In life as in death, he remained an instrument of the dynastic principle laid down by his father, the patriarch. As in old Mayer's last will, so in his own, Nathan charged his sons to remain partners and to preserve at all costs and by every means the unity of the house. As in Mayer's last will, so here the sons were sole inheritors of the firm; the daughters and their husbands would have no part or say whatsoever in their brothers' affairs. (The four girls did receive, in addition to the dowries and huge sums given to them during Nathan's lifetime, a lump sum of 100,000 pounds—over a million dollars—each.)

Like Mayer's will, so Nathan's pointedly avoided any concrete mention of his endless assets. Not only the continuity but the privacy of the fortune must be maintained.

"I would request," said Nathan's last document, "that the executors of the Will as well as any relations in Frankfurt or London unnamed, confine their efforts simply and solely to the due execution of this my Testament and, since it does not pertain to their office at all, not to ask for any further information, or for the production of any books or accounts."

In a letter, Salomon reported how Nathan's sons had pledged to keep the example of solidarity and mutual affection which their father and uncles had set. ". . . there will be no change of any kind."

Inevitably, there was some. The clan closed ranks even more tightly as it moved toward its goals; only the goals grew a little different. For the first four decades of the nineteenth century the Rothschilds had been great conquerors. Afterwards, and into our time, they became great lords. Three of Nathan's brothers belonged to the older school. They were better at swooping than at possessing or savoring. James, the fourth and youngest brother—only ten years older than his eldest nephew—combined both phases and was conqueror and lord in one. Tacitly, but not accidentally, Family leadership now fell to him.

As it happened, shortly before Nathan's death James had built himself a palace befitting the doge of the golden clan. On March 1, 1836, Heine wrote:

> For the beau monde of Paris, yesterday was a remarkable day; we had the first performance of Meyerbeer's long-awaited "Huguenots" at the Opera, followed by Rothschild's first ball in his new house. As I did not leave until four o'clock this morning, and have not been asleep yet, I am too tired to give you an account of the scene of this festival, and of the magnificent new palace built entirely in the style of the Renaissance in which the guests wander, expressing their admiration and astonishment. The palace unites everything which the spirit of the sixteenth century could conceive and the money of the nineteenth century could pay for. Two years have been spent in constant work on its decorations. It is the Versailles of the financial absolute monarch. . . . As at all Rothschild receptions, the guests were chosen strictly for their social rank, the men distinguished for their great aristocratic names or positions, while the women were distinguished for their beauty and elegance. . . .

If amid all this select splendor the Baron ever forgot his Jew Street scrabblings, the world was there to remind him. The rough, rabid urgencies that had shaped his rise remained—in other men. From James's own realm, forces emerged which proved that even for Rothschilds life was not a ball but a jungle.

## 5. *The Grandest Larceny Ever*

A saying claims that great champions breed great contenders. James, improving the wisdom, didn't stop at breeding them; he employed them. The French founder, as Heine remarked, had a rare gift for taking a lease on the talents of other people. But like other first-rate users of people, Rothschild failed to recognize that the human means he hired were, as far as they were concerned, ends in themselves; that a man's ability is more easily put on the payroll than his ego—that, in fact, ego may subvert ability, to result not in talented loyalty but in accomplished revolt. Within a decade James found himself ambushed by two topnotch mutineers.

The first posed the lesser threat, but he struck the lower blow. Among James's protégés a slender young man named Carpentier ranked high. He had a lightning mind for figures and a pleasant, humorous, yet efficient manner which earned him the chief-accountancy of the Chemin de Fer du Nord. Soon he managed to become part of the Baron's personal entourage, or at least the lower fringes thereof. James took the bright youngster along on some of his travels and even invited him to the less exclusive receptions at the Palais Rothschild. In front of ledgers, across the table, during a dull journey, in fact everywhere, Carpentier performed well and looked lively. He could write a balance sheet or crack a joke with equal finesse.

One afternoon in September, 1856, he applied for a four days' leave. James granted it readily. The two had an agreeable chat which has come down to us because the occasion became historic all too soon.

In an expansive mood James remarked that he had just succeeded in clearing the rights for an additional branch line to his railway. When the news became public on the following day, he said, everybody would no doubt assume that Rothschild was now another hundred million richer.

"Monsieur le Baron, a proposal," said Carpentier with his special blend of respectfulness and banter. "Of that mythical hundred million, let me have just thirty real ones."

The Baron laughed, and on the pleasant impulse of the moment gave Carpentier his heavy golden watch chain as a memento of the day. The young man thanked him profusely and went on his leave.

He did not return. At first his absence was not taken too seriously. Then pay day came. Company employees queued up for their wages—and Carpentier had the keys to the safes. The executive in charge sent a messenger to the chief accountant's lodgings. The messenger reported that they were empty. A swift inquiry at Carpentier's brother's brought out that he, too, was puzzled by the sudden disappearance—and by something else. In the mail the brother had received the baronial watch chain, as though it were Carpentier's farewell present.

Now the Baron was notified. He alone had a duplicate set of safe keys. James arrived. With grim foreknowledge he opened the strong boxes. Gone were the entire cash assets of the company, some six million francs.

The Baron, his aides said later, turned pale. But his sangfroid did not leave him for one second. He turned around, issued a two-sentence public statement that a robbery had occurred, then placed a complete embargo on all further details to the press.

The details had only just begun. James ordered a roll-call, and found that five other members of the bookkeeping staff seemed to be missing, too. So were a great many documents. The Baron sensed that this was a conspiracy too big for even six million francs. It took days of concentrated searching to track down all its aspects. Carpentier had been a flawless embezzler. But finally James discovered that his protégé had made the major killing in stock certificates, his own favorite medium. Except that Carpentier's approach was a little different: he didn't bull or bear; he stole.

The company's shares were kept in bundles of a thousand each. Carpentier & Accomplices had removed two to three hundred shares from the middle of each packet, leaving the top and bottom politely undisturbed. After the dainty despoilment of all bundles, the gang sold the stocks in small quantities over a long period of time. This, in the best Rothschild fashion, avoided attention or price fluctuation.

The stock-certificate aspect of the larceny amounted to some twenty-five million francs. If we add the cash booty of six million, we arrive at more than the thirty million Carpentier had asked—not so jocularly, after all—of James. The pleasant young man towered over the greatest robbers of his time. His total haul came to over fifteen million dollars.

James struck back in the only way he could. An unlimited credit was opened for the private detectives who joined the national police forces in the big hunt. But Carpentier had prepared his flight as scrupulously as his crime. A whole year before he struck, he had already started investing in it—with the company's money, of course. The gang had bought an ocean-going steamer for two million francs. Next, under assumed names they had obtained a house somewhere in the United States. When the time came, in September, 1856, Carpentier applied for his four-day leave. He lifted the cash and traveled from Paris to Liverpool. There the get-away ship waited in the harbor. His accomplices had the engines running. His mistress, a certain Mlle. Georgette, waited, smiling, on the gangplank. And so he recedes out of our ken in his own luxurious stateroom, champagne on his lips, Georgette on his lap—uncaught.

James personally absorbed the entire loss. No other man in the country could have survived the sudden disappearance of thirty million francs without even beginning to strain his reserves. For the Baron, the timing of the blow seemed more harmful than its size. The House of Rothschild just then was locked in a desperate struggle with the second ingrate. For the first time since its rise, The Family had to stoop to a fight for life.

## 6. *Monsters' Duel*

Antagonist number two was far more ambitious and dangerous than Carpentier. But at first he was also far more useful. Jacob Emile Pereire, a Jew of Portuguese origin, began his career as a journalist collaborating with his brother Isaac. In the early 1830's he poured out articles on advanced social ideas, on new engineering fields like railroads, and on financial matters. Beau James's first railroad project was running into heavy reactionary weather. He bought up every prorailroad force in sight, including M. Pereire, that fountainhead of progressive energies. The man proved himself powerfully competent during the building of the Paris–St. Germain line.

When James went on to lay a track between Paris and Versailles, he put his find in charge of the entire construction. This line, running along the right bank of the Seine, was also successful. But, alas, it no longer had a monopoly on cattle scaring. Achille Fould, another big financial gun, built his own railway to Versailles on the *left* bank. As a result, Heine began to speak of Rothschild as the Chief Rabbi of Rive Droite, and of M. Fould as Chief Rabbi of Rive Gauche. The rivalry between the two financiers created irreverent thoughts in another mind as well. Emile Pereire, who was now acting as James's proconsul in the creation of the gigantic Northern Railway, always found time to cast glances across the Seine.

There was much to look at in that direction, especially if you had your eyes on the main chance. The 1830's had gone. The 1840's were waning, and so was King Louis Philippe, whom Rothschild owned. Louis Napoleon was waxing, and after the old king's flight he became President in 1848. Rothschild didn't own Napoleon. Achille Fould did. James's rival had lent the new ruler money during his adventuring and playboying years; now Fould was Napoleon's closest financial adviser. On October 31, 1849, the President appointed M. Fould finance minister of the Republic.

Not much later, Louis Napoleon, James Rothschild and Emile Pereire sat in a flower-wreathed steamcoach. The occasion was the opening of the Northern Railway extension line to St. Quentin. "Vive l'Empereur!" shouted the people, anticipating the coronation of the President, which was indeed soon to come. "Vive Rothschild!" they cried, hailing the enlargement of the financier's empire. And yet, as everyone remarked, only Napoleon and Pereire smiled. James remained grave. By then he knew that his chief executive, beaming so sweetly at the populace, was filled with treason. Pereire had deserted to the enemy.

To be more exact, he was about to become *the* enemy—the most vicious, the most determined, the most powerful one The Family would have to face until Hitler's advent. Pereire was no glorified pickpocket, like Carpentier. Nor did he simply switch from a master called Rothschild to a master called Fould. He became a full-fledged partner of Fould's, and soon more than that. The two founded a huge new company, whose specific aim was the slaying of the so-far indestructible giant Rothschild.

Fould supplied his wealth and his status as finance minister. Pereire, assisted by his brother, furnished the fury that drove the thing. He was a veritable whirlwind of schemes and angles that used everything in his experience, from the progressive politicking of his early journalism to the high-powered gimmicks he had learned under James.

His main idea was a marvelous synthesis of socialist sentiment and financial piracy. Why, Fould's propaganda asked, should the credit of the nation be the playground of just a few? Why not democratize it? Didn't a butcher have as good a right to loan a thousand francs to the fatherland as Rothschild with his thousand million? Why not create a people's bank, gathering a myriad tiny trickles into a huge reservoir which would use its power in the common interest and not in favor of one bloated individual?

On December 2, 1852, Louis Napoleon became Emperor. Almost at the same time Pereire's people's bank electrified the national scene. Called Crédit Mobilier, it issued 120,000 shares at five hundred francs each, so that not only the butcher but even his thrifty delivery boy could become a financier. That was the democratic feature of the enterprise. For aristocratic decoration, the names of the Princess von Leuchtenberg and the Duke of Galliera embellished the founders' list. Because of his official position, Finance Minister Fould could not participate in name, but he backed the issue fully. And Pereire sat at the controls. He had created France's most politically lovable profit institution.

The value of a Crédit Mobilier share stayed at 500 francs for only half an hour. At the end of the first day it was quoted at 1,100. Within a week it rose to 1,600. There had been nothing as sensational on the Paris money horizon since the advent of James Rothschild himself. The nation showered its savings on the new bank, and Napoleon III his patronage.

Beau James became Quick James. He appeared in Vienna, where brother Salomon rushed him into an audience with Francis Joseph. The Austrian monarch gave James, his consul general in Paris, a very pleasant courtesy message to Louis Napoleon. It was conveyed, together with the implication that, in contrast to Pereire, Rothschild was a Continental power of the first order; a house through which flowed the good will of the greatest *legitimate* sovereigns; and that this had better be kept in mind by anyone setting himself up as authentic Emperor.

The hint, while pointed, did not have any real effect. More and more of the state's financial business went to the Crédit Mobilier. Meanwhile the Baron had been trying another maneuver, by way of his salon. The drawing rooms of Paris became a theater of war.

A young Andalusian woman named Eugénie de Montijo began to be a frequent guest at James's and Betty's best parties. At first nobody quite understood why. True, she was beautiful. And society gossip knew that Napoleon had tried, unsuccessfully, to invade her bed. But her antecedents were mixed. Her mother, loser in a Madrid palace intrigue, had been forced to resign as lady-in-waiting to the Spanish queen. Eugénie herself had arrived in Paris only in 1850, with few important social credentials. Why, then, did the Baron insist on making her the belle of his receptions?

The answer began to emerge on December 31, 1852. At a secret cabinet council Napoleon III confided his intention of marrying Eugénie de Montijo. He complained of being treated like a parvenu emperor—the great *legitimate* houses prevented him from bringing home a princess worthy of his eminence.

"If I can't contract a political marriage," he said, "I shall at any rate have the comfort of being able to contract a *mariage d'inclination.*"

A number of French ministers considered this pronouncement only a maneuver against the foreign diplomats who had thwarted Napoleon's dynastic wedding plans. This Eugénie What's-Her-Name, this upstart hussy, to be empress? How *ridicule!* And how typical that Rothschild, the upstart of upstarts, should be her sponsor! No, Tout-Paris thought it was a decoy. Why else did his Majesty refrain so carefully from any public display of his so-called intentions?

An anti-Eugénie movement crystallized among the older upper crust. Pereire abetted and financed it. James led the pro-Eugénie forces. The war between Rothschild and the Crédit Mobilier now had a front line running through the finest Empire furniture and the lushest carpets of France. At the Tuileries Ball on January 12, 1853, battle was joined.

Scene: the marshal's room, which only the most privileged were allowed to enter. As usual, Baron James escorted Mlle de Montijo, while her mother leaned on the arm of one of his sons. The younger Rothschild thought he could find room for the two ladies on some settees. Whereupon Eugénie and the wife of an "enemy" minister headed for the same upholstery.

To the tune of a waltz, brief intense hostilities commenced. Eugénie, a tiny bit faster, was gathering up her skirts to sit down when Mme. la Ministre announced, loudly and curtly, that these settees were reserved for ministerial families only. The Spanish lady stood painfully suspended while the ministerial matron took her seat. Even the Rothschilds shifted, pale, from one leg to another.

And then something historic came to pass. The skirmish had been observed from the corner of an imperial eye. Napoleon suddenly interrupted the small reception of which he was the object twenty yards away. In a spectacular breach of protocol he hurried to the embattled settee, offered Eugénie and her mother his arms, and led them to the taborets meant exclusively for the All-Highest family. The waltz kept on playing, but a hush fell over the ball. When the talk resumed a moment later, the whole world knew who had won the palace war.

Eleven days afterwards, the Emperor in a message to the people of France declared that in Eugénie he had "chosen the woman I love and honor."

For once a Rothschild victory was Pyrrhic. James thought he had countered the Crédit Mobilier's fury at the bourse with an attack through the imperial boudoir. But though January 30 marked the Emperor's formal engagement to Eugénie, the ceremony brought an entirely unexpected humiliation for Baron James.

Again the masterful chicanery of the enemy was at work. Pereire had kept his eyes not only on the stock market but on the subtlest nuances of the Paris *haute volée*. For a while now he had watched, and nurtured, a small drama enacted between James Rothschild and Graf Hübner, the new Austrian envoy to France. Hübner did not possess the means of his predecessor. James, still Austria's consul general in Paris, lived on a far more ambassadorial scale than any ambassador. Hübner made futile attempts to treat Rothschild as his subordinate. James sniffed—audibly—that an ambassadorship was meant for a grand seigneur, not a puffed-up little man. This set Hübner seething, and Pereire encouraged him to seethe effectively. When Napoleon's betrothal celebration at Notre Dame was planned, Baron Rothschild naturally figured in the guest list. His invitation was sent in care of the Austrian Embassy. It was not forwarded. Every dignitary in France, including the entire diplomatic corps, appeared at the ceremony, with the blatant exception of Baron James de Rothschild.

Pereire's work was lightning-swift, using one triumph as a steppingstone for another. He already came close to being the financial czar of France. From the Rhine to the Pyrenees he swept everything before him. Yet he well knew the difference between thwarting James and destroying him. Rothschild was a titan straddling five countries. If he was to be annihilated, he would have to be annihilated internationally.

James's failure at Notre Dame did have some international echoes. The ambassadors, ministers and consuls assembled in the cathedral could observe an ugly gap in the hitherto unfailing armor of the house. Pereire considered this a good climate in which to make his first move beyond the border.

And so that very January of 1853, the Crédit Mobilier, barely two months old, wound a tentacle around The Family's Italian fief. The rising Kingdom of Sardinia had concluded one loan with James and was about to contract a second. Pereire distributed some insidiously phrased hints about the clan's decline (*vide* the debacle at Notre Dame). His Crédit Mobilier made a subterranean offer. Possibly he could have clinched the deal—if Fould, in a personal encounter with James, had not boasted of a great Mediterranean coup about to break.

James instantly smelled the correct rat and dispatched his son Alphonse to Italy. The fight for the loan now went on in broad daylight. Young Alphonse Rothschild won it, at a great cost. "You will appreciate," wrote the Sardinian minister Cavour to a friend, "that this competition has been worth some millions to us."

But Sardinia was just a minor prize. All the Italian states together, as a matter of fact, were chicken feed compared to the stakes for which Pereire and Rothschild were now jockeying. The next assault of the Crédit Mobilier focused on nothing less than the Austrian Empire itself.

Again Pereire's timing was ferociously precise. With Metternich's downfall in 1848, The Family had lost its most powerful advocate. Salomon was entering his seventy-ninth year; his grip grew uncertain. Queasy about returning to Vienna, he governed the bank by remote control from Frankfurt and Paris. And because of a new affront, the Austrian ambassador in Paris had reached a serviceable boiling point regarding the Rothschilds.

James still lacked real influence at court, but he had a kind of voluptuous complaint box affixed to the Emperor in the form of Eugénie. Through her, Baron Rothschild stated his grief about the treachery at Notre Dame. In the course of the next court ball, held on March 3, his Majesty went up to James and expressed regret at not having seen the Baron during the betrothal. Napoleon engaged him in warm conversation, all the while ignoring, and thus publicly mortifying, his Excellency, Graf Hübner. Which was exactly grist for Pereire's mill. He knew that the Ambassador, who had more genealogy than money, disliked credit virtuosos like himself. Until now their association had been limited to isolated anti-Rothschild forays. But after this new outrage, the Ambassador was ready for bigger things. Why not form a really important alliance to demolish those archbankers of all time, the Rothschilds?

Pereire and Hübner had a long talk. Both came away edified. Pereire learned what he had vaguely suspected: a huge railroad opportunity was brewing in Vienna. Austria now had an extensive network of tracks, all of which were state-owned except for Salomon Rothschild's line in the north and the Sina road in the south. But the government was again in financial trouble, and one solution lay in the sale of its railroads. The buyer of such assets might well come to dominate transportation and possibly all commerce in Central Europe. Hübner also learned something. Pereire's Crédit Mobilier wanted to help the Sina group purchase the Austrian railways.

A great many negotiations began to sneak and simmer between Pereire in Paris and Sina in Vienna. Conscious of the threat, the Rothschilds tried to counter with purchase offers of their own. They protested that it was they, after all, who had made the first Austrian steam track possible. They argued in a void. Their Metternich had returned to Vienna but not to power, and he was no longer allowed to operate the All-Highest signing machine. The Pereire-Hübner-Sina team forged ahead smoothly. Guided by Ambassador Hübner, a key representative of the Sina interests began to work in the French capital so secretly that not even James knew of his presence, so efficiently that even the imperial family was drawn into the Pereire-Sina net. On the board of the organization which made the railway bid there now appeared not only the two Pereires, Fould and Sina—but also the Duke of Morny, Napoleon's half-brother.

On New Year's Day, 1855, Pereire struck. His outfit bought a great chunk of the Austrian State Railways for a huge but comparatively advantageous price. The Crédit Mobilier, which supplied the money, had won a most powerful stronghold in Austria.

Pereire did not waste one second before trying to convert stronghold into stranglehold. He started negotiations for the two remaining tracks under government control—the Southern Railway, leading from Vienna to Trieste, and the Lombard-Venetian line. At the stock exchange he loosed a series of destructive maneuvers against the Rothschild rail company. His agents separately bought quantities of the enemy stock, then unloaded them together, in a concentrated action to depress the price. Actually it added up to an old trick of The Family's. But now all the cunning and ferocity seemed to be on the anti-Family side.

The black year of 1855 found the Rothschilds as fragile as ordinary human beings, and just as mortal. During that crucial twelve months, three of the four remaining brothers followed Nathan into the grave. Carl of Naples died; then Salomon, head of the beleaguered house in Vienna, and Amschel in Frankfurt. The brothers who had worked and fought together now died almost as one. The cantors wailed burial rites, the women hooded mirrors, during the very months when the *mishpoche*'s strongest foe stalked them in board room and bourse.

Only James, the Parisian, was left—James, and a phalanx of heirs. The year 1855 constitutes a number both funereal and evergreen in The Family's history. It proved what the world had nearly forgotten: that brilliance was the smaller part of Rothschild power; that their greatest talent was (and therefore *is*) iron continuity; and that the dread weapon used by patriarch Mayer would also be handed down to the brothers, to become most potent after their deaths—the weapon called sons.

Pereire was a great expert on, and copyist of, the Rothschild arsenal. But he had forgotten the sons. In particular he had overlooked Anselm, Salomon's boy. Almost by way of camouflage, Anselm presented no very striking figure. By the time he assumed the reins of the Vienna house, he was past fifty. For decades he had led the life of a financial Prince of Wales, with a playboy's escapades in Vienna, Paris, Copenhagen and Berlin, and finally Frankfurt where he had his old orthodox Uncle Amschel for a duenna and the dignity of the Austrian consulship to keep him off the streets at night. What threat could he be to Pereire in full career?

Pereire's Crédit Mobilier now ruled as the financial arm of the French Empire, in the 1850's the first power on the Continent. He had stalemated James, had grabbed the concession for building Russia's railways, had captured most of the Austrian ones and would probably conquer all of them. To cap it all, Pereire was about to launch his own bank in Vienna, based on the triumphant example of the Crédit Mobilier.

Or was he?

Here he received his first shock. When the project reached the pertinent Habsburg ministers, they revealed that an Austrian company of that kind was already being called into existence. It, too, was a "people's bank." It, too, boasted a princely array of names, such as Fürstenberg, Schwarzenberg and Auersperg. It had even had the nerve to borrow the very name of the Crédit Mobilier: it was called the Creditanstalt. And it was organized, led, and primarily financed by—Anselm von Rothschild.

Overnight the spoiled princeling emerged a beast of prey, as shrewd, as swift and hard as any of his forefathers. His company issued no less than a half million shares (compared with Pereire's 120,000). And though the Creditanstalt throve as mightily on the bourse as the Mobilier, it was managed more sharply and yet more circumspectly. It would never, like its rival, hang on the tender mercies of the speculators.

But for the moment Pereire was less concerned with stocks than with rails. Suddenly, Rothschild triggered a counteroffensive in this department too. And "Rothschild" did not mean just Anselm. Lionel had succeeded Nathan in London; Alphonse, James's eldest, was coming to the fore in France. The three cousins constituted the same indivisible crew the five brothers had once been; all three had a hand in the Creditanstalt. Early in 1856 the new trinity made so stunning an offer to the Habsburg government that the finance minister could not turn them down. In return for a hundred million lire (almost fifty million dollars), they received, lock, stock and barrel, Austria's Lombard-Venetian railway tracks.

With one stroke they had outpaced Pereire's gains. At the same time their men began to attack the Crédit Mobilier in all the principal bourses of Europe. While Pereire was kept busy countering dagger thrusts at the stock exchange, the three abruptly came down on him with yet another horde of locomotives: Anselm, Lionel and Alphonse bought the concession for the Austrian Southern Railway and united it with their Venetian-Lombard lines into one formidable system.

Pereire had not yet reached the end of his tether. The Crédit Mobilier could still command large reserves of money. In international credit operations it kept undercutting The Family. During 1859 the Rothschilds were on the verge of a loan to Sardinia, but the Crédit Mobilier smothered the negotiations with its offers and campaigns. The Sardinian prime minister, Cavour, made a famous statement: "If after divorcing the Rothschilds we marry Messrs. Pereire, I think we shall get on very well together." As it turned out, the loan was floated by the Sardinians themselves. The Crédit Mobilier had foiled the Rothschilds in Italy.

But Pereire was running out of ammunition. Those damnable Rothschild sons spearheaded a dozen varieties of assault against him. They kept their big guns booming on the financial and industrial fronts. They also sniped in the diplomatic field. Anselm developed into an insidious puller of Habsburg wires; in 1859 Hübner was replaced as Austrian ambassador in Paris by Prince Richard Metternich, son of The Family's great friend.

The Crédit Mobilier had to fall back from its Austrian and Italian outposts to France alone. Even here the Rothschilds presecuted Pereire without let-up. They pushed him onto slippery ground by a diabolic tactic: on sound investments they leveled a murderous competition of low bids; but when it came to more dubious loans, The Family, after whetting the rival's appetite with a show of fight, always contrived to be nosed out. The financing of Maximilian's doomed empire in Mexico was only one such poisonous plum, gently dropped into the enemy's mouth. Pereire choked, cursed, had to swallow it.

By 1860 the Crédit Mobilier was quoted at 800, a sad descent from the peak of 1,600, yet above the price of original issue. To maintain confidence, it paid large dividends, which came out of capital, not from current earnings.

The Rothschilds kept moving in.

In 1861 the harbingers of Pereire's final doom began to run through Paris. Jules Mires, his indirect ally, fell. This highly gifted charlatan (we have met him before) had gone beyond the wholesale blackmail of doctors or railways. Now he was a member of Louis Napoleon's councils and, by his daughter's adroit marriage, father-in-law to Prince de Polignac. He enjoyed a business alliance with the Duke of Morny, Napoleon's half-brother, and through him with the Crédit Mobilier. The Rothschilds decided to pick off Mires first. Paris' yellow press, with which Mires still worked, could not save his tinselly stock holdings when a billion francs worth of pressure was turned on against him at the exchange. In 1861 the police arrested him for fraud.

The Mires scandal corroded still further the credit health of the French Empire, which had been at a low ebb for years—one might almost say since Baron James had been eased out of the heart of the picture. Napoleon III took a cold look at the money men in his palace. When he had finished looking, Achille Fould, his finance minister and the governmental cornerstone of the Crédit Mobilier, resigned.

A year later Fould regained the ministry. Pereire thought the tide had turned, rushed to his friend and asked for a monopoly on the state credit business. He found that Fould was a friend no more. M. le Ministre seemed very cool and negative and busy. At the same time French government bonds, which had been cutting a sorry picture at the exchange, perked up somewhat through huge anonymous purchases. But France possessed only one force capable of bringing life into so depressed an issue: the Rothschilds.

The Rothschilds helping—that is, conspiring with—Fould? Was it possible? A dozen years ago Pereire had deserted The Family for Fould. Would Fould now desert Pereire for The Family? And could the Emperor, for so long on the Pereire side of the financial front—could he be going over?

He went over indeed, with fanfares, flags and footmen. On February 17, 1862, Napoleon III paid a state visit to Rothschild I, King of the Jews. The spectacle unrolled at Ferrières, James's stupendous new estate.

At the Emperor's entry, the imperial banners were hoisted together with the Family colors on all four towers of the château. Surrounded by a liveried army of lackeys, pedestaled on a thick green-velvet carpet embroidered with gold bees, old James de Rothschild greeted the monarch. He led his Majesty through Renaissance pavilions hung with Van Dycks, Velasquezes, Giorgiones, Rubenses; studded with treasures gathered around the world.

According to Family custom, all visiting crowned heads were asked to plant a young cedar in the gardens. After doing his duty, Napoleon ate off Sèvres porcelain painted by Boucher, listened to music specially composed for the occasion by maestro Rossini, and then went off to hunt in the immense shoots of the Rothschild park—the total score of the party being 1,231 head of game killed on the grounds in one afternoon. When the guests returned to the château, the choir of the Paris opera vocalized a hunting song while a buffet of rarest delicacies was served. And when the Emperor left at night, his coach rode through an espalier of Rothschild torches lighting up the sky to the very edge of the estate.

The British and Austrian ambassadors participated in the festival; so did the Emperor's ministers of the interior and foreign affairs; and so did Achille Fould, in charge of France's finances.

As for Pereire, he sojourned not at the imperial table, but before a judge. The thousand-franc butchers, for whose sake he had launched his bank, had begun to sue him. The full consequences of the Mexican loan disaster were hitting home. Yet a last resort was still open. Pereire and his brother made a desperate appeal to their former friend and protector, Louis Napoleon.

"I shall do everything," the Emperor said, "to support them, because the Empire is deeply indebted to them; but I cannot afford to impede the course of justice or to come into conflict with it."

This was very frigid comfort. By December, 1866, the shares of the Crédit Mobilier stood at 600. In April, 1867, the company had to report a loss of eight million francs. The shares dropped to 350. In October they tumbled to the incredible low of 140. The Crédit Mobilier collapsed.

Emile Pereire, the great financial star, sputtered out into obscurity. As ruthless as the clan, and as well-connected, he had not had their endless solvency nor their instinct for distinguishing between finely calculated risk and florid overspeculation. Achille Fould, despite all recantations, had to resign again, irrevocably this time.

As for Napoleon III— Another Tuileries Ball came along, late in the 1860's. "Entendez vous," said James while the orchestra played still another fateful waltz, "pas de paix, pas d'Empire" (No peace, no Empire).

It became a famous prophecy. James died in 1868 at seventy-six, too soon to see it come true. Two years later Louis Napoleon launched his disastrous war against Prussia. The Germans captured him at Sedan. The French deposed him in Paris. Ironically enough, he was held prisoner of war in Wilhelmshöhe, the very castle which had catapulted Mayer and sons into their enduring power.

Throughout all upheavals, the peacocks, Giorgiones and royal cedars went on multiplying at Ferrières, the Rothschild château. The Third Empire was just one phase in the progress of The Family.

# VII

# *THE MISHPOCHE JUNIOR*

## 1. *Inside Society*

### (a) *Anselm*

THE long-drawn-out vendetta with the Crédit Mobilier obscured another important Family development. Most Rothschilds were getting to be truly at home in palaces. The founders had been, as founders often are, pirates. The founders' sons could, if provoked, let loose some lethal swordplay. But that was a faculty incidental to the fact of being a gentleman. Each Rothschild generation pursued its vocation uncompromisingly. The *Mishpoche* Junior and the *Mishpoche* III gained ultimate chic with the same élan that had gained the dynasts ultimate wealth.

In Austria, where society was most difficult for Jews, the social breakthrough was most significant. Salomon's son Anselm began his reign over the local branch in 1855, not long after Francis Joseph started his over the Habsburg realm. The young Emperor—a strong, aloof personality—was nobody's signing machine. His Majesty brooked no absolute chancellor like Metternich and certainly no absolute banker like old Salomon Rothschild.

Anselm's office, therefore, could no longer use all the bellpulls which had once set off such effective ringing in the Kaiser's Hofburg. But Anselm devised his own forms of power—less direct, more velvety, and as useful in the end. His father had been a court Jew. *He* was a courtly Jew. When Francis Joseph returned after a long journey, Anselm made a gracious gesture, almost, one might say, from one great nobleman to another.

"My dear minister," he wrote to the minister of the interior, ". . . our hearts go out to meet the Father of our country. As some satisfaction to my feelings, I would like to make a small contribution to ease the sufferings of the needy in Vienna, to the amount of the enclosed five thousand florins . . . of which you will make such use as may seem best to you."

We note a significant difference of tone between father Salomon's febrile servilities and this rather elegantly tossed-off largesse. Old Salomon, despite all his colossal wealth and power, had to intrigue for his Viennese citizenship. Anselm, wealthier still, was inscribed in the golden book of the capital and in 1861 became a member of the Imperial House of Lords. He had a perfect, pungent command of the ghetto tongue, but his natural language was Schönbrunner Deutsch—the soft, musical drawl native to Austrian nobility, and by far the silkiest form of spoken German.

Anselm's residences, like his charities, were overwhelming; his vengefulness, on at least one occasion, fragrantly awesome. A casino club near Vienna blackballed him for the usual anti-Semitic reason. By way of reply, Anselm bought a modern sewage-disposal unit for the adjoining village and installed it within sight and smell of the overly impeccable casino. He was quickly sent a membership card. Sanitary construction went right on, however. And the card came back by return mail, scented with the most expensive perfume.

### (b) *Lionel and Brothers*

The most vivid and varied conquest of Vanity Fair took place in England. It was not an instant affair. Nathan had died so suddenly, and comparatively so early in the clan's total rise, that the London heirs had to reconfirm their business eminence before essaying society.

Lionel, as the eldest of Nathan's three sons, assumed his father's place in New Court. But the stock exchange saw his agents rather than young Rothschild in the flesh. The "Rothschild pillar" remained untenanted. Rivals took optimistic note of this and of the fact that, like most upper-class Englishmen, Lionel indulged in a certain amount of education (at the University of Göttingen), in patriotism, and in *noblesse oblige*. Redoubtable Nathan hadn't been handicapped by such distractions. The monster tribe, London division, seemed to be declining into mere virtue. Would it be outpaced by its rivals?

The question soon received conclusive answers. One of Lionel's legacies had been an uncompleted twenty-million-pound government loan reimbursing slave owners in the British dominions after the abolition of slavery. The young man in New Court managed the transaction with the smoothest skill. He was instrumental in raising the eight million pounds with which the British government relieved the Irish famine in 1847. And in 1854 he floated the sixteen million pounds that enabled Great Britain to prosecute the Crimean War.

All these operations still had certain political overtones, masterfully modulated by Nathan's successor. The first item underscored the "sensibly liberal" antislavery stand of the House. The Irish deal constituted a form of very illuminated good works, further spotlighted by the fact that Lionel waived his commission. The Crimean loan deliberately broke with the antiwar policy of the House; to fight the Czar's anti-Semitic government, the Rothschilds shed their pacifist scruples.

Other business was done more strictly for the money. Many of the eighteen government loans brought out during Lionel's career—totaling the vertiginous sum of 1,600 million pounds sterling (almost 25,000 million dollars)—were in this category. New Court played a key part in consolidating the *mishpoche*'s control of Europe's mercury mines. It reached down to South Africa, where Cecil Rhodes was beginning to build a kingdom made of diamonds. It financed vast copper and nitrate enterprises overseas.

The new generation began to play down the habit of clawing wealth directly out of the political arena. The trend was toward more purely economic and therefore less exposed endeavors. In the best circles one does not make history by the sweat of one's own brow. One hires the makers. And meanwhile one rides to hounds.

Lionel knew that well. He tempered supremacy with dignity, a nuance New Court had not stressed before. His younger brother Anthony sat smashingly on horseback and was knighted by the Queen. Mayer, the youngest, bred fine horses, cut a figure at the Jockey Club, and became the first Rothschild to win the Derby. The three—patrician banker, baronet, and sportsman—needed one more elegance to complete the aristocratic gamut. This the fourth brother, Nathaniel, provided. He was an esthetic invalid, living in Paris. Despite a partial paralysis (the result of a hunting accident) he collected masterpieces, kept a brilliant salon, and, since it pleased him to have his own wine label, bought the renowned Mouton vineyards near Bordeaux.

Each of the three brothers resident in England headed a part in the Victorian pageant. To begin with Lionel, we must begin with Gunnersbury Park. In 1835, shortly before his death, Nathan Rothschild had bought the domain as a suburban pleasance. Once Princess Amelia, daughter of George II, had lived there. But the estate did not come into its own until Lionel inherited it and, in the course of years, decked it with such splendors as were unknown in England outside her Majesty's own grounds.

Gunnersbury encompassed, besides the obligatory lakes and swans, a resplendent Italian villa, exquisitely illuminated walks, huge flowerbeds landscaped in the form of baskets and rimmed with heliotropes, climbing rose trees, pergolas and latticed benches. It had an enormous Japanese garden, complete with giant cane, rivulets, stone bridges, palms and temples. "Marvelous," said the Mikado's ambassador on his first visit. "We have nothing like it in Japan."

Lionel's parties were worthy of such backdrops. "The banquet," Disraeli wrote of one, "could not be surpassed in splendor or recherche even at Windsor or Buckingham Palace."

A *fête champêtre* held in July, 1845, in honor of the Duke and Duchess of Cambridge and the Duchess of Gloucester became the social event of the season. Dukes royal and nonroyal, princes, diplomats and the sachems of the City, as well as five hundred other selected guests, sat down to dinner in tents laid out in the huge parks; strolled under the lights of thousands of multicolored lamps; listened to virtuosos, prima donnas and artistes proffering the best music from five capitals.

After the Revolution of 1848, the most rarefied French aristocracy—such as the Duchess of Orleans, the Duke of Chartres and the Comte de Paris—would sweeten their exile here. (Everything and nothing changes. Five months previous to this writing, the present Comtesse de Paris attended a great garden fete given by Baroness Edouard de Rothschild.) Cardinal Wiseman readily accepted an invitation by way of protesting, it was rumored, the law in the Papal States that still confined Jews to the ghetto. The Cardinal, innocently enough, created the one crass outburst of religious prejudice in this Jewish palace: a Protestant refused to share the table with his Catholic Eminence.

In 1857 Gunnersbury saw the nuptials of Lionel's eldest daughter, Leonora. She had, as one commentator put it, "lovely . . . liquid, almond-shaped eyes, the sweet complexion of a tea-rose," and ranked among classic English beauties of all time, like the Duchess of Manchester, Lady Constance Grosvenor and Mrs. Bulkeley. Her bridegroom was, in Family terms, the one young man in the universe worthy to raise her bridal veil: Alphonse, her cousin and future head of the French house. The band of the First Life Guards serenaded the two at their wedding breakfast. All the great world flocked to the ceremony where, under a *chupah* held by her brothers, Leonora de Rothschild became Baroness Alphonse de Rothschild. The French ambassador lifted his glass and his voice in honor of the bride. One past and one future prime minister of the Empire (Lord John Russell and Benjamin Disraeli) followed with toasts.

"Under this roof," said Dizzy, overdoing things with his usual felicity, "are the heads of the name and family of Rothschild—a name famous in every capital of Europe and every division of the globe—a family not more regarded for its riches than esteemed for its honor, integrity and public spirit."

Eight years later Lionel married off his other daughter, Evelina, to the one young man in the universe worthy of the prize: Ferdinand de Rothschild, her cousin and son of the head of the Austrian house. Among the fourteen bridesmaids were included such lofty names as Montgomery, Lennox and Beauclerk. The First Lord of the Admiralty proposed the health of the Rothschild family, and Dizzy, toasting the bride, again overdid things with his usual felicity.

Some piquant overtones distinguished this wedding from the first one. Ferdinand's mother, a British Rothschild (Nathan's eldest daughter), was back in England for good. She had left Anselm because the Austrian chief-of-clan kept collecting railroad networks and mistresses with equal zest. The marital rift failed to diminish the dynastic solidarity, as was shown by the presence of the Austrian ambassador and the Austrian branch.

A second example of Family insouciance materialized in an incident much relished by Jews all over England. Benjamin Disraeli, later Lord Beaconsfield, was a baptized Jew. The father of the bride could not help joshing his friend a bit as the cantor was about to pronounce his benedictions.

"Ben," Lionel called out before the great assembly, "there are so many of you Christians present that our *chazan* [Yiddish for cantor] wants to know whether he should just read the prayers or sing them as in the synagogue?"

"Oh, please let them sing it," Dizzy said. "I like to hear old-fashioned tunes."

What made the second wedding most different from the first, however, was its scene: not Gunnersbury Park, but Lionel's new-built town mansion at 148 Piccadilly. It stood next to Apsley House, the Duke of Wellington's residence, and soon rivaled its neighbor in fame. Six stories tall, this Victorian monster had a tidal wave of a white marble staircase; a ballroom as big as the royal yacht; lusciously embroidered satin curtains the size of mainsails; whole coral reefs of salons and drawing rooms glistening with marble, gold and scarlet. Each chair offered, to quote a contemporary wit, gilt-edged security. The furnishings included, among a host of ineffabilities, a silver table service by Garrard weighing nearly ten thousand ounces; and the famous apple-green service of Sèvres china partly painted by le Bel, a counterpart of which The Family gave to the present Queen Elizabeth for her wedding. The top of the mansion commanded a majestic view of Hyde Park and Green Park—and of the Duke of Wellington's iron chair, placed on the roof of *his* house so that he could sit there and watch the troops march by without being himself observed.

At Lionel's house, Disraeli ate what he gladly admitted to be "the best dinner in London." And it was Lionel's hospitality that brought this high-colored genius some of the greatest private and professional moments of his life.

"Mr. Disraeli," said Baroness Lionel one evening, "will you take Mrs. Wyndham Lewis in to dinner?"

"Oh, anything rather than that insufferable woman!" muttered Diz, and did take in Mrs. Lewis, and repeated the sacrifice during subsequent Rothschild soirees, and married her when she became free, and found in her the indispensable support on which to rest a high career.

A memorable climax of that career also began by way of a Rothschild meal. It was eaten, to be precise, on Sunday, November 14, 1875. Disraeli, Prime Minister by then, was supping with Lionel at 148 Piccadilly, as was his week-end wont. During the main course the butler approached with the telegram salver. The instant Lionel reached for the slip of paper, an episode unfolded which, for concentrated drama, approaches the Waterloo chapter in The Family's history.

The message was from one of the Baron's Paris informants. Rothschild paused for a moment after he had read it, then summed it up aloud: Egypt's debt-ridden Khedive had offered his Suez Canal shares to the French government but had become impatient with France's terms.

Rothschild and Disraeli looked at each other with the same thought. The Suez Canal was one of the world's great commercial and strategic assets. Britain had long wanted to lay hands on it, without being able to pin the Khedive down to a negotiating position. Apparently he was now in such desperate money straits that he would sell his 177,000 Suez shares to anyone who could pay a big enough price fast enough.

At last the Prime Minister said a two-word sentence: "How much?"

Lionel instantly sent a telegraphic query to Paris. The meat grew cold, but neither guest nor host had much of an appetite. Dessert came and went untouched, though Lionel was ordinarily a great lover of sweet fruit. By the time the brandy arrived, the telegram salver made another appearance. The answer was: one hundred million francs, or four million pounds, or forty-four million current American dollars.

"We will take them," said the Prime Minister.

"Ah . . ." said Baron Lionel. For him the suspense was over, though for the world it was about to begin.

At Downing Street the following Monday morning,

Rothschild's information was confirmed by other sources. Both the Prime Minister and his aides agreed that England must strike while the iron was hot. She had to realize her chance before other countries learned of its existence. Speed was as essential as secrecy. Parliament happened to be in recess and therefore could not appropriate the sum. Nor could Disraeli rush off to the Bank of England; a law forbade it to loan money to the government while the House of Commons was not in session. In any case, the Old Lady of Threadneedle Street could not have gathered so many millions so quickly without upsetting the money market. As for the joint-stock banks, their chairmen were empowered to dispose of such a giant amount only after a laborious summoning of the board of directors.

"We have scarcely time to breathe!" Disraeli exclaimed in a note to Queen Victoria.

All this, of course, added up to one inevitability, already implicit in Baron Lionel's "Ah . . ." Disraeli called his ministers together, received their authorization, then stuck his head outside the Cabinet chamber to speak a single prearranged word: "Yes." His secretary leaped into a waiting coach, to be ushered shortly afterward into the Partners' Room at New Court.

There, at the very desk where Edmund de Rothschild sits today, his great-grandfather Lionel reclined, eating muscatel grapes. He went right on nibbling as he was told that the British government would very much like to have four million pounds sterling by tomorrow, please.

For two seconds Lionel chewed a grape. "I shall give them to you," he said, and daintily spat out the seed.

Within forty-eight hours the London *Times* announced that N. M. Rothschild & Sons had credited to the account of the Khedive the sum of four million pounds, and that all the latter's shares in the Suez Canal Company had passed into possession of Her Majesty's Government. These, together with a small lot of stocks already under British ownership, gave England a majority voice. Now she controlled the globe's new lifeline.

"It is just settled!" Disraeli wrote on November 24, 1875, in a jubilant letter to the Queen. "You have it, Madam. The French Government has been out-generalled. . . . Four millions sterling! and almost immediately. There was only one firm that could do it—Rothschilds."

In 1935 the holdings acquired at that price figured in the national assets at more than ninety-three million pounds. And the dividends England received, almost from the start, more than matched the low 3 per cent interest charged by Lionel. In 1936–1937 alone the Canal earned England 2,248,437 pounds, a rate of 56½ per cent on the original purchase money.

Disraeli's evening meal, then, included a uniquely nutritious bite. Even before the occasion, though, Dizzy had thanked the clan for this and other entertainments with a bread-and-butter letter such as only he could write. In *Coningsby*, his most successful novel, the "Sidonias" figure prominently as a rich, powerful, admirable, intelligent, and easily identifiable Jewish family. In fact, they contain—and this always constitutes supreme tribute—some elements of the author's own personality.

## (c) *Country Squires*

Lionel's house at 148 Piccadilly was not the only Rothschild residence in the neighborhood where a prime minister could get a good dinner. At 143 Piccadilly, Ferdinand Rothschild had his Louis XVI *palais* with an exquisite white ballroom. His sister lived magnificently at 142. At

107 Mayer moved into the pioneer West End mansion that Nathan, the founder, had taken. Nearby, Nathan's middle son, Anthony, maintained a ducal household at Grosvenor Place. Not much more than a diamond's throw away, at Seamore Place and Hamilton Place, Lionel's boys began to erect their great establishments. Before long the region was tagged "Rothschild Row"—a fairy-tale re-creation of Frankfurt's Jew Street.

But a Rothschild Grove also came into being as an enclave in greenest Buckinghamshire. It was started by Mrs. Nathan. Like a good Jewish mother, she thought her boys were overworking themselves in the soot of the city. Consequently, she bought some hunting country in the Vale of Aylesbury. Mayer, the youngest, soon caught the bucolic spirit and hired the same Joseph Paxton who had created Prince Albert's Crystal Palace at the London Exhibition. Paxton built for Mayer an Anglo-Norman supervilla called Mentmore Towers, which he filled with several museums' worth of inlaid furniture, tapestries, vases, carpets and *objets;* surrounded it with gardens, parks, pastures, racing stables and a stud farm; and caused Lady Eastlake to exclaim that "the Medicis were never lodged so in the height of their glory."

Thus Mayer, out of devotion to a worried mother, became not a pale pavement-bound clerk but the huntingest, shootingest, ridingest, merriest baron in England. One of the most hospitable, as well. At Mentmore Towers, Delane, the editor of the London *Times*, would volley brilliant dialectics at the above-quoted Lady Eastlake, a famous bluestocking who would volley right back. Prime Minister Gladstone would moderate, Matthew Arnold make measured interjections, and William Makepeace Thackeray sit by silently and politely, as writers will, and occasionally venture a *mot juste*. One of these was so *juste* that it entered public domain and became associated with Talleyrand, who is supposed to have delivered it at a *French* Rothschild dinner. But it was Thackeray's utterance, and it occurred during one of Lady Eastlake's tirades on fashion.

"Female dress," said Thackeray, "is often like a winter's day. It begins too late and ends too soon."

Another Rothschild country house filled Thackeray with a more tender inspiration. Mayer's elder brother, Baron Anthony, had developed an estate at Aston Clinton (just outside Aylesbury), as lush and more tasteful than Mayer's. Its long house parties would attract Robert Browning, Lord Tennyson, Gladstone and Disraeli (the two prime ministers who kept succeeding each other), as well as Matthew Arnold and Thackeray. Baron Anthony's little daughters could take a survey course in nineteenth-century English political and literary history by just walking through their father's drawing room.

To return to the tender inspiration. Heine's infatuation with Baroness James de Rothschild in Paris was no stronger than Thackeray's with Baroness Anthony at Aston Clinton. He sketched this touching portrait of her in *Pendennis:*

> I saw a Jewish lady only yesterday with a child at her knee, and from whose face toward the child there shone a sweetness so angelical that it seemed to form a sort of halo round them both. I protest I could have knelt before her too, and adored in her the Divine beneficence.

Being immortalized is delightful, but when you're in your teens getting gifts is nicer still. And what kind of gift does a Rothschild daughter get? Constance, Sir Anthony's older one, had a passion for teaching. Quite naturally, Daddy gave her—a school. Constance was approaching sweet sixteen when, as she wrote in her journal, ". . . my father asked me what I should like to have for a birthday present. I boldly answered 'an infants' school.' My request was granted and I was allowed to lay the first stone of the new building."

All these splendors were outdone in the end by Baron Lionel's rusticities. Since he already had No. 148 and suburban Gunnersbury Park, he took to the country late in life. But when he made his move, it was on a scale behooving Nathan's eldest and his chief heir. As a start he bought Tring Estate in Hertfordshire, adjacent to the Buckinghamshire properties of his kin. Exclusive of furniture and pictures, the deal cost him a neat quarter of a million pounds (three and a half million dollars), for good reason. Over 3,500 acres surrounded Tring Manor, a lovely seventeenth-century mansion. Sir Christopher Wren, the architect of St. Paul's Cathedral, had designed it, and Charles II had presented it to Nell Gwynn. At Tring, the former orange-seller of Drury Lane, latterly risen to be Britain's Madame Pompadour, had sat and danced and drunk in state.

Here Lionel Rothschild now held his country fetes, with the initials N. G. still blazing from cornices and ceilings. It is reported that the new owner was not always pleased with these curlicued grimaces of England's raffish past. Quite addicted to dignity, Lionel had assumed—and had made his brothers assume—the title of Baron which Nathan had so gruffly ignored. He also converted the Teutonic von Rothschild into the more *soigné* French de Rothschild. Old Nathan, as we have seen, had had himself buried without nobiliary adornment, but his son found a way of ennobling him after death. On the tombstone of the founder's wife Lionel put, "Baroness Hannah de

Rothschild, relict of the late Baron Nathan Mayer de Rothschild."

It is quite natural that such a man would gather around his fireplace fewer of the esthetic types often found at his brothers', and more of Disraeli and Gladstone in their official moods, as well as the greatest magnates, financiers and politicians of the age. And yet those Nell Gwynn initials seemed to sow, now and then, Restoration gremlins in the Victorian grandeur. A story has it that at one Tring stag dinner two cabinet ministers sat next to each other, one bald, one blessed with a full though artificial head of hair. While serving, a footman caught his sleeve button in the toupee and saw it drop to the ground. With more speed than discernment, he picked it up at once to replace it —on the wrong pate. The bald Excellency had suddenly become hairy, the hairy Excellency bald, and the entire dinner company a good deal merrier.

In addition to Tring, the Baron acquired great seats at Halton and at Ascott Wing. All these Rothschild settlements shed on Buckinghamshire a great anecdotal renown. Under the Family touch the livestock of the region throve as never before. Venery flowered: Anthony's partridge shoots and the princely stag hunt at Mentmore became proverbial.

Still, one thing bothered the local gentry at first. Weren't those Rothschilds de-Christianizing Buckinghamshire? Would a velvet Judea displace the Anglican arcadia? Our rich infidels soon dispelled this doubt by restoring churches, installing organs, endowing vicarages more opulently than preceding owners had. When the Bishop of Oxford went confirming in the neighboring countryside, he and his entire retinue were put up at Sir Anthony's Aston Clinton.

Yet what would perfect and confirm Rothschild supremacy in the end was *not* their gestures to the majority faith. In a rather fascinating way, the opposite process turned the trick. An Israelite family clinched pre-eminence in a Christian world by becoming more Jewish than most Jews.

## 2. *Kings of the Jews*

The same Lionel who had so carefully rebaronized his family branch lost all interest in Anglo-Saxon hauteur when it came to his religion. At the Feast of Tabernacles he personally hammered palm branches onto the very gentile architecture of New Court. Let any rabbi marry in London, and a Rothschild wedding gift arrived, usually by truck. At the Jewish New Year great baskets of flowers and fruit were delivered to synagogues "With the compliments of N. M. Rothschild & Sons." New Court, of course, remained closed on Saturdays and often used Yiddish dialect as a kind of code in its cables. (Once one of Baron Lionel's agents, having gotten wind of an impending truce in a South American war, sent a telegram reading, "Mr. Sholem is expected soon"—*sholem* being Hebrew for peace.) Baroness Lionel edited and collected a volume of Prayers and Meditations.

The Baron himself went much further. We will soon see him fighting a dogged and seemingly hopeless battle for Jewish privilege in Parliament. And having wrested, against all odds, a decisive bit of Jewish emancipation out of the Commons, in 1869 he limped, already half crippled by gout, onto the dais of the new Jewish Synagogue, exclaiming, "We are emancipated, but if our emancipation should damage our faith, it would be a curse instead of a blessing!"

He was only following dynastic precedent. His Viennese Uncle Salomon of the founding generation, for example, was an expert lobbyist who knew exactly how much pressure to apply at what governmental level. But on the point of aiding his coreligionists he became almost irrational with solicitude. On one occasion a fellow Jew named Roquirol had brought a fine flock of Merino sheep to Vienna and had asked Rothschild to help him in their sale. Salomon deemed the matter too urgent for mere livestock jobbers, and instantly dashed off a letter to the Chancellor of the Empire.

"I humbly request your Highness," he wrote to Prince Metternich, "to put in a word for Herr Moses Roquirol when there should be an opportunity for doing so, as there is sure to be in the salons of your Highness, which are the meeting place of brilliance and fashion."

It is a little difficult to visualize the Prince promoting a herd of sheep through a drawing room thronged with brilliance and fashion. But it is not easy, either, to imagine Nathan, a tycoon in full career, suspending his conquest of foreign markets to announce that he would honor no bills drawn on any German city which denied Jews their treaty rights. This is just what N. M. did in 1820. Two decades later James Rothschild was embroiled in his great railway duel with Achille Fould. Yet he even interrupted this fight to campaign against sudden anti-Semitic persecution in Syria.

"M. Fould, the chief rabbi of Rive Gauche," wrote Heine, referring to Fould's Left Bank railway, "delivered with the calm of a sage an excellent speech in the Chamber of Deputies while his coreligionists were being tortured in Syria. We must give the chief rabbi of Rive Droit [Rothschild] credit for showing a nobler spirit in his sympathies for the House of Israel. . . ."

Carl von Rothschild would not conclude a loan to the Pope without badgering his Holiness about the abolition of the Roman ghetto in 1850. In 1853 Austria imposed a new restriction on the Jews that kept them from buying real estate. The law didn't touch privileged exceptions like the Rothschilds, yet The Family instantly formed a coalition on the bourses of Paris and London (with the tacit connivance of the Vienna branch) in order to punish Austrian credit. James, in person, tore into the Austrian embassy with such ferociousness that the ambassador (then the not particularly Jew-loving Graf Hübner) advised Vienna "to soothe the children of Israel."

"He is, in a word, beside himself," the ambassador reported of James.

That same year Bismarck, still a Prussian career diplomat in Frankfurt, reported on the same subject to Berlin. "The efforts . . . which Austria made . . . to secure the emancipation of the Jews seems attributable to the Rothschilds. . . . The attitude a government brings to bear upon the Jewish problem . . . profoundly affects the house. . . . There are occasions when other than purely business considerations determine the policy of this family. . . ."

Bismarck did not realize how right he was. Soon after his memorandum, Berlin decided to honor Mayer Carl Rothschild, Amschel's nephew and his successor-elect as head of the Frankfurt house. The Prussian king appointed Mayer Court Banker and awarded him the Order of the Red Eagle, Third Class. It was, however, a Jewish Red Eagle. The normal form of the medal, a cross, had been redesigned especially for Baron Mayer into an oval badge. Evidently Prussia did not think a Jew fit to wear a cruciform emblem, even if it was of honorific and not religious significance.

The Baron hinted his feelings to Bismarck: wasn't it strange to honor a man and at the same time to discriminate against him? The thought did not get through to Berlin. In 1857 the Prussian government imposed on Mayer another segregated Red Eagle, this time of the Second Class, in the form of a second oval. It was like being awarded the Order of the Yellow Star. Obviously Berlin considered Rothschild a very important but not particularly equal person.

Now the Baron's feeling about those ovals was made plain. Pointedly he acted as if he didn't have them. He found flagrantly bad excuses to escape occasions when he would have to wear them and made rather free with his irritation.

At last Berlin woke up. The Prince of Prussia ordered Bismarck, who had other things to do, to compile a detailed report on Baron Rothschild's behavior with his individualized medals.

Bismarck's answer read in part:

> In accordance with the Royal Command of the 27th instant, I have the honor dutifully to inform you that I have not seen Court Banker Mayer Carl von Rothschild wearing such a decoration, since he does not go to big functions, and when he does wear orders, prefers to wear the Greek Order of the Redeemer or the Spanish Order of Isabella the Catholic. On the occasion of the official reception which I myself gave . . . which he would have to attend in uniform, he excused himself on the ground of ill health, it being painful to him to wear the Red Eagle decoration for non-Christians, as he would have to do on that occasion. I draw similar inference from the fact that whenever he comes to dine with me, he merely wears the ribbon of the Order in his buttonhole. . . .

Prussia never desegregated its Red Eagles, and the Rothschilds never forgave—a fact which may have played a part later on, when the Kaiser asked them in vain to establish a Berlin branch of The Family. Nor did they stop expressing and defending their faith in ways Jewry had not known since the Book of Kings.

Ferrières, the French Family's great country palace, featured a private synagogue. The principal Rothschild town mansion in London, Lionel's 148 Piccadilly, had an unfinished cornice to commemorate the destruction of Jerusalem. In imperial Austria the social fall season was marked by the Rothschild stag hunts, which, however, always suffered abrupt interruption on one afternoon. The sundry high-born Christian guests were reduced to chess-playing while the hosts left for the Vienna synagogue. There they fasted and prayed through the Day of Atonement before resuming horse and hound again.

All over Europe the greatest chefs began to learn, if not a downright kosher, at least a baconless cuisine. And a curious new custom began to spread from the Family fetes to great soirees in a dozen countries: after dinner the gentlemen did not adjourn from the smoking room to join the ladies in the salon; instead, the ladies had to come to the gentlemen. Rothschild practices were often followed before they were understood, and many people failed to grasp that this arrangement was the elegant outcome of a male-centered patriarchal philosophy.

And of course the clan took great care to implant Judaism in the young, often through full-time religious tutors. The result was more than a formalistic respect for Hebrew tradition. A child's diary has preserved how aristocratic English diction, naïve misspellings, a Talmudic delight in soul-searching, leaping high spirits and grave religious devotion were spontaneously intermingled in a

Rothschild girlhood. Annie, Sir Anthony's younger daughter, wrote in her journal:

> How I should like to paint like a genius. . . . To have an innate genius, to be selftaught, to see masterly drawing developed under my own pencil. Yes, I should like it, but it is good that I have not been thus favored, that I have only a little natural talent, for it does not give rise to the love of superioty [*sic*] characteristic of me. I like to show my superioty in playing some pieces of brilliancy, my superioty in my little knowledge of Hebrew, my superioty of reasoning powers in geometry. It is a very difficult fault, this, to cut out, so difficult do I find it not to exult in the little I know. . . . But with all my faults I have an innate respect for love for religion and enthusiastic adoration for the holy creed of Judaism. May God forgive me, but even in this I did not wish to be inferior to anyone. I heard with envy of Clemmie's [her cousin, the daughter of Mayer Carl Rothschild] sudden [religious] zeal. Is that the way to show my reverence to him who hath said Love Thy Neighbor Like Thyself? Oh Almighty God, hear my prayer, make my heart soft and charitable to all those around me, then I may be worthy of being one of those chosen ones, for Thou hast said through thy prophet Moses that we shall love our fellow creatures. . . .

The little enthusiast grew up to write, with her sister Constance, a stately tome called *The History and Literature of Israelites*. At twenty-nine she became the wife of the Honourable Eliot Yorke, M.P., son of Lord Hardwicke and prominent member of the Church of England. A generation earlier, her Aunt Hannah had also married a high-born Anglican. But whereas Hannah's union had once pained Jews, Annie's now scandalized Christians. For the first time a British aristocrat took as his wife a girl who remained after the wedding exactly what she had been before—a practicing and pious Jew. Quite contrary to the usual process, the Rothschilds embraced their faith more firmly with each generation.

Lionel himself set all old and new members of The Family an example with the single most dramatic adventure in his life.

## 3. *Storming Parliament*

By the middle of the nineteenth century most of the restrictions on British Jews had been done away with. One remained: they were permitted to obey the law, to practice it, but not to make it. They were not admitted to Parliament. The vanguard of English Jewry, including the Rothschilds, had long chafed under this disability. Petitions were submitted, the sympathy of leading journals enlisted, press and pamphlet campaigns conducted. Parliament would not be moved.

The head of the English Family then took prejudice by the horns, a decision that could not have come easily to a man of his rather prim and sedentary bent. Since he did not have the legal qualifications to run for Parliament, he began to storm it. In August, 1847, Lionel de Rothschild mounted the hustings as Liberal candidate for the City of London. The City, being the capital's financial district, had long stood for freedom of trade, a principle to which Rothschild astutely added freedom of religion.

"My opponents say that I cannot take my seat," he told

the voters. "That is rather my affair than theirs. I have taken the best advice. I feel assured that as your representative, as the representative of the most wealthy, the most important, the most intelligent constituency in the world, I shall not be refused admission to Parliament on account of any form of words whatsoever."

The "form of words" became critical before long. Lionel was elected. Prodded by this *fait accompli*, the Commons passed a bill permitting the seating of a Jew. But the House of Lords rose in revolt. Many of the usually absent peers rushed to London. From the remotest demesnes of Cornwall and Wales, viscounts and earls hurried to vote down Hebrew insolence. Lionel, accompanied by his brother Anthony, stood in the august chamber, listened grimly to the wrathful speeches, would not withdraw even while the division was taken—and saw himself defeated.

But his grandfather, the patriarch Mayer, had been no more stubborn in stalking the Hessian court than Lionel was in besieging the Mother of Parliaments. He formally vacated his seat, thereby forcing another election in his constituency. In 1849 Rothschild's renewed candidacy was broadcast in handbills and advertisements.

"I do not hesitate again to solicit your suffrage," he said, "because in my person a principle can be vindicated and because I believe that you are prepared to maintain the great constitutional struggle that is before you with the same vigour and earnestness that you have heretofore evinced. . . ."

Once more he was elected. Once more the Upper House cast him out. Lionel determined that the time had come for a direct and personal assault. He would take physical possession of the seat for which his constituents had chosen him, and to which he had every moral right.

On July 26, 1850, his wife leaned forward in the gallery

of the Commons and watched the House simmer with excitement. The Sergeant-at-Arms announced that a new member wished to take the oath. Lionel advanced to the Table of the House. The clerk rose to administer the Oath of Admission in the usual form and with the usual book, the Holy Bible.

"I desire to be sworn on the Old Testament," Baron Lionel said in a loud, clear voice.

The House exploded. "Sir," thundered Robert Inglis, leader of the opposing faction, "from the time that this has been a Christian nation and that this house has been a Christian legislature, no man—if I may use the word without offence—has ever presumed to take his seat here unless prepared to take it under the solemn sanction of an oath in the name of our common Redeemer. I for one will never give my sanction to his admission."

After a long heated debate, an adjournment and three divisions, the Commons at last permitted Lionel to be sworn on the Old Testament. The following day he stood again before the Table. Now the battle of the "form of words" was properly joined. Among the admission ceremonies was the so-called Oath of Abjuration, with which the new M.P. must renounce all allegiance to the long defunct Stuart dynasty. A historical leftover, the Oath constituted the chief instrument of the anti-Jewish party because it ended with ". . . upon the true faith of a Christian."

From gallery to front bench a hush fell over the House as Lionel repeated the formula after the clerk. Everybody waited for the last phrase. Here Lionel said, "I omit these words as not binding upon my conscience," and concluded the Oath in the Jewish fashion, using the Hebrew formula and covering his head. He was about to sign his name on the members' roll when, pen in hand, he was arrested by a voice from the dais.

"Baron Lionel de Rothschild, you may withdraw," the Speaker said, and a moment later Lionel had to leave the House amid an uproar.

But the Baron was only warming up. At the next general election, in 1853, the City of London doggedly returned him as its member. Again the House, after violent controversy, passed a bill to remove the oath difficulty, and again the Lords threw it out. The argument engulfed the nation.

"If you destroy the groundwork of Christianity upon which this legislature is based," inveighed the Bishop of London, "in order to gratify for a time a handful of ambitious men, you will destroy Christian England."

An Anglican M.P., on the other hand, said that "he should be sorry to have so indifferent an opinion of his religion as to suppose that the introduction of a Jew into Parliament would weaken or affect the principles of Christianity."

Henry Drummond, a famous sectarian leader, railed against the election of a Jew "by the rabble of London, acting partly out of love of mischief, partly from contempt of the House of Commons, and partly from a desire to give a slap to Christianity."

It was whispered that Rothschild money had paid for the election of Lord John Russell, the Prime Minister, to win him as a friend. The Bishop of Oxford and other ecclesiastics dignified the rumor with their names, whereas a number of eloquent voices within the Church championed the Rothschild party nobly.

"We may guess," said one of these, ". . . how many of the clergy will spend Christmas . . . the sacred time petitioning against Jews. Two courses will be served before the mince pies: the roasted heretic and the disenfranchised Jew. We shall be told of angels singing peace on earth by those who would prolong the reign of discord and persecution. Whose birth is it that the church commemorates? Is it not the birth of a Jew?"

And the London *Times* declared in a leader: "If the qualities of any single candidate must, perforce, be associated with the merit of the principle he maintains, we think that those of Baron Rothschild will bear the comparison as well as any that are now before the public. . . ."

The peers of the realm did not see it that way. Altogether Lionel was elected six times by his stalwart constituency. Six times he marched up to the Table, demanding to be sworn according to the tenets of his faith. Ten times the Liberals introduced a bill revising the Oath of Abjuration. Ten times Disraeli crossed his own party, the Conservatives, and unsheathed his oratory in the revision's favor. Ten times it was passed in the Commons, and ten times the Upper Chamber tore it up.

The eleventh time the Lords had to relent. In 1858 they consented to a bill allowing each house to modify the oath for its own members. On July 26, 1858, Lionel went through the old dramatic scene with a new ending. He stood before the Table and took the oath with his head covered according to Jewish tradition, then signed his name to the rolls and proceeded to his seat unhindered.

For eleven years this pampered nabob had chosen to live outside the palatial seclusion to which he was born. For eleven years he had made himself the butt of national argument, of caricature, scurrility and abuse, and possessed no martyr's nature with which to absorb it all—only the gouty, crotchety temper of a multibillionaire. "For eleven years," the Baroness is reported to have said, "we've had the M.P. question screaming in every corner of the house."

For eleven years he had fought the good fight, disarrayed his emotions, snapped at his butlers, spent huge sums on electioneering, stirred up England to the far corners of her Empire. And after he had finally, painfully, moved the mountains that barred his way to parliamentary privilege, he gained it—to do nothing. Not a single speech or overt action was recorded during his entire tenure of over a decade and a half. It seems, in his case, a logical paradox. He was no more a simple politician than a mere capitalist. He was a Rothschild, *ergo* a living principle. The principle had wanted vindication, as he had said in his early election appeals. Vindication had been achieved. That seemed enough. The main thing was that he had thrust the gate open to others of his creed.

Inevitably, however, the door of the Commons must lead to the portal of the Lords. If a Jew was good enough for the Lower House, was he not fit for the Upper? Gladstone thought so in 1869, and the Jew he had in mind was the same Baron Lionel, M.P. But now only one elector figured: the Queen. In this matter, as in several others, she chose to be more Victorian than her age. To Lord Granville, her Lord-in-Waiting, she wrote a letter bristling with italics.

"To make a *Jew a peer*," she said, "is a step she *could not* consent to. It would be ill taken and would do the government great harm."

At the Prime Minister's suggestion, Lord Granville prepared another brief. "The notion of a Jew peer is startling," he conceded to her Majesty, ". . . but he represents a class whose influence is great by their wealth, their intelligence, their literary connections." He then went on to the real reasoning behind the suggestion: the government felt that Rothschild's appointment would check republican sentiment, which seemed to be developing in some powerful financial circles.

Her Majesty, though, thought the monarchy could survive *without* help from the grandson of a Jew Street peddler. Thereupon Gladstone made a personal attempt to disarm those royal emphases:

> 10, Downing Street
> October 28th, 1869
>
> . . . As the head of the great European house of the Rothschilds, even more than by his vast possessions, and his very prominent political position . . . Baron L. de Rothschild enjoys exactly the *exceptional* position, which disarms jealousy, and which is so difficult to find. . . . It would not be possible, in this view, to find any satisfactory substitute for his name. And if his religion were to operate permanently as a bar, it appears that this would be to revive by [the implication is, royal] prerogative, the disability which formerly existed by statute, and which the Crown and Parliament thought proper to abolish.
>
> Mr. Gladstone has now troubled Your Majesty to the full extent incumbent upon him, and will not think of pressing Your Majesty beyond what Your Majesty's impartial judgement may approve.

Victoria sat tight. It was not until Suez had become British through Jewish money; not until Disraeli, baptized in faith but very unbaptized in sympathies and passions, had won her heart; not until Lionel had died in 1879; that she yielded to Lionel's weapon, that same old Rothschild weapon, his son.

On July 9, 1885, Nathaniel Mayer de Rothschild walked into the great house in Westminster and did in the Upper Chamber what it had once forbidden his father to do even in the Lower. The new Lord donned the Jewish ceremonial headgear, the three-cornered hat, and on a Hebrew bible swore his holy Jewish oath.

"It was the first time," an awed historian noted, "that the Peers of the Realm had looked on while one of their number took the oath covered, or on another book than that which Christian practice and English tradition prescribed."

But there was a second unique feature attending the ritual, which pertains to the uniqueness of the new Lord's generation, the next one.

## 4. *Three Suns at Noon*

Of Nathaniel, Lionel's eldest, the story goes that he once met at the stock exchange a fellow banker puffed up with pride. The man had just received a patent of nobility from the Italian king, in return for a favor, presumably financial. Natty listened to him go on and on about his new distinction, took a good look at the lire exchange rate—which had been especially favorable to the pound that week—and then, as usual, spoke his mind. "Congratulations, Baron," he said. "I knew you wouldn't fail to pick up a bargain."

It is interesting that in the second half of the nineteenth century a Rothschild was already in a position to jest at the *nouveaux* riches of somebody else. It is even more significant that Lionel's three sons ignored their own baronial distinction and chose to become misters. The very title from which their grandfather had so warily kept his distance, and which their father had been so careful to use, *they* let lapse out of indifference. It became immaterial in the face of their prestige.

The three brilliantly illustrated an old truth. Wealth or honors may be achieved in a lifetime, but, due to some perverseness in human nature, social position cannot be conquered by *one* man. It must be inherited several times over before it truly begins to exist. Society, like virginity, may be lost at any moment but will be gained only at birth.

Natty, Alfred and Leo had the right kind of birth. In the case of another family the question might be asked: was it right enough? They were, after all, only two generations removed from the ghetto. In their case, no doubt ever arose, not only because of their incomparable fortunes, but also because of their superb casualness. It was this last flair which exempted The Family from the awkward stage of the *arrivé*.

An *arrivé* is a clumsy imitation of the long-arrived. There is nothing more vulgar than trying not to be. But the Rothschilds, with their Yiddish jests framed in Cantabrigian flawlessness, with their proud observation of Sabbath on Buckinghamshire lawns, with their pictures of old Poppa Jews plastered across manor walls—the Rothschilds were always strictly themselves. They conformed to no earl, duke or marquis. They sported the kind of free-swinging eccentricity, the self-indulgent truthfulness unto their basic fiber which comes to another family only after five butler-born generations—assuming the basic fiber hasn't been refined away by then.

In the instance of the Rothschilds, the basic fiber was (indeed, still is) remarkably sturdy. But some special factors set apart the trio of scions who made up the third generation in England. Of Lionel's brothers, only Nathaniel, the Parisian invalid, had sons, and they chose to become French Rothschilds, a somewhat different regal tribe. Lionel's three boys were, therefore, in complete possession not only of the London bank but of all the vast

Family domains in Great Britain.

In terms of time, they occupied a double zenith: no one before them had been as rich as they; no one after them who was as rich could escape the egalitarian fervor or strangling taxes of the leveler known as the twentieth century (in which, as a matter of fact, they had to spend their last years). In terms of place, the three scintillated among English nobility—an élite which has survived into the space-age culture more intact than its counterparts on the Continent. Natty's, Leo's and Alfred's universe, while exotic in its lushness, has come down to us with many of its trappings and meanings still present.

### (a) *Natty*

When good Queen Victoria raised Lionel's eldest to the dignity of a Baron of the United Kingdom and thus to a peerage in 1885, she came up against something of a surprise. It was an almost invariable custom that all men so honored abandon their names for a different, more lordly and, of course, Anglo-Saxon style. Benjamin Disraeli became Lord Beaconsfield. Marcus Samuel became Lord Bearsted. But Nathaniel Mayer Rothschild elected to be Nathaniel Mayer Lord Rothschild in the simplest, haughtiest fashion of all.

His choice is a clue to his whole life. He inherited not only limitless wealth but also the accumulated supremacies of three generations. Plain old-fashioned loftiness was so much his natural element that it strikes us today almost as an endearing quality, the way noble savagery does in *The Last of the Mohicans*. Lord Rothschild wore his top hat and boutonniere no less convincingly than Chingachgook once did his feathered headdress and tomahawk.

Victoria did not initiate "Natty" into public life. That began in 1865, when he ran for Parliament. But he refused to electioneer in a business district after the manner of his father. No, he picked the countryside, the very best gentlemen's pleasance—namely, Aylesbury in Buckinghamshire, whose importance was certified by the fact that The Family owned most of it.

Needless to say, he carried the district. Needless to add, he was victorious in contest after contest, the voters offering him their ballots as yeomen had once offered fealty to their suzerain. Later, of course, he relinquished the Commons for the Lords. But no matter what his title, he was Parliament's most qualified, most impressive, most ornamental spokesman of reaction. He sniffed at social services, suffragism, old-age pensions, and everything else malodorous with progress. His speeches on the subject were not only immaculately phrased but well fortified with reason and example, proving that there was an inordinate amount of mind under the top hat.

"Whenever I want to know a historical fact I always ask Natty," confessed Disraeli, himself one of England's most retentive brains.

But Natty could do more than speak. He put up formidable opposition to politically forward legislation.

"I ask you," cried Lloyd George in 1909. "Are we to have all the ways of reform, financial and social, blocked simply by a notice board: 'No thoroughfare. By order of Nathaniel Rothschild'?"

His grandfather, Nathan, had favored the liberal wing of the Liberal party. Lord Rothschild, though nominally Liberal in party affiliation, was actually the showpiece and often the moving force of the Right. The same evolution took place at the Rothschild bank. Under its founder New Court had been the boldest organization in the City. Under

Natty it became, and could easily afford to be, the most conservative, exclusive and selective. His one innovation was aristocratic. He began the practice of stationing the visitors of the day in various anterooms. He would enter the first one, watch in hand, announcing the number of minutes at the interviewer's disposal. He listened and replied courteously enough for the stated time, but not a second longer; then he moved on to the next audience in the next chamber. His own office was reserved for the highest personages in the land. As a result, the Partners' Room in New Court retains the incensed air of an inner sanctum even today.

He was truly the King of the Jews. There is the anecdote of the emigrant from Poland who, shortly after his arrival in London, spent the Day of Atonement in the East End synagogue. Suddenly he heard all prayer stop, and an unearthly hush fell over the congregation. "The Lord has come!" whispered a neighbor to the Pole, who prostrated himself instantly before the Messiah. But then he saw a famous top hat and realized it was human divinity in the form of Lord Rothschild, awing the flock with his appearance.

On June 23, 1897, Cardinal Vaughan congratulated Queen Victoria on her Diamond Jubilee in the name of all the Catholics in her Empire. It was Natty, naturally, who did the same on behalf of the Jews. And when he came through Baghdad on one of his great tours, the Jews there received him with the same honors their forefathers had once accorded the Exilarch, that legendary, long-extinct sovereign over all the Israelites of the Diaspora.

Indeed, Natty watched over his people the whole world 'round. No persecution or pogrom occurred anywhere without thunder from New Court against the oppressors, without aid to the victims. To cite only the most impressive example: Because of Russia's cruel attitude toward her Jews, she was usually turned away from New Court's doors when she came asking for money. In 1891 a special financial mission from St. Petersburg did sit down with a New Court delegation for some serious negotiating. But at a new outburst of government anti-Semitism, Natty dispatched a runner, and the Rothschild people, who had warned the Russians of just such an eventuality, walked out without so much as a word.

Virtue is its own reward. In 1917, when the Czarist treasury defaulted because of the Revolution, the Rothschilds were not as hard hit as other banks. And virtue is not always its own reward. When the short-lived democratic government floated a "Liberty Loan" in St. Petersburg, New Court immediately telegraphed one million rubles, and naturally was never repaid a single one from Lenin, whose government followed.

Natty was buried by then, but had he lived he would have written off that million as intended good works. His charitable donations were of nothing less than imperial dimensions. To handle them, he developed a special, amply staffed department at New Court. He was the chairman of three London hospitals, the treasurer of a fourth and, for good measure, the chairman of the British Red Cross. His specifically Jewish charities were legion. A single one of them, the upkeep of the Jews' Free School, cost him a reputed hundred thousand dollars a year.

Natty's manner, even in the very act of benefaction, was consistently gruff. His grandfather, we recall, used to make beggars run by giving them a guinea. Natty never refused beggars, either, but was sometimes noticed to run himself, for fear he'd have to hear their thanks or form his lips into a smile.

With larger philanthropies he could be proportionately

more acrid. At the turn of the century many thousands of Russian Jews came to England, where their coreligionists facilitated further emigration to the United States. Natty and other money men took care of these displaced masses. But one day there was such a desperate overflow from the docks that all communal resources of the East End seemed exhausted. Hermann Landau, a philanthropist specializing in the problem, found the streets filled with homeless families. They would need instant help on a scale generous beyond his own means. Landau drove straight to New Court. The Partners' Room, taboo to many business people, opened readily to him, as it did to others on charitable errands. Landau explained that 25,000 pounds were needed immediately for the construction of temporary shelters. Before he could finish his plea, Natty pushed toward him an order he had just written. It placed 30,000 pounds at his credit.

"You didn't understand me," Landau said. "I only need twenty-five thousand."

"Listen to him, Leo," Lord Rothschild said wrathfully to his youngest brother. "Landau is having *rachmones* on us!" (*Rachmones* is Yiddish for "pity," something Lord Rothschild was accustomed to give, not receive.)

But Landau got better treatment than some of Natty's social equals. There was one duchess whom the Baron heartily disliked and whom he persecuted by inviting all her friends but not herself to his best parties. When that couldn't reduce the enemy to tears, he conceived a strategem diabolical enough to be worthy of his demon grandfather. He held a banquet in his mansion at 148 Piccadilly and seemingly honored her Grace by seating her on Gladstone's right and his own left. These were the sides on which the respective men were deaf. The lady had to spend hours between two table companions who would not respond to a word she said.

Natty seldom bothered to be so wily. At Tring Park, his country estate, another distinguished person, Lady Fingall, dared to pick one of her host's famous muskroses without asking his permission. Before the entire company of guests, Lord Rothschild gave her hell. Later he apologized indirectly by placing an enormous bouquet in her carriage. Yet the saying remained in force that Lord Churchill and Lord Rothschild were the two rudest men in England.

## (b) *Sweet Leo*

The youngest brother balanced the eldest beautifully. Natty was a haughty lord; Leo was a kind sport. Not that he forgot the implications of his name. He maintained no less than four palatial residences. At 5 Hamilton Place—back of Rothschild Row at Hyde Park Corner—he built himself a town house with the following conveniences: a hydraulic lift which was so expensive to operate that it cost more to go from the first to the second floor than to travel by horsecab through all of London; for those who wanted to save money, a serpentine staircase completely hand-carved and perhaps the finest of its kind in all of England; a huge library, also entirely hand-carved, in maple and mahogany, on which forty imported Italian artisans worked for two years; a kitchen that could roast a whole ox on a spit; conduits under every windowsill and table surface to keep the food warm; and a great number of barely credible etceteras. The whole marvel survives intact as the plushiest private club in London.

Another Leo household was many-splendored Gunnersbury Park, inherited from his father. In addition, he bought Palace House near the racing course at Newmarket, where the King of England and similar types were glad to be his guests. Finally, he owned an estate at Ascott Wing, a lovely country manor with miles of gardens and views. This, by far the most tasteful and probably the most pleasant of all Rothschild realms in Buckinghamshire, is the only one inhabited by The Family to this day.

Ascott abutted on South Court, his stud farm and dearest passion. Racing was handed down to him as a legacy from his Uncle Mayer. Leo bred horses ingeniously, without regard to expense, and cheered them on without regard to English reserve. Sometimes it was hard to choose between spectacles: Mr. Leo's blurring thoroughbreds on the track, or his Oriental exuberance in his box. Uncle Mayer had won the Derby once; Leo won it twice, in 1879 and in 1904. In between, he led into the paddock literally hundreds of champions.

That he did not win the Derby three times may be laid to *rachmones* of a very rarefied kind. The Prince of Wales, Leo's good friend, entered the Derby of 1896 with a virtually unknown animal named Persimmon. The blue-and-yellow Rothschild silks were represented by St. Frusquin, possibly the greatest four-legged celebrity of the *fin de siècle*. Leo had once been offered sixty thousand pounds for this horse, which had walked away with almost every important turf event in England. But in 1896 His Royal Highness happened to have rather more mistress trouble than usual. He stood in need of cheer. Somehow it happened that Persimmon came in first.

Leo's compassion, if it was a factor here, extended to the humblest citizens as well. It was said of him that the more races he won, the more money he lost. To celebrate, he gave away not only the winner's purse but its multiples. Often he would gain a cup—and some hospital an entire wing.

Off the track his benevolence was no less active. Petitioners who did not dare come near Natty, or were fazed by Alfred's peculiarities, sidled up readily to Mr. Leo. He became the welfare minister of New Court. A cold day would, for some reason, give his openhandedness a special impetus, and he was especially touched by children. One winter Sunday, when he took a somewhat absent-minded stroll on Natty's lawns at Tring, he noticed a little shape before him. Instantly, automatically, he reached into his pocket. Only the frantic intervention of a butler saved him from a transcendental *faux pas:* he had been about to press a half crown on one of the royal dukes of England.

Mr. Leo became a byword of spontaneity and good-nature. In a clan that, for all its remarkable qualities, has never been notorious for sweetness, he stands out as a kind of darling mutation.

> Of men like you
> Earth holds but few:
> An angel—with
> A revenue.*

## (c) *The Incomparable Alfred*

In the manor of Edmund de Rothschild's great estate at Exbury today there are hundreds of family heirlooms. Visiting Family members, though generally quite inured to that sort of thing, never tire of asking for one specific item—"Alfred's baton." This is a staff of pure white ivory banded with a circlet of diamonds. The instrument had a very solid, practical use. Alfred needed it to conduct the symphony orchestra he kept as a private hobby.

* A quatrain taken from Cecil Roth's account of the three brothers.

The baton is symbolic of a way of life unique even among Rothschilds. Alfred, in age the second of the triumvirate, never married, and by his bachelorhood alone he departed from clan tradition. (Natty had wedded Emma Louisa, a Frankfurt Rothschild; Leo, an Italian-Jewish beauty named Marie Perugia.) Alfred's physical appearance was even more radically different. In the English *mishpoche*, Jewish genes carefully interbred, and an ancestral sense solicitously nourished, produced generation after generation of the same portly, generously nosed, Frankfurt Semitic type. Alfred, however, was a slim, blond Ariel, of a dainty countenance delicately shrubbed with sideburns.

His brothers' indulgences were properly luxurious. His were dizzily sybaritic. Often he had a personal train standing by for him in full steam. He maintained the private Philharmonic mentioned above, whose concert master submitted each morning the selections to be rehearsed for dinner music that night. He also had a private circus to which—beautifully accoutered in blue frock coat, whip and lavender kid gloves—he would play ringmaster, to his friends' amusement. And he simply adored driving his zebra four-in-hand.

Small wonder that he rusticated not like a squire but like an emperor. His Halton House was a vast pile of the most expensive ornamentation hundreds of thousands of pounds sterling could buy. It clashed luridly with the simple glory of the Buckinghamshire beeches around it, exciting outrage and, just possibly, envy, among various sensibilities. One spoke of "an exaggerated nightmare of gorgeousness and senseless and ill-applied magnificence." "A combination of French château and gambling house!" cried another.

Notwithstanding such towering excess, Alfred had flair.

In the country, where an exquisite would feel out of his depth anyway, he didn't bother with esthetic harmonies and let the zebras caper. In the city his connoisseurship came into its own. At 1 Seamore Place, a renowned (now razed) London address, he built a suitable roof over his head. It, too, constituted an immense grotto matted and jungled with treasures. A single mantel would hold 300,000 dollars' worth of objects. And yet there was rhyme, reason and rhythm to it all, if a number of stunned witnesses are to be trusted. Seamore Place confirmed Lady Dorothy Neville's edict that Alfred was "the finest amateur judge in England of eighteenth-century French art."

Lord Beaconsfield thought so, too. A widowed ex-premier, he moved out of 10 Downing Street into Seamore Place in 1880. "The most charming house in London," Dizzy said, "the magnificence of its decorations and furniture equalled by their good taste."

Alfred's taste was most dextrously exercised in his favors and hospitalities. To his very good friend, Lord Kitchener of Khartoum, he presented two items, both masterpieces of resourceful giving. The first was a replica of Reynolds' "Lady Bampfylde" (one of Alfred's most cherished possessions) executed so well that it could hardly be told from the original; the second, a parade set of ornate saddle steels made for Philip III of Spain.

He was not only the most lavish giver, but the most cunning impresario of parties. Friends often wondered why he bothered to subscribe to his great box at Covent Garden, when all the stars appearing there also performed for his private soirees. Rubinstein, Liszt, Melba (whose financial affairs he managed), and Mischa Elman (whom he discovered) enchanted his music rooms. The moment they entered his house they were talented friends, not professional artists—a convivial impression he could create with the utmost deftness. He never seemed to realize that the jeweled trifle with which he thanked them for their courtesy was worth far more than the highest concert fee.

This was his forte and made him the greatest host of the era: unparalelled attention to the visitor's well-being. Cecil Roth recounts the breakfast ritual, which began with an infinitely capacious dumbwaiter standing at the ready in the guest's bedroom, and the footman announcing the menu: "Tea, coffee, or a peach off the wall, sir?"

Let us assume that the guest, unprepared for such unprecedented matitutinal variety, chooses tea.

"China tea, Indian tea or Ceylon tea, sir?"

"China, if you please," decides the stranger.

It is poured out. The litany continues. "Lemon, milk or cream, sir?"

The guest indicates that he will take milk.

But the inquisition is not yet over. "Jersey, Hereford or Shorthorn, sir?"

The day passed in this fashion. When the company repaired to their dressing rooms toward evening, they found baskets filled with a rainbow of sprays from which to select boutonnieres or corsages for dinner. If the burden of choice engendered a headache, a delightful remedy was at hand; throughout the night broughams and drivers waited to soothe insomniacs with a moonlit ride. If the chill of dawn gave them a cold, they could resort to a medicine chest as magnificently stocked as the wine cellar. And when they had to go home at last, their luggage would be larded with little mementoes of their stay. The men would find boxes of the host's famous guinea cigars (that is, fifteen-dollar cheroots, which became so renowned among gourmet smokers that at least one manufacturer tried to exploit the cachet with a brand called Alfred de Rothschild cigars). The ladies came away with such perishable treasures as chocolates, exotic fruits and hothouse blooms.

A specialty of Alfred's was the "adoration dinner." This was a miniature banquet, attended by only one woman—the lady in whose honor the affair was given—and three or four men "she might like to meet." A beautiful actress of turn-of-the-century London—Lily Langtry, for example—would be "adored" in the lushest possible circumstances by, say, the current Prime Minister, the world's foremost tenor, and a legendary general like Lord Kitchener. This function, too, culminated in a "little" present which the gentlemen joined in laying at her feet (the choreography here must have been interesting). The male guests were consulted on the gift beforehand, but its purchase was the host's monopolistic privilege.

Alfred, the most urbane and delightful of men among inhabitants of his own stratosphere, always acted a little awkward before the lower classes. He seldom mixed with his beneficiaries (as Leo liked to) or with the common ruck of tycoons (as Natty did). Aloofness only added to his aureole. Inevitably he became one of the favorite targets of Max Beerbohm's pencil. And yet, dandy, fop, dilettante though he was, he remained a Rothschild. He was not an idler. With all his many silken divertissements, he still found time for the three Family vocations: business, Jewry and charity.

Of course, he interpreted all three his own way. Even Natty, the despot of the City, could not get him to show up at New Court on time. He came late and stayed late, and instituted a whole "Bohemian shift" of clerks to be his staff. At twenty-six he was elected the first Jewish Director of the Bank of England. The job is not a sinecure. Even a Rothschild needed both ability and application to keep on being re-elected for twenty-one years. When he resigned in 1889, a bit precipitously, it wasn't lack of financial gifts that had tripped him up, but excessive curiosity as a collector. He had paid a great deal of money for a picture he had long wanted. The dealer in question banked at Threadneedle Street, and the profit he had made could be gleaned from his account. Alfred gleaned. Alfred cried out, a bit too loudly. The dealer lost a client, and Alfred his directorship, but London gained another first-rate Rothschild story.

No such mishap occurred when he performed his Jewish duties. He attended synagogue as punctiliously as his brothers, though Natty often had to make sure his boutonniere was properly subdued. And despite his strong inclination toward the decorative splendors of Renaissance paintings, he disciplined himself not to buy them, because of their religious content (another proof of how hard it is to be a Jew).

Also in a Judaic context, Alfred is associated with a deathbed mystery about Disraeli. The great statesman had been baptized at the age of twelve but never hid his racial pride. He claimed descent from the Marranos, or secret Israelites of Spain, whom fifteenth-century terror had forced into an artificial Christianity but who redeclared their faith at the final hour. Now, Disraeli's dying words, according to some biographers, resembled the phrase "*shema Yisroel*," the Jewish deathbed confession of faith. And Alfred de Rothschild was among those in charge of the last rites over the body. It all added up to a rumor which has been neither proved nor stopped.

To the public, Alfred's name blazed most brightly in connection with philanthropic fetes. Here he was an endlessly industrious and accomplished impresario. No other man could have masterminded the unique gala night in Covent Garden on behalf of the Boer War charities. For his sake alone, the great Patti abandoned her iron prejudice against performing at benefits, and with Alvarez

—imported especially from New York—she sang the great duet from Gounod's *Romeo and Juliet.* Only Alfred could have managed to book the massed bands of the Queen's Household Cavalry and the Brigade of the Guards. Only at his bidding would the *haut monde* of London pay such exorbitant prices: 250 pounds (or four thousand dollars) per box, fifteen pounds (or 230 dollars) per seat. And this particular affair aside, it is probable that mainly he, the most magnificent of the three magnificos, animated the august friendship on which the triumvirate based much of its eminence and to which we will turn now.

## 5. *At Marlborough House*

The greatest social triumph of The Family came to pass—by now a traditional irony—through their stubborn Jewishness. During a good part of the nineteenth century the two major British universities did not care for foreign faiths. They required that every academic candidate declare allegiance to the Church of England. At Oxford one had to do so before matriculation, at Cambridge not until the awarding of a degree. Therefore Natty, Leo and Alfred attended Trinity College, Cambridge, to study though not to graduate. Even today, long after the removal of religious restrictions, the Rothschilds read at Trinity as a result. In the 1850's this circumstance brought them together with a chubby, merry Cambridge boy named Bertie. He was also known as the Prince of Wales.

The friendship between the future King of England and the grandsons of a ghetto apprentice was instant and intimate. It remained permanent and astounding. Bertie's chumminess with Natty, Leo and Alf—and, before long, with Ferdy (the Austrian Rothschild, Ferdinand)—was unheard but not untalked of. It produced newspaper headlines, upset court chamberlains, and roiled protocol. Some of her Majesty's ministers worried lest the heir apparent pass on state secrets to a commercial firm. As it turned out, his Highness, primed by the Rothschild information service, often knew more than the fretting ministers. But generally the friendship intrigued every walk of life and thrilled Jews all over the world.

Day after day the court circular announced that the Prince of Wales had stayed with Lord Rothschild at Tring Manor, joined Mr. Leopold at the Rothschild shoot in Leighton Buzzard or yachted with Mr. Ferdinand at Ramsgate. It was the Rothschilds, more often than the oldest ducal clans, who could send out cards with the magic phrase, ". . . to have the honor of meeting Their Royal Highnesses, the Prince and Princess of Wales." On a darker occasion, after Bertie's appearance in the witness box of a divorce court, it was Alf's piano that beguiled the Prince through a sleepless night at the Amphytrion Club.

More usually the friends sojourned at Marlborough House, where Bertie held his un-Victorian court; where one toasted, waltzed, placed bets together, occasionally lent one another money, and made the silkiest whoopee in the Empire. The "Marlborough Boys," of whom the Rothschilds were a vital part, became *the* set in Europe. A motley galaxy, the set was not without a certain historical impact. It did something about Lytton Strachey's complaint that royalty had been unfashionable in England since Charles II. The Hanover line had put a beery vein into Majesty. Victoria—respected, revered though she was—could not be admired as the quintessence of chic.

But long before he became Edward VII, her son managed even his naughtiness with an Edwardian flair. At Marlborough House Bertie reigned more smartly and practiced a much more democratic snobbery than Mrs. Astor did on Fifth Avenue. Society went through a healthier house cleaning than anywhere else on either continent.

Let the courtiers raise their eyebrows sky-high—joviality began to outrank genealogy in London; wit took precedence over etiquette, the colorful over the emptily decorous. The Rothschilds scored on every count. In addition, they were always ready to help a chap out with a few thousand pounds, even if his Mater's name was Victoria. Natty, Leo and Alfred played their part in running the wax figures out of Mayfair, in revitalizing the élite and thus adding to the viability of the country, in glamorizing the Crown.

The Queen herself came to recognize this, despite her rather ingrained earlier thoughts about the place of Jews. However, it took more than the combined luster of the three brothers to sway her Majesty at last. It was a fourth Family personage who induced her to make the initial public move.

Ferdy, the Austrian, turned the trick. We must go into his history a little to understand how. He had married Evelina, a sister of the three brothers, in the 1865 wedding described earlier. Eighteen months later she died in childbed. Ferdy decided to remain in England. He became an English Rothschild in residence, maintaining at Rothschild Row that town house with the famous white ballroom; English in political allegiance, becoming a subject of the Queen and, when Natty left the Commons for the Lords, taking over The Family's parliamentary fief by becoming the new M.P. for Aylesbury; English in his charities—he founded the Evelina de Rothschild Hospital for Sick Children in London and the Evelina de Rothschild School in Jerusalem. At Christmas he sent a brace of pheasants to every busman in London; as acknowledgment, the drivers ribboned their whips in yellow and blue, the Rothschild racing colors. And Ferdy was English in his eccentric willfulness. He would give a ball at such short notice that his female guests would not have time to prepare their dresses, whereupon the hasty host made amends by ordering them new couturier creations at his own cost for the next function.

A typical Ferdy whim produced one of the greatest sights of southern England. In 1874 magic began to transpire at Lodge Hill, as desolate and deserted a spot as could be found in Buckinghamshire. Ferdy had bought it and 2,700 acres of environs from the Duke of Marlborough for some 200,000 pounds. Ferdy happened to like the view. To make the vantage point habitable, the entire top of the hill was sliced off. Water must be hauled from fourteen miles away. A special steam tramway with a track fourteen miles long had to be built to transport materials from the nearest rail station. Numerous driveways with a manageable gradient were hewn into the slopes. Teams of Percheron mares, imported for the purpose from Normandy, toiled up the rise with building stuff.

A wilderness was coerced into a park through topographical surgery, drainage, irrigation, and the wholesale planting of shrubberies. Acres of flowerbeds were sown. Since Ferdinand placed his woods as conveniently as other people place their ashtrays, he had hundreds of trees transplanted. Since he liked large chestnuts, sixteen horses were needed to move each one; the telegraph wires by the roadside must be lowered for their passage. The whole thing was rounded out with the customary terraces, aviaries, rookeries, fountains, and groups of seventeenth-century statuary by Girardon, an important Versailles sculptor.

What house could fit such an estate? Ferdy decreed a select anthology of his favorite French castles. Into his mansion of mansions he incorporated the two towers of the Château de Maintenon, the dormer windows of Anet, the chimneys of Chambord, two versions of the staircase of Blois (slightly smaller, and glazed to fight off the English climate)—all "suitably combined, edited and improved," one expert thought.

As to interior decor, Ferdinand sometimes had the paneling specially carved to accommodate outsize paintings like Guardi's two vast views of Venice. More usually he contented himself with ready-made wares—that is, with the finest *boiseries* (decorative paneling), extracted from the most luxurious Louis XV and Louis XVI Hôtels in Paris, brought across the Channel, and integrated artfully into the various apartments. The furniture consisted largely of peacock pieces made for the royal family in France. The carpeting constituted the world's largest collection of Savonneries, so named after the workshop of their origin, whose products went exclusively to the Bourbons. The ceilings, Beauvais tapestries, Sèvres porcelain, and *objets* (including a big musical elephant) matched the foregoing and each other. Canvases by Reynolds, Gainsborough, Cuyp, Pater, Van der Heyden—not to speak of those by Watteau and Rubens later added by heirs—were almost legion.

After more than a decade of creation there rose above the English countryside an immense French Renaissance mirage, glistening in white marble, resplendent with 222 rooms. Ferdy rested, and thought it good. He called it Waddesdon Manor. To this day it remains an absolutely stunning circumvention of coziness.

All the world came to see and to gasp. At his Saturday-to-Monday parties (the week end was practiced but not yet invented in the *fin de siècle*) the host would entertain the Shah of Persia, the German Emperor, Henry James, Robert Browning, Guy de Maupassant. (*The* Agha Khan and a series of prime ministers from Balfour to Winston Churchill are also found in the guest book.) Bertie honored one of the Blois staircases by breaking a royal ankle on it.

Rumors of the phenomenon reached Victoria's ear. On May 14, 1890, Her Majesty did a nearly unprecedented thing. She called on a private individual. She had to see for herself what this Rothschild had wrought out of a bare hill. A small incident marred her reception. Lord Hartington, later Duke of Devonshire, committed the inexplicable gaffe of shaking Madam's hand instead of kissing it. As a result she kept it to herself during the rest of the introductions. But after a pony had driven her about the grounds in a Bath chair, after she had strolled through the galleries, vestibules, drawing rooms, she couldn't help agreeing with all other visitors. "The host was delightful," she said, "as the place was beautiful."

The day warmed her heart toward the Rothschilds. When on the Continent, she began to drop in familiarly at the French estate of Alice, Ferdy's sister. She even used Rothschild couriers for some of her private mail, finding it a more discreet channel than the diplomatic pouches. (The extent of Family discretion became evident after her death, when Natty, appointed trustee of the Disraeli estate, discovered a number of "very private" letters from the Queen to the very dearest of her prime ministers. Natty took one look at them and sent them to King Edward, who for once expurgated his mother and not vice versa: he had the letters burned.)

Even this supernal fellowship the Rothschilds conducted without damage to their Jewishness. On the contrary, sometimes the Church of England seemed in greater danger. On January 19, 1881, the Prince of Wales drove through a horrendous blizzard to appear at the Central Synagogue in Great Portland Street for Leo's wedding. He loved the kosher food served at the reception. He roared at the Jewish jokes. These gradually became his passion. Since Natty shared the weakness, the House of Rothschild became a great international center not only of finance but also of stories about Moe and Ike.

"At least one foreign diplomat, Baron von Eckardstein," reports a biographer, "had standing orders from the Rothschilds to collect and report all good Jewish jokes he heard abroad—especially stock-exchange puns from Berlin. On more than one occasion . . . he even dispatched bon mots by wire to New Court whence they would find their way before long to Marlborough House."

The archivists at the London bank today, who guard so many secrets, also guard a treasury of Jewish jokes relayed in telegram language by a Prussian nobleman.

Later the Jewish theme would emerge more seriously on a more august level. By 1908 Bertie had become His Britannic Majesty. The Rothschilds had long fought for the betterment of their coreligionists in Russia. And now that the King was to meet the Czar in Reval, there ensued a correspondence between the members of the Marlborough set on what exactly could be done about Russian intolerance.

Something was done. Jewish persecution became an important item on the Reval agenda. "From my report," the British ambassador in Petrograd wrote to Natty shortly afterward, "you will see that the Russian Prime Minister contemplates amelioration for the lot of the Jews in Russia."

It was about this time that a London rabbi is supposed to have said that the Jews, unlike the Christians, did not yet know a Messiah—but they did have a holy family.

They had, if his simile be accepted, more than one. There were other Rothschilds in the world just as Rothschildian as the English ones. It is the only rich clan without poor relations. To round out the splendors of the *mishpoche*'s *fin de siècle*, we must travel to France and Austria.

## 6. *Naughty Bismarck*

In France the clan's social eminence was perhaps most easily established. Eighty years of intermittent revolution had demolished the Bourbons, dethroned the Orleanists, discredited the Bonapartists. Only the Rothschilds kept their scepter. After the smoke of the Paris Commune cleared in 1871, Baron Alphonse emerged as the head of the family with the most unbroken ruling record.

Genealogically, the French branch was the closest of all to the ghetto. It skipped a generation. James, the dynast, was the youngest of the five founding brothers and did not have offspring until comparatively late in life. His children were the contemporaries of his brothers' grandchildren. The four sons—Alphonse, Gustave, Salomon and Edmond—cut as luminous a track through the social history of their country as did their counterparts across the Channel. But of the Paris quartet, the first- and the last-born left the strongest impress.

Alphonse, as small and stout and cannily relentless as *père* James, was even more suave and *comme il faut.* It was said of him that he owned the best pair of mustaches in Europe. Altogether he made an awesome, handsome standard-bearer of the name.

A railroad journey with a fabulous mishap conveys something of the aura of that name in France. One of Alphonse's clients, the King of Belgium, had asked him to a strictly private dinner at the Belgian capital. To avoid publicity, Alphonse took a simple first-class train ticket to Brussels. But a few miles from the border the express stopped and rolled to a siding. Inquiries revealed that the main track had to be cleared for a private train.

Now, the Baron was not accustomed to being on the short end of someone else's priority. Furthermore, he arrived in Brussels too late for the royal soiree. The telegraph wires between France and Belgium quivered with his wrath. Finally, sheepishly, they disclosed the root of the trouble. Alphonse's valet, having forgotten to pack the baronial dinner clothes, had used the master's name to send them after him via private train. His own dinner jacket had shunted the Baron to a side track.

On more important occasions Alphonse managed to be in the right spot at the right time. His career intertwined with a great French cataclysm—the destruction of Louis Napoleon and the violent birth of the Third Republic. Through it all, Alphonse manned the traditional Rothschild station: right behind the scenes.

On July 5, 1870, an imperial adjutant summoned the Baron hastily and brought him to the palace at St. Cloud. The Emperor was deeply disturbed. He explained that Prussia had overdone it at last. She had made one long sore out of the Franco-German border, and now she was foisting a Hohenzollern onto the throne of Spain, to get at

France from the back. Her persistence must mean war. Only England might be able to restrain Bismarck, and England must be asked to act immediately. But since the English happened to be without a foreign minister—the incumbent Lord Clarendon having just died, and a new one (it was to be Lord Granville) not yet appointed—Napoleon wished to make use of Rothschild channels.

Alphonse read between his Majesty's words. An official French request for British mediation might smack of French weakness. In this case, a discreet Rothschild hint would be more diplomatic than a diplomatic move.

The Family, of course, was an old hand at this sort of thing. On the same afternoon a cipher telegram flew from rue Laffitte to New Court. The same night Natty decoded Alphonse's message. The next morning he reached the Prime Minister's residence just as the P.M. was about to leave for Windsor Castle and an audience with the Queen. The two drove together to the station, and Natty conveyed the message from Napoleon. Gladstone listened, pondered. Finally he said he did not think his government was in a position to influence Prussia.

With that brief conversation Napoleon's empire began to fall. Again the wires buzzed between New Court and rue Laffitte. Hours later the Emperor knew that his bid to save both face and peace had failed. Bismarck had his way. Twelve days afterwards, on July 19, France unmuzzled her feeble cannon against Prussia. On September 1, Napoleon capitulated at Sedan.

Within a week the monarchy was erased, the German armies ringed Paris, and the House of Rothschild prepared for the next round with history. The Family was about to play a particularly neat trick. It had failed in its intervention on behalf of the victim. But it was to best, rather entertainingly, the victor.

By the middle of September the siege of Paris began in earnest. On September 19, Wilhelm I, General Moltke and mighty Bismarck established their high headquarters at Ferrières, the principal *mishpoche* country seat. The Prussian monarch wandered through the Renaissance vasts of the château, admired the thoroughbreds teeming in the stables, smelled a lake of orchids in the hothouses, tasted the Goshen-sized fruit, surveyed a whole private landscape of parks and gardens—and was frank enough to be thrilled.

"Kings couldn't afford this," he said to his staff. "It could only belong to a Rothschild."

Bismarck did not feel quite so exhilarated. It was his misfortune that King Wilhelm regarded Ferrières' owner as a very powerful colleague. His Majesty therefore refrained from commandeering Baron Alphonse's munificent bedroom, using a modest chamber instead. Wilhelm issued, besides, a strict edict to the General Staff, who were billeted with him: even touching the various art treasures was *verboten*. And Bismarck—Bismarck himself!—received orders not to indulge his hunter's passion in the gorgeous shoot.

Baron Alphonse's chief steward, as the enforcer of these nasty prohibitions, was the bane of the Iron Chancellor at the hour of his triumph. Today, in the château's blue drawing room, Baron Guy still keeps a copy of the steward's report. The stout fellow refused to serve Bismarck, who wanted to mitigate his annoyance with a few good drops, any bottles from the famous Rothschild cellar. When Bismarck, enraged, forced the steward to sell him a case for good payment, the latter lodged a complaint with his master in Paris.

Baron Alphonse was amused by the German bogyman who must fight for his wine at Ferrières while the rest of Europe cowered before him. The Rothschild amusement became the property of the *haut monde* in besieged Paris. In December the Prussians shot down a balloon containing a letter to the Countess de Moustier with the following words: "Rothschild told me yesterday that Bismarck was not satisfied with his pheasants at Ferrières, but had threatened to beat his steward, because the pheasants did not fly about filled with truffles."

These lines, relayed to Prussian headquarters, upset the Iron Man no end. He saw in them a hint that he had breached the King's proscription. And, to be petty about it, he *had* sneaked a tiny bit of pheasant shooting on the sly.

"What will they do to me?" he is quoted in his collected works. "They won't arrest me, for then they won't have anybody to arrange peace."

They did have him to arrange the peace. They also had, on the French side, the eldest Rothschild brother, who would not stop trying the Chancellor's nerves. For one thing, Alphonse consistently scooped German news services on the armistice by sending pigeon post from rue Laffitte to New Court; thus the Rothschild system overcame even the rupture of telegraph connections. When it came to actual negotiations, he was not easy to deal with, either. The little Jew squared up very calmly to the huge Prussian. He even insisted on speaking French, though Bismarck reminded him angrily of the German origin of The Family and harped on his own friendship with old Amschel of Frankfurt.

Alphonse, adamant, stuck to his guns, his language, and his indispensability. No one but Rothschild could guarantee a food supply to starved, beaten Paris (in London Alfred, Leo and Natty headed the French relief efforts). No one but Rothschild could underwrite the five-billion-franc indemnity to Prussia. No one but Rothschild, aided by his foreign cousins and the bankers in his group, could have paid off this monstrous sum so much less ruinously than Bismarck expected—and two years ahead of schedule.

It was this performance, above others, which assured the continued eminence of the Paris house throughout the newest French republic. Bismarck ruled and thundered, receded and departed. Rothschild ruled and whispered—and remained. Ferrières still stands as the mightiest Family château.

## 7. *The Plushiest Pilgrim*

The youngest sons of great European families often resort to the army, where they make do with colonelcies, or to a church career sans true vocation, or to an untalented expatriatism. The Rothschilds know no such case in all their ranks. Their youngest sons get so much more to start with, and, as Edmond's example shows, they can make so much more of what they get.

This baby brother of Alphonse (he died only in 1934, at the age of ninety) engaged in the customary activities on the Family program. He sat behind his desk in the Partners' Room at rue Laffitte (his specialty was dividing the world's oil with Shell and Standard Oil); he built a great town house; he married another Rothschild, Adelheid of the German branch, in a round of festivities which were both religiously orthodox and religiously splendid. He had powerful cultural interests. If his brother Alphonse gathered rare goldsmith work of the Renaissance, if his cousin Willy in Frankfurt became a celebrated bibliophile and cousin Nathaniel in Vienna specialized in late eighteenth-century bijoux—he, Edmond, assembled a sumptuous collection of engravings and left no less than twenty thousand of them to the Louvre.

But Edmond also turned to an interest that gradually consumed his long and characteristically energetic life. It began as charity and ended, in our time, as history. It can be summed up in one word: Palestine.

The story starts on September 28, 1882, with an incongruous interview in Edmond's office. Behind his desk sat the Baron with his manicured imperial, his velvet bow tie and fragrant buttonhole. A strange apparition faced him, wreathed in wild prophetic whiskers. The Grand Rabbi of France, who acted as the Baron's appointment secretary in such matters, introduced the man as Reb (Rabbi) Samuel Mohilever, and endorsed his mission: to raise money for the support of new Jewish colonies in Palestine. Reb Mohilever did not look like a fund raiser, though; he certainly didn't act like one.

The conversation began with an inquiry. Would the Baron mind if he, Reb Mohilever, did not discourse in the modern manner, but employed the tone of voice used by a rabbi in front of the congregation? All right, to the first main point. Why was Moses, who was tongue-tied and stuttered—why was he picked to be the leader of the Jews and to take them from Egypt to the land of Israel?

After discussing the pros and cons in the Talmudic manner, the Reb disclosed to the astonished Baron that the reason lay in this: God deliberately avoided a smooth talker for the revelation of His word. He chose a stutterer to show that what was so compellingly convincing in Moses' mouth was not a clever tongue but the Voice of the Lord.

A series of similar sing-song reasonings led Reb Mohilever to the conclusion that he, too, was a poor speaker; but that perhaps his smallness had been chosen to demonstrate the greatness of his cause: to show that the soil of Zion was the one haven for his persecuted brethren in Eastern Europe. He had come to Paris hoping to commit to Palestine the innermost fiber of Baron Rothschild's soul.

Edmond answered that he was prepared to contribute the necessary sum—which his visitor had not even mentioned. But Mohilever's Talmudic dialectics steered the interview straight back to the soul again. The Baron, not prepared for a spiritual set-to, kept stressing his willingness to give money; the Rabbi would not let go of the innermost fiber. At last the deep black eyes of the old man won out. Edmond promised ". . . to consult myself and make a trial to see what will result from it."

Grand Rabbi Kahn, who played interpreter whenever the Baron's Yiddish gave out, has handed down the phrase. It turned out to be no mere politesse. For the remaining fifty years of his life Edmond made a trial of the question, and it made a trial of him.

He became the greatest activating force in Jewish colonization prior to Zionism. He began by financing the settlement of exactly one hundred and one Russian Jews not far from Jaffa. Gradually he went on to subsidize needy Jewish colonies and to create others. His funds drained swamps, dug wells, ploughed land, built houses, surveyed terrains. Of the seven new Jewish agricultural communities existing in Palestine in the middle 1880's, three escaped bankruptcy only through Rothschild. A fourth was altogether of his own making. The rest benefited vitally, if more indirectly, from his help. The initial colony of Rothschild-propelled emigrants was soon followed by many hundreds and later thousands of such settlers.

All that constituted Edmond's outward involvement. It didn't really harmonize with a rather fastidious, saturated, retiring inner nature. Gladly he would have let just his checks speak for him. In fact his first contribution was signed "Nadev Hayeduha," the Hebrew term for "anonymous benefactor."

A contradiction developed in the man. Chaim Weizmann noted it the first time he met him. "Everything about him was in exquisite taste," Weizmann recalled later, ". . . his clothes, his home—or rather his homes, his furniture and paintings. . . ." And yet there he was—this aloof, immaculate dandy—hip-deep in the economics of irrigation, manure and soil rehabilitation.

Apparently the eyes of Reb Mohilever remained fixed on him, demanding the innermost fiber of his soul. Some force always pulled him out of the drawing room into the heat of the Jewish battle. His princely reserve, fostered by secretaries and assistants, always lost to the Rothschild drive that must conquer definitely whatever it casually touches.

Before long Edmond found himself intervening with the Turkish government, at that time in control of Palestine, in favor of Jewish colonization. He did diplomatic backstage work. And he was sucked into the internecine strife among the settlers. The distant donor changed into the querulously loving father and finally into the fond, familiar tyrant.

When a deputation of Russian Zionists called on him to discuss the need for reform in some of his settlements, he grew purple like David mortified by Absalom's treason: "These are *my* colonies, and I shall do with them as I like!"

Few of his friends in the Jockey Club would have recognized M. le Baron.

It was an awful spectacle, this combination of paternal ire and Rothschild autocracy. Often he threatened to withdraw his immense subsidies and thus to wither all Jewish Palestine with one stroke. How seriously he meant such threats became plain later on, when some other Rothschilds began to show a tentative interest in Palestine.

"What!" he said furiously to Weizmann. "After I've spent tens of millions on the project, while they made fun of me, they want to come in now with a beggarly few hundred thousand francs and share the glory? If you need money, you come to *me!*"

The degree of his embroilment reached touching and tragicomic heights in 1889, a so-called Sabbatical Year. (Orthodox Jewish law, based on certain passages in Leviticus and Deuteronomy, forbids the tilling of Jewish land during every seventh year.) Edmond thought that idleness for so long a period would ruin most of the young settlements. He remonstrated with the rabbis of Jerusalem, who remonstrated right back. Edmond flew into a fatherly Jewish fit, the worst fatherly fit there is. He forsook racing, banking, collecting and all his other superb leisures. To combat one fanaticism, he had to assume another.

For months on end he plunged into ferocious theological maneuvers. He convoked a series of secret conferences of rabbis friendly to his position. It was decided that the Sabbatical Year must be worked through, but without breaking orthodox tradition. Edmond's counselors devised a method to have this kosher cake and eat it too: all the Jewish land in Palestine had to be sold, for that one year only, to people of another faith. In the eyes of God the settlers would then be working for non-Jews—which was permissible—and not for themselves.

The rabbis of Jerusalem cried out at this as a blasphemous fraud upon the Eternal. They threatened to excommunicate anyone caught working. They promised to take up collections to support all those who abstained.

They were dealing with a Rothschild. Edmond laid a powerfully worded brief of his argument before Rabbi Isaac Elchanan of Kovno, Lithuania, famed throughout the world as the greatest orthodox authority. After considerable coaxing on the Baron's part and deep study on the part of the savant, Reb Elchanan issued his verdict: under such safeguards as Edmond's rabbis proposed, the soil of Zion could be tilled during the Sabbatical Year.

Thus Edmond won another victory. But the innermost fiber of his soul was sore. The very man who had first sensitized it, Reb Mohilever, had not spoken up for Rothschild's side of the controversy.

A remarkable document survives from that time. It is a letter written by Edmond to the Grand Rabbi of France but meant for Reb Mohilever. The Baron, too hurt to address the Reb directly, asked the Grand Rabbi to bring the letter before the true object of his emotions. Edmond's indignation was such, in fact, that he even abstained from French. He wanted to berate Mohilever in Mohilever's own idiom. And so this outburst is innocent of the polished perfections of the secretariat usually in charge of the Baron's correspondence. Composed by Edmond himself, it consists of Jew Street jargon, a sort of Yiddish. And Edmond's halting Yiddish seems a good deal more pathetic than the primitive German once used by his ghetto-dwelling grandfather. With his poor German old Mayer Amschel pursued the success he fully achieved; while with his beginner's Yiddish the baronial grandson reached for a folk identity he could never quite attain. The missive, scrawled painfully in Hebrew letters, is an explosion of fond disappointment, overflowing with fury and love, and culminating tremulously: ". . . Herr Oberrabiner, do you know what I think? I will tell you the truth. . . . These colonists want to take the land and the houses away from me and then scoff at me. . . . Let Rabbi Mohilever know that I will send the colonists . . . and all their families back to him and then we will see what he will do with them. And besides traveling expenses, I will not give them a cent."

Needless to say, the threat was never carried out. Reb Mohilever could conclusively prove that he had worked undercover for Edmond against the hostile rabbis; had, in fact, clinched the supertheologian's favorable decision. He and Edmond resumed their curious friendship. The colonists did work through the Sabbatical Year and, for all their spasmodic rebelliousness, came to regard Edmond as their protector-king. His name merged with the designation "Nadev Hayeduha" under which he had first given money for their cause. At the end of the nineteenth century, Jewish Palestine knew him as Baron Rothschild, the Anonymous Benefactor.

This particular wound healed. But there was another Palestinian problem Edmond could never quite resolve. The Rothschilds, in all their branches, kept their distance from Zionism. Official Family policy held that they and their coreligionists were European citizens of the Jewish faith, who must refrain from anything that might jeopardize emancipation. Most of the *mishpoche* looked at Edmond's Palestinian obsession with what was at best astonishment.

Theodor Herzl, the political founder of the Zionist movement, sensed an opening. He considered The Family "the most effective force our people have possessed since the dispersion." If only it were a force sympathetic to his aims! Albert von Rothschild, head of the house in Herzl's native Vienna, had not even deigned to answer a request for an interview. But perhaps this Paris Rothschild, this Palestine-prone Baron . . .

Herzl pulled a hundred wires to achieve an appointment with so great a prize. But Edmond closed his doors. His activities in Palestine were a matter of philanthropy, not of nationalist politics. Thereupon Herzl, in a letter to the Grand Rabbi of France, declared that he would resign Zionist leadership in favor of the Baron the moment he turned Zionist. Edmond agreed to a meeting. It took place on July 18, 1896, and ended fruitlessly. For the Baron, Palestine was a refuge for oppressed brethren, period.

When Herzl met Lord Rothschild and his brothers later on, the encounter turned out even less happily. Natty, Leo and Alfred liked the man (they even helped to support his family after Herzl's death), but they were impervious to most of his ideas. "How is one to negotiate with this collection of idiots!" Herzl exclaims in his diaries.

New Court, in fact, launched the bitterly anti-Zionist League of British Jews. Nothing seems odder, therefore, than the following letter by the British foreign minister, a letter known to the world as the Balfour Declaration.

Foreign Office
November 2nd, 1917

Dear Lord Rothschild,

I have much pleasure in conveying to you, on behalf of his Majesty's government, the following declaration of sympathy with Jewish Zionist aspirations which has been submitted to, and approved by, the Cabinet:

"His Majesty's government view with favour the

establishment in Palestine of a national home for the Jewish people and will use their best endeavours to facilitate the achievement of this object, it being clearly understood that nothing shall be done which may prejudice the civil and religious rights of existing non-Jewish communities in Palestine, or the rights and political status enjoyed by Jews in any other country."

I should be grateful if you would bring this declaration to the knowledge of the Zionist Federation.

Yours sincerely,
*Arthur James Balfour*

The Lord Rothschild apostrophized here is, of course, no longer Natty but Lionel Walter, his heir, in The Family's eyes a dangerous maverick because of his weakness for Herzl's dream. Yet not even he approached one tenth of Edmond's ostensibly non-Zionist efforts toward the realization of Israel. Thus the historic strangeness of the Balfour Declaration and the paradox of Edmond's own position.

In his memoirs Chaim Weizmann, Israel's first president, recalls a remark by the "Nadev Hayeduha": "Without me, Zionism wouldn't have succeeded, but without Zionism my work would have been struck to death." A pregnant statement, it contains both the implied separation between Edmond's "work" and Zionism and his crucial connection to a cause he could never quite bring himself to espouse formally. (To Edmond is ascribed the saying that a Zionist is an American Jew who gives an English Jew money to get a Polish Jew to Palestine.) He considered Palestinian Jewry not as a polity but as his own obstreperous yet passionately loved family, whose duty it was to love him, its father, in return. But Zionism?

The national goals, the propaganda apparatus, the official trappings of a political organization? That sort of thing dismayed him. After all, he, Edmond de Rothschild, was there, ready to take care of it all benevolently and privately.

"Why must you people go around making speeches and attracting attention?" he once asked Menachem Ussishkin, a Russian Zionist leader.

"Baron Edmond," the man answered, "give us the key to your safe, and we promise not to make any more speeches."

Actually the Zionists had it both ways. They went on making speeches. And they did get the key to the Baron's safe, at least to one of his larger ones. The money went on flowing throughout the Baron's long life.

In 1931, at the height of the depression, Zionism was out of funds. Dr. Weizmann was dispatched to the Baron. As soon as the Jewish leader reached Paris, the grippe struck him down. This most chronic of Zionist speech-makers was flat on his back when, surrounded by a panic of bellhops and concierges, the eighty-six-year-old Baron came in. In his hand he carried a check for forty thousand pounds.

"This should help bring your temperature down," Edmond growled, put the piece of paper in Weizmann's hand and stalked out again.

Never has an ideological shirker been more generous to the cause he shirked. Palestine flourished in a hundred places under his touch. His money helped start new soil cultures in the Holy Land: almond trees, mulberry bushes, jasmine, mint, tobacco. He not only pressed the introduction of viticulture, but guaranteed its financial survival by purchasing the entire grape crop of all Jewish settlements year after year—and at a higher price than the quotation on the world market.

He also sparked the industrial development of Israel-to-be. His funds facilitated the formation of the Palestine Electric Corporation Ltd., the Portland Cement Company's "Nesher Ltd.," the Palestine Salt Company and the Samarita Water Company.

And still this was not the end. He even made sure that the colonies he bought clustered strategically across Judea, Samaria and Galilea, to serve as strongholds in time of need. The time of need came, four decades later.

At one point it puzzled Weizmann why Edmond spent such huge sums of money on excavating and exploring the Mount of Zion. The Baron claimed he was interested in finding the Ark of the Covenant.

"I asked very seriously," Weizmann says, "what he hoped to achieve with the Ark. He answered, '*Les fouilles, je m'en fiche: c'est la possession.*' Excavations be damned, it's the possession that counts."

The Arab armies can deem themselves lucky that there weren't more such non-Zionists as he.

Following Edmond's money came Edmond himself. The Baron and Baroness began to visit Palestine, perhaps the plushiest pilgrims the Holy Land had ever seen. The couple liked to travel in their own yacht, weighing anchor in Marseilles and docking at Jaffa.

It was on May 5, 1887, that the "Nadev Hayeduha" first walked on Zion's soil. That day marked, in an observer's phrase, "the historical meeting between a prince and his people." Trailed by a great following, he prayed at the Wailing Wall and—he was, after all, a Rothschild—quickly undertook to buy it from the Arabs. Not only that; he aimed at the conversion of the surrounding neighborhood into one huge Jewish shrine. To meet Moslem objections, he made a second commitment: he would purchase another, equivalent plot of land; here he would accommodate, in much more comfortable houses than they had near the Wall, all the Mohammedans who must be evacuated.

Edmond appropriated three quarters of a million francs. The Pasha of Jerusalem had already given his approval. Yet the whole scheme died mysteriously of the opposition from Jerusalem's Chief Rabbi.

Nevertheless, this and subsequent baronial visits were splendid occasions. The velvet bow tie was seen everywhere—in hospitals, schools, farms, industrial installations, workshops. Naturally Edmond took a *cognoscente*'s interest in things familiar to him—the wine cellars, for example, or the perfume factories, or the display of horsemanship by young colonists. (Today his grandson, the present Baron Edmond, and England's Lord Rothschild jointly continue the administration of his huge Israeli interests. They also continue the tradition of pet luxuries: their special hobby is the development of Caesarea into a fashionable golfing resort.)

No matter how occupied, Edmond did not forget the innermost fiber. Once, at Tel Aviv, he said publicly and bitterly, "Never before did I regret so much as now that I cannot speak Hebrew."

Another time—it seemed the eyes of Reb Mohilever, now dead, would never release him—he called out his conviction "that if you abandon Judaism, all our people will suffer shipwreck . . . for you are the pride and hope of Jewry. . . ."

Two days after this speech, settlement leaders were invited to dinner on the Rothschild yacht. They found great wonders there. The ship had a complete, specially fitted kosher kitchen, and a kosher Escoffier who created meals such as Solomon must have served Sheba. The satin-lined cabin used as a prayer room was in the stablest part of the ship. And all the doors of all the sumptuous staterooms had *mezzuzahs.*

The story goes that one of the settlement elders, greatly taken with the prodigies of the vessel, kept walking its decks and almost missed the tender that took his colleagues back to shore.

"Don't you want to return to Zion?" one of them twitted him.

"*You* go to the Promised Land," he is supposed to have answered. "*I'll* stay on the Promised Yacht."

## 8. *Hoffähig*

In Austria, Salomon's grandchildren had come of age and helped to spangle the evening of the Habsburg Empire. Of this *fin-de-siècle* generation we already know Ferdinand, the Anglicized lord of the palazzo at Waddesdon and member of the Marlborough House gang. Ferdy's two brothers administered the Family fortunes along the Danube. Both covered Vienna with their philanthropies. They founded, among many other things, a General Hospital, an orphanage, an Institute for the Blind, an Institute for the Deaf Mute, a neurological clinic and hospital, and a botanical garden.

Both brothers raised Rothschildian palaces. Albert, the youngest (chosen by his father to take over the bank), conjured up an enormous Louis XVI mansion on Prinz Eugenstrasse. Inside, the "Albert Memorial," as some of the English Family dubbed it, teemed with magnificences; we will mention only the silver dining room and the gold ballroom, with their heroic chandeliers of over half a thousand candles each.

As for Nathaniel's *palais* in the Theresianumgasse, it

ran the gamut from four Van Loo paintings commissioned by Madame Pompadour to a unique porphyry table of Marie Antoinette's, and held the clan's most extensive collection of Louis XIV, XV and XVI treasures anywhere. When this building was demolished after World War II, both principal art museums in Vienna had to rearrange their collections thoroughly in order to absorb the massed gorgeousness given them by Baroness Clarice.

The care of such treasures demanded regiments of servants. Among the endless personnel of the Rothschild households were the hereditary positions of silver-polisher and marble-polisher. These functionaries consecrated their entire lives to caressing Rothschild cutlery and stroking Rothschild stone and jealously handed on the privilege to their sons.

Baron Albert savored the rugged side of life as well. A dedicated mountaineer, he was the seventh man to climb the Matterhorn, and neither he nor his brother neglected the chief bucolic pleasure of the aristocrat. At Schloss Langau, at Enzesfeld, and particularly at the castles in Schillersdorf and Beneschau, the great Rothschild hunts were staged. Here the poorer of the major nobility would sometimes arrive with suitcases full of dirty laundry. Two good reasons accounted for this habit: 1. It increased the bulk and weight of one's luggage, bringing it in line with that of other guests; 2. One unpacked one's clothes and left them casually about one's room, as though they had just been soiled. The maids picked them up automatically and brought them to the Rothschild laundry, 130 men strong, which washed thousands of garments without asking a single question. In the end, alas, Baron Albert stopped the practice. Instead, boxes of brown soap were put in the luggage of his unlaundered friends on their departure.

In Vienna, the height of the spring season was the Derby held on the first Sunday in June (here, as in England, the *mishpoche* won it three times), the social highlight of the day being the Rothschild tea given after the race. But the greatest show was the Family progress along the Hauptallee, the long tree-lined avenue connecting city and race course. A mechanical wonder figured in the procession: the Rothschild electric auto. All of Austria-Hungary hardly knew its like. Gliding along silently in the Family colors of blue and yellow, it was a final landmark of *Alt Wien*. But on the Hauptallee it always suffered a jovial indignity. Frank, one of the most famous *Fiakers* (horsecabbies) in town, would overtake it; youthful Rothschilds leaned out of the galloping cab, hooting at the slow galvanic monster.

*Fiaker* Frank rates an explanation. He was the living badge of nabobery. Old Vienna's other immortal horsecabbie, *Fiaker* Bratfisch, was Crown Prince Rudolf's. Both the Habsburg and Rothschild families had fleets of their own vehicles, but, in addition, each hired a special independent taxi for its exclusive use and for the whole season. The Crown Prince always had Bratfisch ready to take him to tender appointments best concealed from the regular servants manning Habsburg carriages.* The *mishpoche*, acting with less amatory enterprise but with equal lavishness, engaged Frank because of his celebrated speed.

In *Fiakers* and in some other respects Rothschild and Habsburg ran parallel. But to many it seemed impossible that the two should ever meet. Rothschild doing business with a cabinet minister, or even Rothschild entertaining a duke—well, all right, it couldn't be helped. But Roth-

* It was Bratfisch who discovered the bodies of Rudolf and his mistress after they killed themselves at Mayerling.

schild breaking bread with Habsburg, Europe's greatest imperial symbol—*Himmel!*

In 1887 *Himmel!* happened. Emperor Francis Joseph "by a special act of grace" forgave the Rothschilds for not being descended from four lines of high-grade nobility and for being unbaptized. They were declared *Hoffähig*, or courtworthy. The dispensation admitted them to levees, receptions and private gatherings attended or given by the imperial family. Henceforth the *mishpoche* moved among a circle boasting a longer continuity of rule, and a far haughtier inaccessibility, than the courtier society surrounding Queen Victoria or the Prussian Kaiser.

Francis Joseph himself was correct—no more, no less—to the people he had just appointed his friends. Every Rothschild funeral or wedding received an All-Highest personal telegram. To one Family party the Emperor lent the Court Opera ballet and permitted it to dance through the torchlit Rothschild gardens in the Theresianumgasse—a singular imperial favor. Yet the sovereign's private exchanges with Rothschilds seldom went beyond comment on the weather or common health problems.

A story, perhaps apocryphal, suggests reasons for this attitude. Once, when his Majesty had involved Baron Albert in longer conversation than usual, the *haut monde* swiftly teemed with the rumor that the monarchy was in need of a new loan. Perhaps his Majesty felt that such intimacies were too damaging to Habsburg credit.

His wife Elizabeth, Austria's strangest, loveliest and most intellectual empress, didn't have to bother with such considerations. She liked the female members of the clan, with their many esthetic interests. A close friendship began between her and Albert's sister Julie, a cosmopolitan Rothschild, sumptuously typical of the *fin-de-siècle mishpoche.* Born of the Austrian house, married into the Naples one

(Adolph von Rothschild was her husband), living in Paris and a frequent visitor to her brother Ferdy's English splendors, Julie had her favorite residence in Switzerland—a fairytale villa in Pregny on the shores of Lake Geneva. On September 9, 1898, she and the villa became linked with a dark hallmark in Habsburg history.

That day the Empress of Austria came to visit, not in an Austrian vessel of state, not in the Rothschild yacht Julie had offered, but by ordinary steamer. She arrived in her customary deeply veiled, discreetly hatted, strictly incognito fashion (she traveled as Countess Hohenembs), attended by a single lady-in-waiting.

As so often, Julie managed to cheer her high guest. The magnificent dinner was served with subtle regard for the dietary laws of both ladies: Julie ate kosher; while Elizabeth was the first low-calorie Empress, with *Vogue* cheekbones and, despite her sixty years, an infinitesimal waistline. The concealed orchestra played a sweet Italian air. The hostess steered the conversation to Heine, her guest's favorite poet; and before long the All-Highest lady proposed a champagne toast, a levity rare in her melancholy later years.

Afterwards the ladies adjourned to the gardens and then to Julie's hothouses. Arranged by countries and climates, the plants constituted the finest private conservatory in Switzerland. As an exquisite bouquet of petals and aromas enveloped the Empress, she brightened still further. All was smiles until the time of departure. Then Elizabeth signed the visitors' book and, still in her pleasant mood, turned it a few pages back. She stopped, pale. There was the signature of Crown Prince Rudolf. Her son, too, had been a guest at Pregny, shortly before his suicide at Mayerling.

When the Empress left, Julie noticed tears in her eyes.

And later the lady-in-waiting recalled that on the way back, again by ordinary steamer, Elizabeth had talked about nothing but death. The subject was apt. Less than fifteen hours afterward, in front of her Geneva hotel, she died of an anarchist's dagger. The Empress of Austria had spent her last full day in Julie von Rothschild's home.

Happily, most fraternizings between royalty and the Austrian *mishpoche* were not ominous. Other sisters of Albert and Ferdy had other friends with scepters. Mathilde, who had married Wilhelm von Rothschild of Naples, is one example. One day her husband's namesake, Wilhelm II (grandson of the admirer of Ferrières, and Kaiser Bill of World War I), invited Mathilde to dinner. The occasion almost induced apoplexy in the court chamberlains at Potsdam and inflicted a historic *Schrecklichkeit* on Prussian protocol. For Mathilde von Rothschild refused to touch a morsel on his Majesty's table. The Kaiser had forgotten to cook kosher.

Last, not least, there was Alice, youngest of Albert's sisters, who lived until 1922. She and Lord Natty were beyond doubt the most formidable individuals yet produced by the House of Rothschild. Alice never married (an even greater rarity among Family females than among the males), perhaps because a lady so overwhelmingly independent in income and mind wasn't fit for mere wifehood. Who was man enough for the woman who cowed Victoria, Queen of England?

By way of introduction to this feat it should be said that Alice inherited miscellaneous Austrian fortunes, including Ferdy's Waddesdon Hall. But the apple of her eye was her great estate at Grasse in the South of France. Here she, too, kept elaborate gardens. In contrast to Julie, however, she wielded one of the gruffest green thumbs in horticultural history.

Victoria, after her first taste of Rothschild hospitality at Waddesdon, became a frequent, often daily guest at Grasse during every royal stay in southern France. These visits put Alice into her fiercest fettle. The memoirs of Lady Battersea (née Rothschild) vividly described Cousin Alice ". . . walking miles up and down hill, giving orders to the Inspector of Police, the royal coachmen, the foremen and workmen, with the manner of Napoleon. As a surprise to the Queen she ordered a mountain road to be levelled and widened, and this had to be done in *three* days which means building small walls, picking out huge stones, covering small ones with macadam, turning a stream. . . ."

Alice never failed to welcome Victoria with courtesies such as custom-made landscapes. She even beguiled her august friend into throwing flowers from a hidden villa window at passers-by, and almost changed the venerable monarch back into the tomboy princess she had been three quarters of a century before. But when the Hanover heel trod on a Rothschild petal, all bets were off. A dread moment saw Victoria trespass on a newly planted flower bed.

"Come off at once!" Baroness Rothschild thundered at the Queen of England and Empress of India.

The Queen came off. After that she referred to Alice, perhaps only half in jest, as "The All-Powerful One." Their friendship endured. So did the epithet. "The All-Powerful One" became Alice's nickname to her kin.

But weren't they really *all* all-powerful, all-enduring? The Family colors fluttered from the finest towers in Europe. It seemed impossible that they should ever be hauled down.

# VIII

## *NO MORE PLUMED HATS*

### 1. *Two Kingdoms Resign*

THE mathematically inclined reader may have noticed that recent chapters spoke only of three Rothschild banks—in London, Paris and Vienna. But the five founders established five houses; which leaves us, at the beginning of the twentieth century, with a deficit of two.

The disappearance was not accompanied by convulsive changes. In fact, the two casualties managed to dismantle themselves with the same stately *savoir-faire* with which the other branches flourished. In 1861 Garibaldi's Red Shirts stormed southern Italy. What had been the Kingdom of the Two Sicilies became part of unified Italy. The Rothschild bank at Naples closed its portals because there was no longer a Neapolitan monarch to loan to. Adolph, son of the founder, Carl, did not care to do business with lesser principals and followed the royal family into France. A nice difference obtained between the two expatriates. In Paris the king became an ex-king, but Rothschild was not an ex-Rothschild. His exile proved no less noble than his former native household. The Empress of Austria (who became so intimate with his wife Julie) was only one of many illustrious guests in his several residences.

But Adolph had no children. His brother Wilhelm had three; brother Mayer, seven. All ten were—supreme frustration—girls. In this unrelieved femininity lay the demise of the Italian branch and, as a matter of fact, of the German as well.

Strictly speaking, the Frankfurt house had stopped with the death of Amschel, who was not blessed with offspring. After him the excess boys of the Naples branch, Wilhelm and Mayer, assumed the Frankfurt reins. Yet the river Main, by whose shore the original patriarch had sired those five titan scions, seemed to have bedeviled the newer Rothschilds: They had daughters, daughters, daughters only! The lack of sons soured and withered Mayer and Wilhelm, just as it had once withered and soured Uncle Amschel. Like Amschel, they buried themselves in orthodoxy (Wilhelm wouldn't shake a man's hand unless assured his fingers had not touched pork that day) and in collecting (Mayer's silver collection and Willy's library represented Frankfurt's greatest private treasures). To business the two didn't pay much more than mechanical attention. Why should they, with no young men to carry it on?

In Berlin the government tried to provide incentives. The Kaiser's newly constituted Reich wanted to benefit, as had the other great European powers, from a thriving Rothschild House. Mayer was appointed to the German House of Lords. Bismarck forgot the confounded cheek of Ferrières' wine steward and attempted several times to lure spare Rothschild sons from other capitals. The *mishpoche*, however, was, and is, a hard family to beguile. One cannot promise the moon to people who own the moon. The Frankfurt Rothschilds stayed sonless. The foreign Rothschilds stayed put. The inevitable came to pass.

In 1886 Mayer was found dead, his head sunk across a column of figures. In January, 1901, Wilhelm was buried. Three months later Edmond (son-in-law of Wilhelm) and Natty (son-in-law of Mayer) sent out a historic announcement to all friends and business acquaintances of the original House in Frankfurt:

> It is our sad duty to inform you that in consequence of the decease of Baron Wilhelm Karl von Rothschild, the Banking House of M. A. von Rothschild und Söhne will go into liquidation. The liquidators are 1) The Right Hon. Nathan Mayer, Lord Rothschild, London. 2) Baron Edmond de Rothschild, Paris.

There are two postscripts to this ending. Until the advent of Hitler, the Family name survived in Frankfurt in hyphenated form. Minna, Wilhelm's youngest daughter, married the banker Maximilian von Goldschmidt and for a dowry brought him not only a fortune but the ten magic letters. After his wedding and until his death her husband was known as Maximilian von Rothschild-Goldschmidt.

The second postscript concerns an interesting nautical vignette. According to the diary of the then French ambassador to Berlin, it occurred on the blue Mediterranean in April, 1908. Two luxury vessels happened to be anchored in the harbor of Palermo. One was the *Hohenzollern*, Kaiser Wilhelm's great seagoing limousine; the other, the yacht of "a young French Rothschild" (possibly Edouard, Alphonse's son). The imperial ship signaled an invitation, and soon afterwards the young Baron was piped onto the Emperor's deck. His Majesty greeted his guest with warmth and almost instantly launched into the argument for a Rothschild return to the *Vaterland*. The Kaiser praised the greatness and fruitfulness of The Family; asserted that he had no racial or religious prejudices, nor would he tolerate any in his court; and pledged that a revived German house would enjoy a position actually superior to the London, Paris or Vienna branches.

Though it provided a pleasant occasion, the Kaiser's cordiality was no more successful than Bismarck's. The Paris, London and Vienna branches were too busy being their refulgent selves, too occupied with enjoying and radiating the ultimate splendors of an age that died of shellshock in 1914.

## 2. *The Golden Momentum*

All the balls and soirees did not stifle a fundamental Rothschild instinct. Bismarck had called it "the absurd desire to leave to each of their (often numerous) children as much as they themselves inherited."

Business was business, and business continued to be prosecuted by the three remaining houses. In England, N. M. Rothschild & Sons invested hugely in Indian mines; it financed Cecil Rhodes' diamond dominion in South Africa (a burly uncut diamond still lies on the mantel of the Partners' Room in New Court, and the house is still connected with de Beers); its banking and loan operations covered most of South America. In France, de Rothschild Frères went into electrical industries, developed the Mediterranean Railway, branched out to North Africa and exerted such control over the Baku oil fields in Russia that the French Family was for a number of years a principal competitor of the Rockefeller trust. In Austria, S. M. Rothschild und Söhne extended its scope into Hungary through the famous 6 per cent Gold Loan of 1881; the Credit-anstalt, invented as weapon against the Crédit Mobilier, grew to be a species of giant subsidiary of the Family bank and became a financial force in every corner of the Habsburg realm.

Thus the *mishpoche* maintained a good deal of the octopus tradition. It also retained, and much more painstakingly, a much more fundamental habit. Take Anselm's testament, written in 1874 by a sophisticated, cosmopolitan Viennese grand seigneur. In its instructions and emotions it is still an exact echo of the first patriarch's will composed under a ghetto roof nearly three quarters of a century before. Anselm wrote:

> I charge all my dear children to live constantly in perfect harmony, not to allow family ties to loosen, to avoid all disputes and unpleasantness and legal actions; to exercise forbearance and tolerance to one another and not to let themselves be carried away by angry passions; . . . let my children follow the example of their splendid grandparents; for these qualities have always insured the happiness and prosperity of the whole Rothschild family, and may my dear children never become unmindful of this family spirit. In accordance with the exhortations of my father, the grandfather who so sincerely loved them . . . may they and their descendants remain constantly true to their . . . Jewish faith.

Then follows a refrain common to so many Rothschild testaments, from Frankfurt Jew Street onward:

> I forbid my children most explicitly in any circumstances whatsoever to have any public inventory made by the courts, or otherwise, of my estate. . . . Also I

> forbid any legal action, and any publication of the value of the inheritance. . . . Anyone who disregards these provisions and takes any kind of action which conflicts with them shall immediately be regarded as having disputed my will, and shall suffer the penalties for so doing.

In London, Natty went his father one better and resurrected his grandfather's custom of leaning against the "Rothschild pillar" at the 'Change. It was purely an ancestral ritual.

Not that Rothschild had stopped being the great specter of Europe's bourses. But now The Family usually bulled or beared by messenger and telegraph. Its name was still a thunderclap. In 1873 the Vienna stock market ran wild with shares issued by imitations of the successful Creditanstalt. Prices rose with speculative passion—then fell with dangerous speed. Finally a Rothschild agent appeared on the floor. A broker, anxious to sell, made a beeline for him and asked whether he was interested in acquiring half a million's worth of bank securities.

"Half a million!" the Rothschild man said within hearing of a crowd. "All your banks together aren't worth that much today!"

This single remark, uttered with Family authority, massacred prices, mowed down a dozen pseudo-banks, and helped set off the crisis of 1873.

But the name could enchant as well as terrify. In 1889 the London house made available for public subscription shares of its Burma Ruby Mines operation. The day after the announcement, Lord Natty's carriage could not enter St. Swithin's Lane. This rather narrow street leading to New Court was choked, wall to wall, end to end, with people. It was the first time the bank had offered subscriptions to a mining enterprise, and from all over London investors had rushed to sink their savings into a Rothschild project.

Natty's driver and footman formed a prow through this veritable overflow of confidence. His Lordship followed, swearing into his buttonhole. Matters got worse at the bank building proper. The crush blocked access to every door. Finally a ladder was lowered from the first floor, and Lord Rothschild—top hat, beard, watch chain, morning coat, carnation and all—clambered up the wall and through the window, like a thief in the night.

Natty's dislike of ladders stopped him from getting into many more such public share offerings. The Rothschilds were (still are) big individualistic operators, who would rather do business with their own kind. Kings do not as a rule clog St. Swithin's Lane, and the *mishpoche* preferred one monarch to a hundred thousand grocers. (The classically favorite money customer in Family history remains Leopold I of Belgium. In 1848 he entrusted the French house with a nest egg of five million francs. When he died in 1865, they had parlayed his worth—for appropriate commissions—into over twenty million.)

Alas, the nineteenth century grayed into the twentieth. The kings dwindled, while the shopkeepers multiplied. On this increasingly important clientele the joint-stock banks battened. And while The Family controlled at least one important grocer-conscious institution in the Creditanstalt, neither their hearts nor the core of their business went out to the idea.

And so gradually, and in full panoply, they seemed to retire toward the sidelines. After all, they could afford everything even a Rothschild could want. Their fortunes grew automatically even while they slept or danced or missed chances. They were bored by risk. Not long after his climbing tour at New Court Natty confessed his philosophy on all kinds of speculation: "When I say 'no' to every scheme and enterprise submitted to me, I return home at night carefree and contented."

On another occasion a royal duke asked him if there was a certain technique for making money on the 'Change. "There certainly is," Natty answered. "It consists of selling too soon."

In Vienna, Albert kept quoting the advice of his grandfather, the founder Salomon: "One must go into the market as into a cold shower—quick in and quick out."

The showers, it appeared, had become a lot colder lately. The next generation showed signs of not wanting to get their feet wet at all. They had other interests, such as animals. Lord Natty's eldest, Lionel Walter, established the great Tring Zoological Museum on the Family estate. Eventually the museum held—mounted, arrayed and captioned in exemplary fashion—more than a quarter of a million birds and over two million insects, including specimens not found in any other collection. Walter, a Cambridge-trained natural historian of the first rank, financed a number of expeditions; he published several important scientific papers as well as *Novitates Zoologicae*, a periodical highly regarded in the field.

The flea collection at Tring was particularly famous and intrigued not only scientists. A wag claimed that the most precious specimen in the collection had cost the owner ten thousand pounds but, on nearer examination, turned out to have escaped from the Family bank.

Another, more authenticated, development made the incongruity between bugs and business painfully clear. Walter, of course, had his bank duties to perform. But the museum began to engulf his energies, his time, and finally his pocketbook. The allowance he received from his father was fittingly generous. Still, it did not quite cover the stuffing of several hundred thousand animals. Hopefully he speculated on the market. But he did not know how to sell too soon. The money vanished. After that he knew only one resort—to borrow a large sum and secure it with a life-insurance policy for 200,000 pounds made out, secretly, on his father. Unfortunately his scientific ardor outran his commercial circumspection. He had forgotten that insurance companies often divide their large risks with other firms. In this case the other firm happened to be the Alliance Insurance Corporation, founded by N. M. Rothschild, with Lord Rothschild as chairman of the board.

One day milord looked at recent accounts of the corporation, and discovered the munificent policy on his life, contracted by his own son. From that moment on, Walter was excused from all further work at New Court. Yet in the end The Family had reason to be proud of Walter's taxidermist career; he became the first of several important Rothschild scientists.

Other members of his generation ended tragically, however. Walter's brother, Nathaniel Charles, died by his own hand, as did his Viennese cousin Oscar; while Oscar's brother, Georg Anselm, spent his final years in a private asylum. Family rivals wondered whether the fiber of the *mishpoche* was weakening. Some thought that Rothschild, the erstwhile lion, had become a dozing decadent. They began taking liberties with him—and reeled back, bloodied. The lion could leap from his cushions to kill as competently as ever.

In France a former right-wing Deputy named Bontoux was the first to rediscover the Family claws. In 1876 he invented the Union Général, a shrewd combination of bank and anti-Semitic crusade. The incorporation prospectus announced the intention "of grouping and transforming into a powerful lever the capital of Catholics. . . ." Wasn't it time to make an end of the republican finance system sucked dry by Hebrews? All the moneyed Christians who detested the palatial Jewry in their midst were attracted to the concept. Each reactionary element paid Bontoux its dues. Soon he had coined four million francs out of prejudice—sufficient initial capital. The Union Général allied itself with the powerful Banque de Lyons et de la Loire, floated shares which rose from 500 to 2,000 to a great deal more, and promptly spread the holy war on Rothschild to Austria.

Here Bontoux closed ranks with the Länderbank, a rival of the Creditanstalt. And here he followed the ominous precedent set by Pereire's Crédit Mobilier. As with Pereire, the Rothschilds gave way to Bontoux for months, even years. Grimly the clan watched him overextend himself.

In 1881 all Rothschild banks began to strike back in their orthodox, irresistible fashion. They acquired scattered piles of enemy shares, then rid themselves of everything at once, with one single price-depressing blow. The first big slash of the Rothschild paw brought down the Banque de Lyons. Bontoux cried out. He invoked the mercy and the money of all Catholics against the enemy—to no avail. Between January 5 and January 20, 1882, the Union Général fell 2,090 points from a high of 3,050 to 950. On the so-called Black Sunday at the Vienna bourse, Bontoux and most of the banking houses allied with him were wiped out.

The panic that ensued on Europe's money markets could be stopped only by the force that had started it: Rothschild. And Rothschild was the first to buy again. Bontoux perished, but the *mishpoche* and Christendom survived together.

Eight years later this Continental spectacle repeated itself, with some modifications, in the British Isles. The rival in London was the House of Baring, not a fly-by-night like Bontoux, but the oldest and—next to the Family house itself—the biggest merchant bank. Lord Revelstoke, head of the firm, had long wanted to show those New Court parvenus where to get off.

The great Argentinian boom of 1886 seemed to be an excellent opportunity. He excluded the Rothschilds from this bonanza by summoning all Baring reserves; or, rather, oversummoning them. There was, for instance, a port-construction project billed at ten million pounds, underwritten by Baring but despite all efforts unsubscribed by the investing public.

This time The Family didn't have to slash. It just bided its time. In the autumn of 1890 the Bank of England received news that Baring had accumulated liabilities to the tune of twenty-one million pounds sterling and saw no way of covering them.

The importance of the firm was such that its fall would drag with it much of the credit of London. Something had to be done. The merchants and financiers of the City began to raise a guarantee fund for Baring creditors. No less a sponsor than the Bank of England provided the auspices for the scheme. And yet it was doomed without the help of the biggest private money power in the Empire.

All eyes turned to the Partners' Room in New Court. Would The Family come through to help its own worst competitor?

The Family came through, not only on one but on two vital levels. It added the name of Rothschild, plus a Rothschildian sum, to the guarantee. (The exact amount of the various private contributions was never revealed in this ticklish affair.) It also exercised its incomparable foreign connections in favor of the failing rival. Through Natty's intervention, Alphonse in Paris was alerted; and through Alphonse, the guarantee fund picked up an additional three million pounds, in gold, from the Bank of France.

London's credit remained unblemished. On November 15, 1890, the Governor of the Bank of England could announce that Baring would be in a position to liquidate all its commitments.

"When you thank the Bank of England," he said, "it is very important to bear in mind the willing and cheerful aid we have received from others, in the first place from Lord Rothschild, whose influence with the Bank of France was of such assistance without which . . . we could not have rendered the aid we were enabled to give."

In brief, the clan continued as a paramount presence not only in the drawing rooms but also on the money markets of the world. Until the shots of Sarajevo, it remained almost majestically unchanged.

## 3. *The Great House and the Great War*

### (a) *Peacemongers Again*

There is a difference between stately old-fashionedness and utter ossification. The house took powerful pains to stay itself, but it was not insensitive to the drifts of history. From 1850 on it had recognized the awakening new national identities in Europe and made gradual, probably unconscious adjustments. Once upon a time the *mishpoche* had stationed members in England, Austria and France. Over the decades these turned into very English Rothschilds, very Austrian Rothschilds, very French Rothschilds.

In France, Baron Edouard (Alphonse's son) built a typical Frenchman's daydream. As companion piece to his Versailles at Ferrières, he thought he'd like a Petit Trianon, a small and playful country palace. His Manoir Sans Souci at Chantilly (today still one of the residences of his widow) therefore has a mere ten guest rooms and requires a gardening staff of only three. There is no mistaking its Gallic quintessence, from the *chaises percées* in the powder rooms to the Picasso drawings along the corridors to *objets de frivolité*, such as ostriches made of downright feathery porcelain and fluffy tortoise-shell bureaus with twinkling rubies for drawer pulls. The squat concrete swimming pool scooped out by Göring during the occupation only points up the manor's Frenchness by contrast.

As for the Vienna house, it has loved music with a profligacy distinguishing Austria even today. (The budget slice spent in another country on missiles is spent here on Mozart.) The most lavish entertainments by the Danubian part of The Family were the musical soirees. Footmen in knee breeches and powdered wigs ministered to these affairs into the teens of the twentieth century. And, as we have noted, through the Rothschild garden there would dance the Vienna Opera ballet.

And in England? Constance Rothschild perfected in her butler the reflexes of immaculate Anglo-Saxon understatement. During the bombings of World War I he would enter after the first detonations and say boredly, as though announcing the arrival of a tedious ducal couple:

"The Zeppelins, my lady."

Well before 1900 the Rothschilds had divided into three separate groups that never for a moment forgot their common connection, yet whose first allegiance went to the countries of their birth. Such allegiance became more urgent. While the several houses lived more nationally, Europe smoldered more nationalistically.

Of course, The Family tried as hard as ever to preserve or at least to finance peace. Each year this became a harder task. A great state no longer need rely on some few big financiers—a war minister could simply tax an army into existence. But when Prussia and Austria went to war in 1866, the *mishpoche* applied every form of pressure. At one point the Paris house even descended to returning the Austrian ambassador's check for a mere five thousand francs, on the grounds that his Excellency did not have sufficient funds to his credit. The *haut monde* gasped. Wasn't the ambassador a Metternich and therefore perforce an old Family friend? Rothschild's slap at Habsburg diplomacy became the talk of Central Europe. Nevertheless, the war went off on schedule.

It was a comparatively brief and small clash. But the *mishpoche*, into whose very nerves was bred a dynastic hatred of cannon, smelled a much larger conflagration far ahead, long before the smoke began to bother other nostrils.

That same year, on September 12, 1866, Anthony de Rothschild (Lionel's brother) expressed a heavy premonition. The jockeying among the powers over colonial aggrandizement weighed on his mind. "The sooner we are rid of all our colonies," he said, rather remarkably for a man with a bankful of overseas investments, "the better for England. We want peace at any price. . . . What do we care about Germany or Austria or Belgium?"

The key word here is Germany. After its triumph over Napoleon III, it had become a burgeoning bullying empire of Prussians. Each year the sabers of Berlin were heard more loudly in the capitals of Europe.

In 1911—four and a half decades after Anthony's warning—his daughters, Constance (Lady Battersea) and Annie (Mrs. Yorke), cruised together in the latter's yacht, *The Garland.* Sailing through the Baltic, whom should they run into—it's a peculiarly small world if you are a Rothschild—but the Kaiser in *his* yacht, the *Hohenzollern?* As in the harbor of Palermo, so here Wilhelm made a great show of hospitality. Constance's journal describes, with a wary and prophetic eye, the lunch his Majesty served them.

"He sits on a raised seat in the officers' mess," she observes. "We listened to his band of forty strong he had on the yacht with him. . . . He spoke quite respectfully of Grandmamma.*. . . He said: 'We should remain friends, but don't like our toes trodden on.' . . . I hope we see him again, but not as our conqueror."

The threat was plain—and The Family was not the kind to just sit and sigh. Random yachting encounters would not avert a global conflict. Bald pressure could not be used as in the old days. But perhaps one could catalyze preventive negotiations?

It was only logical that England, the inveterate intermediary, should have had the Rothschild house most keenly sensitive to the handwriting on the wall. The surprise lies in the particular Family member who was most actively and ingeniously pacifist. Not until it was all over and the memoirs, often the secrets, of statesmen and politicians saw print, did the public discover the identity of the Rothschild who made such remarkable attempts to arbitrate among the powers.

Who would have suspected that Alfred, the most eccentric of sybarites, the driver of zebras, ringmaster of his private circus—that just he, the hothouse flower of the mauve decade, would turn out to be a very quiet, subtle,

* The Kaiser is speaking of Queen Victoria, his grandmother.

efficient diplomat on the sly?

He was, let it be remembered, Imperial and Royal Austro-Hungarian consul general in London. (The dignity, like so many others embellishing the *mishpoche*, was an heirloom handed down through three generations. Nathan Mayer had been the first to receive it. From him it had descended to his son Lionel; from Lionel, after his conquest of Parliament, to his brother Anthony; and from Anthony, who had no sons, to his nephew Alfred.) But Alfred's consulship was almost as purely honorary as his knighthood of the French Legion of Honor. It served only as the vaguest framework for the efforts he began in the 1890's. Possibly he deployed his Austrian office as counterweight to the fact that his first loyalty went to the English Crown. For Alfred made a soundless art out of being impartial and yet solicitously agile, out of being a private individual who commanded resources and connections matching a prime minister's.

His base of operations was his great town house at Seamore Place. Here, at cunningly composed dinners, German dignitaries and British statesmen mingled without the encumbrances of protocol or official implications. Here, under the influence of the rarest vintages, the best cigars, the choicest food, they could warm to each other's jokes, each other's wives—and, just possibly, each other's viewpoints.

It was on the nap of Alfred's sumptuous carpets that an early English-German crisis subsided. In 1898 Berlin and London were at loggerheads over the ownership of Samoa in the South Pacific. Alfred, a good friend of Count Hatzfeld, the German ambassador, received word that the Kaiser wanted to thrust a very bluntly phrased note at Whitehall. The public effect of such truculence was incalculable. Rothschild undertook to furnish a more civil channel. At Seamore Place shortly afterwards Ambassador

Hatzfeld and Joseph Chamberlain, Her Majesty's Secretary for the Colonies, sat next to each other in great soft leather armchairs. They drank demitasses and clicked crystal cognac glasses. Then the German informed the Englishman, in terms as pleasant and elegant as the setting, of the gist of the complaint. Later Chamberlain conveyed it, in similarly courteous form, to Lord Salisbury, the Secretary for Foreign Affairs. Salisbury could then respond, without losing an ounce of British dignity, to the Kaiser's satisfaction.

Alfred was equally adept when it came to sweetening London's tone toward Berlin. In 1900, after the outbreak of the Boer War, the German steamer *Bundesrat* was detained by British naval craft and thoroughly searched. A violent German protest followed. It evoked a no less violent reaction from British newspapers, particularly the anti-Teutonic *Times*. Berlin flew into an uproar. The situation bordered on the critical until Seamore Place resumed its sumptuous arbitration. Over some five-star bottles, Alfred found a way of letting the Germans know, discreetly, that the prime minister neither shared nor necessarily approved of newspaper passions in London. Her Majesty's Government was unable to strong-arm a free press, but conveyed its position through the good offices of Alfred.

"Baron Rothschild," reported the acting German ambassador, "has confidentially informed me that this journalistic attack has displeased the Foreign Office. . . . A Cabinet minister has urged him to make every effort to bring pressure to bear on the *Times* in this affair. Baron Rothschild was shortly to meet Mr. Buckle, the editor-in-chief of the *Times*, and he told me he would speak to Mr. Buckle very strongly on the matter."

Victoria died shortly thereafter, which made Alfred's ticklish task somewhat easier. Now his good-fellowship with the new king could be enlisted. He would get

Edward VII to agree with his desire for a less irascible press, then have the *Times* chaps to dinner and impress on them the viewpoint "of an august person."

About this time the Boxer Rebellion broke out in China against Shanghai's European settlements. An international expeditionary force was dispatched to suppress it. Alfred, in shrewd estimation of the Kaiser's military pride, moved every lever at his disposal to give Germany the ceremonial honor of the top command.

It seems strange that the Rothschild who lived most glitteringly distant from the world's daily cares was also the Rothschild most concerned about war, the greatest daily care of all. One of his letters sums up the constancy, the tact and the doggedness of his conciliations. It was written by him to the German diplomat von Eckardstein for transmission to Count Bülow, the Kaiser's chancellor. Essential extracts read as follows:

> Your friends (my dear Eckardstein) know from experience that I have had the interests of the two countries at heart for many many years; although during this period various subjects of discussion have arisen between the two Governments . . . great good will has subsisted with regard to Germany in the highest circles, in the Ministry and in the country itself. . . . I can prove personally that this is the case, for I have always been more or less behind the scenes, and I have always done my best to produce satisfactory results. When Prince Bismarck was Chancellor he wanted to have representatives on the Egyptian *Caisse de la Dette*, and this was immediately agreed to; later he embarked upon a colonial policy which was also approved by the British government (on the Samoa question an agreement was reached in accordance with Germany's wishes, and

quite recently . . . British troops in China were placed under the supreme command of Count Waldersee). In a word, as far as I can recollect, the British government has always done everything possible to meet the wishes of the German government.

What is the position now? For some months, it might indeed be said for some years, the German press has constantly written against England; indeed, to such an extent that authoritative circles are beginning to wonder what is the aim of this aggressive policy, and whether Count Bülow or the German government cannot do something to prevent it. I am well aware that the Press in Germany is free, as it is in England, and that it will not have its policy prescribed . . . but when the Press of a country spreads rumors about a friendly Power that are absolutely false, the Government could well have taken the first convenient opportunity of stating how much it regrets that such false statements have been given such currency.

. . . Such allegations have not merely made the Germans resident in this country indignant. . . . People here would have been glad to hear that the caricatures of our royal Family, which were sold in the streets of Germany, had been confiscated by the police. In a word, of recent years Germany's policy toward England has been a kind of "pinprick" policy, and, although a pin is not a very impressive instrument, repeated pricks may cause a wound, and, since I hope and pray with my whole heart that no serious wound may result, I am venturing to address these lines to you in the hope that you will clearly explain to Count Bülow how difficult my position in this matter has become with regard to the British government, since I have done everything possible over such a long period of years, and that I feel now that you do not fully appreciate the great advantage of a genuine understanding with England. Possibly Count Bülow does not know that various German Ambassadors have often met famous English statesmen at my house, and it is not very long since the deceased Count Hatzfeld frequently met Mr. Chamberlain at my house, and they both shared absolutely identical views regarding the general policy of the two countries, in their mutual interests.

In referring to these details in a very private way, my dear Eckardstein, I do so in order to show that I am not speaking *sans connaissance de cause*, and I should be infinitely sorry if the small *refroidissement* which at present obtains and has absolutely no *raison d'être* should continue and possibly increase. . . .

Possibly you can prevail upon his Excellency to send me a few lines in reply to my observations; I would naturally show these only in the highest circles, and make the most discreet use of them; I am convinced that a friendly *éclaircissement* would produce the most satisfactory result—and immediately. If you should have the opportunity, my dear Eckardstein, assure the Emperor of my complete devotion; you know how greatly I esteem His Majesty.

Yours,
*Alfred von Rothschild*

This sensitively worded, delicate reproach was reinforced by more open displeasure from Alfred's brother, Lord Natty. How important Rothschild sentiments were to the Wilhelmstrasse, how close The Family may have come —during one phase of the early crisis, at least—to avoiding the great catastrophe, may be gauged from a subsequent communication between Chancellor Bülow and the Kaiser.

"I venture most submissively to suggest for your Majesty's consideration," Bülow wrote to Wilhelm, "whether your Majesty's Ambassador in London should be specifically asked about any possible action to be taken with a view to dissipating any ill feeling that the Rothschilds may have, or about any other points arising out of the Eckardstein report."

And yet in the end it all came to nothing. The velvet suasions of Seamore Place, Alfred's *soigné* French diplomatic locutions, his expert soothings—even his tiny ingenuity of changing the Family particle from "de" to "von" in his signature on the letter to Eckardstein—they were all blasted by the explosion at Sarajevo in July, 1914. The Kaiser moved from yacht to battleship. It would have been better for him, for the Rothschilds and for the world if Alfred's noblest pursuit had not been a lost cause.

## (b) *The War*

The holocaust spread from the Austro-Serbian border across the world. Not since the Napoleonic campaigns had the world found itself in so great a war. This time the Rothschilds were the losers, not the gainers. For one thing, the front line split the Austrian branch from the English and the French; theoretically a Vienna Rothschild in uniform was obliged to shoot his poilu or Tommy cousins.

This possibility, though chilling, was small. Another factor grew more important. A century before, during the forging of their greatness, the Rothschilds had been a tough, hard-fisted, fireproof band who waded in and out of the heaviest odds. Now success had smoothed the calluses away. For many decades The Family's favorite arena had been the board room or the salon conference. There its means and its mettle found few peers. But at a time when nations ripped and starved one another to death, it was the machine gun in the trench that did the most effective negotiating. A few pages—and a whole world—ago Alfred was still writing his suave peacetime prose to Eckardstein. The difference between that communication and a wartime letter of his two years later dramatizes the clan's alienation from the raw new realities.

The supply of pit-props for dugouts had become desperately short. Alfred, now seventy-five, tethered to his fireside at Seamore Place, thought of the glorious beeches on his country estate and, a little confusedly, tried to help. His message really belonged on some assistant's desk in the War Ministry. But Alfred had no connections on such a level, and therefore addressed himself to his Majesty's first minister.

"I am not an expert," he wrote Mr. Asquith on February 28, 1917, "as regards what sort of timber would be suitable for 'pit-props,' but I cannot help thinking that, as there are so many fine trees in my woods at Halton, some of them at least would be suitable for the purpose. May I ask you very kindly to send down your expert who would very easily be able to report fully on the subject, and I should indeed be proud if my offer should lead to any practical result."

The Family of a hundred years before had stormed through Armageddon in great forays of self-aggrandizement. Now they were encumbered not only with wealth but with scruples. War had become more a matter of service than of profit. Each Rothschild gave his flag whatever the flag demanded of him.

Alfred donated all his most beautiful trees. Natty

sacrificed some treasured animosities. An old political enemy, David Lloyd George, was chancellor of the exchequer at the outbreak of the war. Among his key duties figured the prevention of a financial panic, and without advice and help from Lord Rothschild he would not easily succeed. Accordingly, his Lordship was asked to come to the treasury. Lloyd George looked forward with some twinges to the meeting. After all, he had once publicly included Natty "among Philistines, not all of whom are uncircumcised." He had called him still other words which were, as he himself later admitted, "not of the kind to which the head of the great House of Rothschild had hitherto been subjected." That Jewish peer would not be an easy visitor.

"Lord Rothschild," said the Chancellor of the Exchequer as they shook hands, "we have had some political unpleasantness . . ."

The other man brushed that aside with his celebrated curtness. "No time to bring up such things. What can I do to help?"

"I told him," the statesman recalls. "He undertook to do it at once. It was done."

But Natty did still more. He let many of his staunch prejudices go up in smoke. Natty, in his middle seventies, the rudest, deafest opponent of social service, of suffragism and of every other kind of progressive flim-flam, Natty the most gorgeous avatar of reaction—Natty instantly suppressed every impulse which might obstruct England's victory. How could His Majesty's Government best raise money for the war effort? "Tax the rich!" snapped milord. "And tax them heavily!"

To the end Leo remained the most charitable of the three brothers. He contributed his son. On November 17, 1917, Major Evelyn Achille de Rothschild fell fighting the

Turkish army in Palestine. Leo himself died the same year; and before the war ended, Natty and Alfred lay buried in the Jewish cemetery at Willesden.

In France, the Paris clan's loyalty to the cause produced an unexpected result. After spending some intensive months nursing the wounded in a hospital carrying her name, Baroness Maurice de Rothschild took a few days' leave. She called one of her favorite hotels, the Palace at St. Moritz, to ask if there were any Germans there. The manager swore that nothing Teutonic would offend her eyes. Yet the first sight that greeted the Baroness was a well-known German champagne manufacturer. Mme. la Baronne turned on her heel.

When the Rothschilds are disappointed with a resort, they do not simply patronize another; they create their own. Baroness Maurice embraced a cause with a determination recalling her father-in-law, Edmond, in Palestine. Single-handedly she developed the village of Megève into the most chic French winter playground. (Today her son, Edmond de Rothschild, is the principal owner and controlling power in the resort; it admits very rich champagne manufacturers of any nationality.)

Megève notwithstanding, the great war was a grim affair for the Rothschilds too. Everywhere the Family branches enlisted their great fortunes and their young men. Major Evelyn de Rothschild did not remain the only casualty. On the Austrian side of the front, his cousin Eugene had his leg shattered by a Russian bullet. When the last gun ceased in 1918, nothing was the same, not even the Rothschilds.

## 4. *Aftermath*

It is reported that in the bad fall days of 1917 an English Rothschild chatelaine approached her chief gardener, whose staff had been decimated by the draft boards. She asked him, with an innocence no less sublime than sincere, how he had managed to scatter so many fine-colored leaves all over the walks this year?

In postwar autumns the exotic litter reappeared and remained in many Rothschild bowers. Now their budget kept the chief gardeners short of help; here and there the gardens themselves began to fray away. Suddenly the world turned into a meaner place. How simple being rich had been! Suddenly it was complex and so expensive. Taxes rose, rocketed, became murderous in the *mishpoche*'s bracket. Revenue officers assaulted the Family safes far more successfully than the most vicious rivals. It became increasingly difficult to live like a Rothschild.

"I've got to keep on breathing," Natty is supposed to have said in his last year. "It'll be my worst business mistake if I don't." One of his characteristically rough jokes, characteristically true. Being completely Family-owned, the Rothschild banks rested not on the money of a hundred thousand stockholders, but on the private fortunes of the partners. These became subject to immense death duties. Natty did make the mistake of dying. Within two years, as we know, both brothers repeated it. Thus the state tore three consecutive, titanic chunks out of the clan's assets.

The loss was compounded further by Alfred's testament. As a bachelor without commitments to wife or children, he had left a fortune still larger than his brothers'. Even after taxes a great estate remained, but the major part of it—Alfred steadfastly non-conformed, down to his last will—

did not go to other Rothschilds. It was left to Almina, Countess of Carnavaron. With part of the money, his heiress financed a great archeological venture in the Nile Valley; at Thebes this expedition made the momentous discovery of the grave and the treasures of Tutankhamen. Alfred's testament upset two dynasties. It disturbed the sleep of the Pharaohs and, even more, the reserves of the Family bank at New Court.

Ultimately, though, it was not exterior inclemencies which made the 1920's and 1930's the feeblest phase of the house; it was a matter of internal poise. The Rothschilds had played so triumphant a part in the *fin-de-siécle* idyll that they could not quite adjust to the new backdrop which history had slammed so boorishly over the old. Some of their best friends had lost crowns, courts and kingdoms. Some of their best servants seemed to have socialist afterthoughts. Some of their best balls began to be haunted by a horrid cacophony called jazz. And of course much of their best income fell to the government.

For a while they stood uncertain amid the shambles of a world they had helped create. Quite a few among them turned inward. Particularly in England, they seemed to use their hobbies as hiding places. Two pairs of brothers replaced the three British magnificos, and with one exception they did not possess the hardy business energies of their forefathers. Lord Lionel Walter, Natty's first son and successor, became immured in the Zoological Museum at Tring. It developed, at a cost of more than half a million pounds, into one of the finest of its kind in the world. Walter's brother Nathaniel was also a gifted natural historian. Conscientiously but unhappily, he performed his duties at the bank until his suicide in 1923.

Leo's elder boy, Lionel, surrounded himself with the vast rhododendron and orchid pavilions at Exbury, "a gardener by profession, a banker by hobby." His younger brother Anthony, excellent scholar though he was (he took a Double First at Trinity, Cambridge), stood out as the most practical and forceful of the current Rothschilds. For him attendance at the Partners' Room in New Court was neither perfunctory nor painful. But he was the youngest, and for a long time his voice remained small.

The aggressiveness of the tax, and the passivity of the taxed, brought about a great dying of palaces. Founder Nathan's West End mansion at 107 Piccadilly succumbed to the demolition squad. The huge estate at Gunnersbury turned into a public park. Alfred's famous manse at 1 Seamore Place died literally of the twentieth century: to ease Mayfair traffic congestion, it was razed so that Curzon Street could have direct access to Hyde Park.

The magnificence of these mortalities is best dramatized by the demise of 148 Piccadilly, where Baron Lionel and Disraeli had once plotted the purchase of the Suez Canal over dinner. In 1937 the great town house expired, with a lush art book of an auction catalogue whose 250 pages included sixty-four plates and gatefolds. A single item of furniture—a tulipwood *secretaire* with Sèvres porcelain panels, made especially for Louis XIV—fetched fifty thousand dollars.

And the revenue department reached out to the Family demesnes in Buckinghamshire. In 1932 the second Lord Rothschild had to sell his collection of over a quarter of a million birds to the New York Museum of Natural History; on his death Tring Park became empty and the museum public property. Aston Clinton lapsed into a hotel. In Alfred's gorgeous manor at Halton a great training center for the Royal Air Force was installed.

The important French Rothschilds had sense enough not to die in the years after World War I, and thus postponed the fiscal penalty for being flesh. But if their substance didn't shrink, their manner stiffened. Baron Edouard had been in charge of the house since the demise of his father Alphonse in 1905. Under his aegis the family fortunes were phlegmatically administered rather than actively deployed.

The same stasis appeared to apply to the clan's social life. It was a time when the Jazz Age jangled down on the world's drawing rooms, when wealth began to shimmy and shake off inhibition, when the upper class in one sleek swoop jumped out of the landau into the sports car. "The very rich are very different from you and me," Scott Fitzgerald wrote, tremulous with glamor. But for a while the Rothschilds seemed very different from the very rich. They had become "old money" at a moment which did not value age of any kind. This dazed them still further, and further removed them from the new diversions of their peers. They looked quite rigid, odd, venerable.

Then a few among them remembered that being modern was one of the Family traditions. Suddenly some of the younger Rothschilds became expertly wild. Henri (the invalid Nathaniel's grandson) began to cruise through the 1920's in his yacht *Eros*, whose passengers often did honor to her name; wrote smart plays under the pseudonym André Pascal; built the Theatre Pigalle; and gave some of the most glittering and curfew-defying parties on the Côte d'Azur.

James Armand popped up—a top-hatted, monocled cross between Fred Astaire and Charlie Chaplin, almost as intriguing a dissonance as jazz itself. To begin with his national disparateness: "Jimmy," as the son of Baron Edmond, was French by birth; as the principal heir of his eccentric Viennese Aunt Alice, largely Austrian by fortune and by monocle; by citizenship and membership in the

House of Commons, English. He was also a frail man. His left eye had been knocked out by a golf shot of the Duke de Gramont. He went through so many abdominal operations that The Family came to believe he grew a new gall bladder as soon as the old one was removed. And as he was not an especially fortunate rider, the saying developed that "whenever Jimmy has time between surgery, he sneaks in a quick fall." Yet he practiced sports, politics, philanthropy and art collecting up to the age of seventy-eight with great vigor.

And with a contradictory élan. His frock coat, stiff collar, sideburns, Tout-Paris inflections combined with Oxford accent, made him the almost clownish epitome of Anglo-French elegance. At the same time he had an accomplished career as a Liberal in the Commons, was often seen with labor leaders like Aneuran Bevan, and talked fluent Hebrew to workers in Palestine, where he carried forward the colonization projects of his father.

At the racetrack he resembled a Damon Runyon caricature dolled up in spats and monocle. And he had priceless hunches. A typically incredible Jimmy performance took place at the Cambridgeshire Handicap in 1921. Minutes before post time he began to rage up and down the line, putting bets on a 100-to-7 shot called Milenko until the bookies refused to accept any more. The grandstands laughed. Milenko won by a length and a half. Jimmy made some 200,000 pounds that afternoon.

With women, too, Jimmy had a bizarre but felicitous way. At thirty-five he suddenly decided to marry and inquired about a suitable bride at—where else?—the secretary's office of one of his golf clubs. The secretary glanced over the golf scores of various members. What about young Miss Dorothy Pinto, who had been making such good progress on the links? Soon afterwards a rabbi solemnized a union which lasted forty-three happy years, through all the many-faceted phases of Jimmy's career, until his death in 1956. Today Mrs. Jimmy administers capably her late husband's philanthropies in Israel.

Jimmy's brother Maurice was a wild Rothschild in a somewhat different way. Apparently Maurice realized that The Family, great as it was, had not yet produced a single decent black sheep. To the filling of this gap he dedicated himself with huge and by no means untalented energies. In his spare time he played banker. It also pleased him to be a senator in the French parliament. But mainly he excelled in being a black sheep. His bite, it might be added, was just as bad as his bleat. Some people went so far as to claim that, to count in the *haut monde* of the 1920's and 1930's, one had to be seduced or at least pinched by Baron Maurice if one was a woman, or affronted by Baron Maurice, if a man. No other personage surpassed him in enriching the delicious scandal of his times.

Among the more mentionable highpoints of his career figures an interlude at the Hotel de Paris in Monte Carlo. The hotel quite justifiably considers its cuisine one of the finest in the world. The day came, however, when a dish displeased M. le Baron. He promptly rented an apartment with a huge kitchen, summoned his chef from Paris and installed him there. Maurice himself kept his suite in the hotel, but repaired demonstratively to his "eating apartment" in town during mealtimes.

He could behave quite differently when seriously crossed. In Cannes a haberdasher sold him a pair of bathing trunks which, on their first immersion, turned out to be most scratchy. M. le Baron stopped swimming and abandoned them to the fish. He walked on shore exactly as God made him. In the immense uproar that ensued, he told press, police and anyone else who cared to listen the name and address of the culprit haberdasher and the quality of the trunks which had led him to expose his grief in so natural a fashion.

Of course he was best (or worst) known as Don Juan de Rothschild. His favorite fields of operation, apart from the dressing rooms of Paris theaters, were Deauville and Biarritz during their respective seasons in August and September. It was in Biarritz that a particularly illustrative event transpired.

One of the great *femmes fatales* began to hold court there in the middle 1920's. Every man who enjoyed her favors she subsequently either survived or divorced, or at any rate relieved of most of his worldly goods. A number of people thought her to be quite worthy of Maurice. They arranged an introduction. The lady was achingly beautiful and glitteringly poised. The Baron appeared to be agog and quickly undone. He lost all his proverbial rudeness. Smitten, he danced with her all evening at the Hotel du Palais. He drenched her in roses. Again and again he declared in the presence of the whole table that he must bring together the most beautiful neck in France—he bowed before the minx's decolletage—and the most beautiful necklace in Biarritz. Everyone, including the neck's owner, considered this an adorably phrased pledge.

Against her usual C.O.D. practice, the lady became Maurice's that night. On the morrow he ushered her into his most impressive car and drove straight to the resort's leading jeweler. In the window hung a necklace worth 300,000 dollars. Maurice escorted her up to the plate glass.

"Voilà, ma chère," he said, kissed her hand and, having brought neck and necklace quite close together, turned on his heel to drive away, alone.

While the Family banks receded into the background,

Henri, Jimmy and Maurice kept impressing on society the continued presence of the clan. The three showed that the old dynamism, however oddly expressed at the moment, was still there. Perhaps they were an intimation that the clan would survive in style even what was to come. For the House of Rothschild, which had started as epic and con tinued as extravaganza, was approaching tragedy.

# IX

# *HITLER VERSUS ROTHSCHILD*

## 1. *The Depression and Baron Louis*

SHORTLY after the turn of the century, a story goes, two hoboes went walking through Vienna's Stadtpark. There was a click-clack of hooves, and one asked the other who that tiny tot was, being driven about in a huge carriage all his own?

"Look at the livery," the second hobo said. "That's little Baron Louis taking the air."

"So young!" the first hobo said admiringly. "So young—and already a Rothschild!"

Neither he nor anyone else knew it, but that golden coach drove toward the depression, toward the Anschluss, toward a Gestapo prison and World War II.

Little Baron Louis grew up. He was twenty-nine when his father Albert died, shortly before World War I. Now, it is a peculiarity of the Austrian house to invest all business authority not in partners (the usage at New Court or rue Laffitte), but in a single person. Alphonse and Eugene, Louis' brothers, dedicated themselves to their high leisures. Louis assumed the helm of all Rothschild affairs in Central Europe. And so a rather poetic appositeness came about, the kind in which Family history abounds. The Austrian branch, more than any other, was to be battered by the vicissitudes of the new century. Louis, more than anyone else in the whole *mishpoche*, was the classically polished foil to all the brute newfangledness.

The mettle of the man became apparent quite early, through an incident with, curiously, a Manhattan background. It seems that the New York agents of The Family participated in the financing of the New York Interborough Rapid Transit Company. Young Louis, who had been sent over to soak up America, had a hand in the project and helped inaugurate it by going on one of the earliest subway rides. This particular journey ended with a breakdown of motor and ventilation systems. When the sweating, choking passengers were finally helped out into the fresh air, there was one odd bird who had kept on not only his jacket but his overcoat. In fact, rescuers swore that he emerged with not a bead on his brow: the Baron.

Others who came up against Louis' inviolable composure often didn't know what to make of him. Icy insouciance or simply cold fish? At any rate, the young head of the Vienna house matured into the silkiest, most stoic, most smoothly and untouchably finished grand seigneur yet sired by The Family. There had never been a Rothschild quite like this one before; circumstance made sure there would never be one in his image again. He himself apparently refused to marry, and neither of his married brothers produced surviving sons. He was the last head of the Austrian Rothschilds.

This helped cast an extra glow over a life all the more romantic because of the reticence of the man who lived it. The Manhattan accident—that strange confrontation between a last Rothschild and a first subway crush—contained prophecy. Other distempers of modernity were in store for him, much more vicious ones, and he would face them with the same spectacular tranquility.

Nature had equipped Louis well for his role. Slim, blond, handsome, the image of the Anglo-Saxon aristocrat for all his synagogue-going, he could give his spareness of speech a disarmingly simple or forbiddingly aloof nuance. Despite a minor heart ailment (what's a thoroughbred without a small, piquant complaint?) he had extraordinary energies, extraordinarily if frigidly groomed. A fierce polo player, a formidable huntsman, a rider of the famous white Lipizzaners of Austria's "Spanish" State Riding School (even under the Republic, a privilege granted only to the best horsemen of the best circles), he was also an acute scholar in anatomy, botany and the graphic arts.

Last, not least, he was a lover accomplished and discriminate. To his great bachelor *palais* in the Prinz Eugenstrasse, or to his Renngasse office, wallpapered in dark red silk, Vienna's loveliest women came calling. It may be a measure of the man's discretion that this private office had three entrances, one camouflaged so well that only he, his secretary and selected visitors knew its location.

But it wasn't only luscious ladies that came toward Baron Louis. Often it was black news. He steered his house through an increasingly ugly era. Before 1914 the Vienna bank had been the chief financier of a great imperial realm, prime mover in the financial nerve center of Southeast Europe. After 1918 Austria dwindled to a pauperized fraction of its former self. Inevitably, the Austrian Rothschild firm diminished as well.

As the leading, almost "official" private banking institution, S. M. Rothschild und Söhne was tied to the fortunes of the faltering little fatherland. Loyally it had bought state securities by the million and saw inflation devour its investment. In the mid-1920's it could not, like its great Viennese rival Castiglione, undermine the government by speculating on the fall of the Austrian Krone. The Krone fell, of course. Castiglione towered and threatened to overshadow Rothschild.

Castiglione went on to speculate on the fall of the franc. His allies dumped and dumped French currency on the market. Down plummeted the franc, up zoomed pound and dollar. And Rothschild? Experts began to write off The Family's Central European pre-eminence. It had grown very quiet in the silken study at the Renngasse. Then, all at once, the franc backed up startlingly, began to rise, in fits at first, then with an absolute fury that put Castiglione out of business. The financial world was stunned. Baron Louis, with a cool smile, went to Italy for a bit of polo.

What had happened? Actually an old, old Rothschild story which unrolled once more in 1925. The various *mishpoche* banks in England, France and Austria had secretly realigned their tentacles. With the French house in the lead (Baron Edouard was a director of the Bank of France), they had organized a noiseless international syndicate that reached from J. P. Morgan in New York to the Baron Louis-controlled Creditanstalt in Vienna. Everywhere, at a prearranged signal, the Rothschild syndicate began to depress pounds and push up francs. As in the past, nobody could withstand such wealth juggled with such split-second skill. Baron Louis returned from his Italian polo tanned and barely smiling.

There were further trials in store for him. The 1920's

had been tricky. The 1930's were treacherous before they turned tragic. In 1929 the depression broke out. The fragile young republic was least equipped to deal with it. It toppled Austria's business. It undermined Austria's banking. And it began to move toward the Family palace.

In 1930 the Bodenkreditanstalt—the country's key agricultural credit institution—was in desperate straits. Louis, panicproof as usual, demonstrated calmness by hunting deer at one of his game preserves. The government was much more excitable. The federal chancellor entrained personally to the Rothschild estate. As he himself later put it, "I aimed a gun at the Baron's chest." He forced Louis to bail out the failing bank. "I'll do it," Herr Baron said, "but you'll regret it."

The Creditanstalt, Austria's greatest public bank (Louis von Rothschild, President), took over the liabilities of the agricultural credit institution. Austria regretted it. As a result of this overextension, the Creditanstalt, too, had to suspend payment one year later. Now the financial structure of the entire country tottered. It was the government itself which must come to the rescue, with funds drawn from the state treasury. And the House of Rothschild contributed thirty million gold schillings to help the Creditanstalt back on its feet.

Mitigated though it was by considerable subterranean help from the French Rothschilds, this was a cruel drain on the Family reserves. The Baron sold some of his country places and moved from the huge mansion in the Prinz Eugenstrasse to a somewhat smaller residence nearby.

He was still the richest man in Austria. His own bank, S. M. Rothschild und Söhne, stayed intact, a giant in Austrian terms. He remained one of the large landed proprietors in Central Europe, retained control over immense investments in textile factories, mining industries and chemical companies.

To the north the storm troopers began to beat their drums, but he kept dictating in his red-silk office, into the teeth of fate.

## 2. *Windsor at Enzesfeld*

So came Louis von Rothschild's final years as the last great gentleman of Central Europe. Between 1931 and 1938 the Baron's life unrolled like the final act of a sumptuously produced suspense play. The initial shock had been shaken off. The dark climax lay still veiled. A brief calm reigned, ornamented with butlers and enlivened by a glamorous intermezzo.

In 1936 Edward VIII abdicated for Mrs. Simpson. On the day before his momentous act the King talked on the long-distance wire to the world's most famous divorcee. The British government had arranged a haven for him at a Zurich hotel, but Wallis strongly opposed the choice. A hotel was much too fragile a shelter against incursions of the insatiable press. And so was, for that matter, the telephone connection between his London and her Cannes.

"David," Mrs. Simpson said, wary of eavesdroppers, "why don't you go to the place where you had that cold last year?"

"The place" was Schloss Enzesfeld near Vienna, a castle belonging to Eugene von Rothschild, Louis' brother and a good friend to the two parties involved. Here David could enjoy complete seclusion; here he could play his beloved golf on the Baron's private links; here he could speak

Austrian German, his favorite foreign dialect; here, where he had gotten rid of a minor cold the previous year, he might best survive the major crisis of his life.

"Indeed I will," said the King.

The next day, December 11, he was king no more. Less than forty-eight hours later the gates of Rothschild's estate parted to admit, in a black limousine, the man who had just renounced the crown of the greatest monarchy for the most romantic possible reason. The curiosity of five continents converged on Eugene's house. Enzesfeld became as famous a word as Mayerling.

A garland of fables was quickly woven around it, some of them quite amusing. For example, one claimed that the newly created Duke of Windsor tossed incredibly luxurious parties behind those castle walls; that the bills for all such entertainments were sent to the host; that the Barons Eugene and Louis, tired of the elongation in their accountants' faces, had resorted to a typically ingenious Rothschild device: that through the village council they had the Duke elected "Master of Enzesfeld" and then instructed all tradesmen to direct their bills to the personage so honored.

Actually the Duke lived—and golfed—very quietly on the estate. The day was organized around six thirty P.M., when Eugene had the telephone room ready and all local lines cleared so that David could call Wallis long distance at Cannes.

Nonetheless, the stay of so mythic a personage had its effect on the Central European landscape of manners. When the Duke joined the Rothschilds and their other guests for dinner, it was discovered that he wore his black tie with a soft, not a starched collar—a fact which fomented something of a sartorial *Putsch* in Austrian society. David was also responsible for another innovation. In the words of Baron Eugene, "he invented brunch." That is, the Duke favored a late and rather heavy breakfast, which often led to the omission of the midday table. This meal, too, found its place in the repertoire of inside sophisticates.

For the last time Austria enjoyed something of the imperial glow it had once radiated. And for the last time ever, an Austrian Rothschild exercised a hospitality commensurate with his name.

## 3. *The Ides of March*

The Enzesfeld interlude was a loud contribution to The Family's social éclat. Meanwhile Louis' career continued to embody the quietly seignorial. In 1937, not long after the Duke's departure from Enzesfeld, the Baron attended a dinner party at a friend's home. A mewing was heard outside the window, and before anybody could stop him, Rothschild had opened the window, stepped out onto the sill, edged along a crevice of the wall, retrieved the kitten and jumped back into the room.

This sort of thing had happened before. Louis always had a remarkable physical as well as emotional sense of balance. Like his father Albert (the Matterhorn pioneer), he had climbed many peaks and, if no peaks were at hand, even buildings. But in 1937 he was fifty-five years old; the night was dark, and the apartment five stories high.

"Baron!" said one of the guests. "This is a job for the fire brigade. Why risk your life?"

The Baron replied with one of his cool smiles. "I suppose it's become a habit," he said.

Everyone knew what he meant. The German armies were massing at the border. Most people in his position found travel attractive. His brother Eugene had moved to his Paris residence. Alphonse, the eldest, went back and forth over the Swiss border. But Louis stayed put in the Austrian capital.

Calmly, almost dashingly he draped the cape of doom about him. His secretaries still worked away in the silken suite at the Renngasse. In fact there was, rather inexplicably, more activity in the bank than ever. Each Wednesday the curator of Vienna's Kunsthistorisches Museum still came for breakfast at the Baron's house and held with him a sort of two-man art seminar. Each Friday morning a professor from the Botanical Gardens still appeared to bring and discuss interesting new specimens. Each Sunday the head of the Anatomical Institute dropped in with charts and books. Twice a week Herr Baron still rode the great Lipizzaners. Life went on as usual though friends at the Jockey Club shook their heads. As the chief of the Austrian house, as the epitome of the Jewish capitalist, Rothschild was the Führer's favorite abomination. Why must just he remain? Why provide so inviting a target in such a parlous area?

Two good reasons accounted for his obstinacy. Both were dynastic. One remained secret, revolved around the muffled hubbub in Louis' office and would not emerge until many months later. The other reason was public and obvious. As head of The Family, Louis moved in the Austrian limelight. Any motion smacking of flight would upset still further an already wobbly ship of state. The head of a Rothschild house (we have encountered instances of this before) is a human being second, a principle first.

In the cool perfectionism of the Baron's mind, principle congealed to dogma. He did not go near the border. When the Austrian chancellor was summoned before Hitler in Berchtesgarden, Louis left Vienna—for a bit of skiing in the Austrian Alps. And when on March 1, 1938, a courier from the French house knocked at his door in Kitzbühel with an urgent warning, he did not hurry away to Zurich. He put away his skis—and returned to Vienna.

On Thursday, March 10, a last alarm was telegraphed from Switzerland. The following morning German troops flooded across the border. The ship of state had sunk. The presence of principles could no longer save it. On Saturday afternoon Louis had himself driven to Vienna's airport along with his valet Edouard, their ostensible destination being Louis' polo team in Italy. At the barrier, a short distance from the plane, an SS officer recognized the Baron and confiscated his passport.

"After that," recalls the valet, "we went home and waited."

It did not take long. In the evening there appeared before the Rothschild *palais*, as before hundreds of other Jewish homes, two men with swastika arm bands.

The butler, however, would not tolerate the unmannerliness of an arrest. He first had to see whether the Herr Baron was at home. No, he told the callers two minutes later, the Herr Baron was not. The two bravos, stunned by this ambush of etiquette, retreated first into a stutter and then into the night.

But on Sunday they were back with six steel-helmeted daredevils, all drawing pistols against further high-society tricks. This time Herr Baron received the senior henchmen. He accepted an invitation to come along—after lunch, which was about to be served. A confused consultation ensued among the steel helmets. The upshot was: Well, eat.

The Baron ate, for the last time in full baronial splendor. While the gang dandled their pistols two yards from the table, the butlers bowed and the dishes filled the room with the scent of sauces. The Baron finished in leisure; used, as always, the finger bowl after fruit; dried, as always, his hands on the fresh damask napkin held out for him; enjoyed his after-dinner cigarette; took his heart medicine; approved the next day's menus; then nodded to the pistols and departed.

Very late that night it became plain that he would not return. And so, in the small hours of the morning, the good valet Edouard packed his master's special bed sheets, his toilet kit, a careful selection of outdoor and indoor clothing, some books on art history and botanical lore—in fine, the customary assortment for the more tiresome sort of week-end invitation. Soon afterwards he presented all these items at police headquarters enclosed in a crested pigskin case. He was sent away amid furious laughter.

But the valet's performance made the Nazi police commissioner become even more intrigued with his prisoner. Louis' first interrogations were designed to satisfy perfectly understandable curiosities.

"Well, so you're Rothschild. Just exactly how rich are you?"

Louis answered that if the entire staff of his accountants were summoned, and provided with up-to-date reports on the world's commodity and stock markets, they might come up with a reasonable answer after a few days' work.

"All right, all right. How much is your palace worth?"

Rothschild gave the inquisitive gentleman an ever so slightly amused glance. "How much is the Vienna cathedral worth?" he replied, quite accurately.

"*Impertinence!*" roared the commissioner. From his viewpoint, he was perhaps not wrong.

Guards pushed the Baron down into the cellar. There Louis carried sand sacks beside the Communist party chiefs who happened to be fellow inmates. "We got on rather well," Louis recalled later. "We agreed that this was the world's most classless cellar."

Other unusual things occurred. Odd letters reached a Rothschild executive in Switzerland. The authors were three of Central Europe's foremost whores, who enjoyed excellent rapport with the Nazi police in Vienna. The ladies offered themselves as middlemen in ransom discussions. The Rothschild houses—traditionally adept in extraordinary negotiations—might have come to terms even with these partners, if not for a sudden but actually inevitable turn of events.

## 4. *Hermann Göring Says Hello*

At the end of April Berlin began to pay attention to the importance of the prisoner. Overnight Louis was separated from the Communists and the sand sacks and found himself at the Vienna Gestapo headquarters in a cell next to the deposed Austrian chancellor. His case had been lifted from the local police level to the highest and most conspiratorial circles of the Reich. Now he had twenty-four guards—a booted, belted horde, "my grenadiers"—whose familiarities he quashed by teaching them, like a bored professor, geology and botany.

As successor to the foremost whores, a new emissary appeared in Switzerland: A man named Otto Weber identified himself as an "associate" of a Dr. Gritzbach, who in turn was personal advisor to Hermann Göring. Slowly it became evident who was calling the tune now. Slowly, after many shadowy precautions, the terms emerged. Herr Baron would go free if Marschall Göring were given 200,000 dollars for his trouble and the German Reich got every remaining asset of the Austrian house, particularly Vitkovitz, the largest iron-and-coal works in Central Europe, located in Czechoslovakia.

This was stern news. It involved the highest ransom in the history of the world. But Eugene and Alphonse, who did the negotiating in Zurich and Paris, had a trump of their own. And it was a beauty: Vitkovitz, though owned by Austrian Rothschilds, had by some queer magic become English property. In the prewar days of 1938 that meant it was immune to Göring's claws.

All the tiptoe hurly-burly in Louis' office during 1936 and 1937—just before it was too late—had centered around this transformation. Together with a canny old banking executive named Leonard Keesing, Louis had sneaked the Union Jack around some twenty-one million dollars. It was financial cloak-and-dagger in the best Rothschild tradition.

How had Louis Rothschild done it? His underground work had started with one paramount fact: plants of such enormous size could not change citizenship without consent on the highest governmental level. Therefore the Czech prime minister was persuaded very discreetly, in 1936, that continued Austrian control of Vitkovitz would constitute a danger to Czechoslovakia in the event that Vienna fell under German domination. Simultaneously, and under separate secrecy, the Austrian chancellor received intimations that the anti-Austrian and anti-German bent of the Czech authorities might lead to a seizure of Vitkovitz as long as it was Austrian-owned. Thus both Vienna and Prague, for opposite reasons, assented to the change.

Next came the transfer itself—an intricate, accomplished exercise in fiscal and legal craft. It made expert use of the fact that the Rothschilds were not the exclusive but only the majority stockholders in Vitkovitz. The minority owners, another great Austro-Jewish family named von Gutmann, had recently become depression-ridden. To pay their debts, the Gutmanns must sell their shares; and to do that, a revision of Vitkovitz' corporate structure had become necessary. Under cover of this reorganization the nationality of the multimillion-dollar enterprise was incidentally transmuted.

All that sleight-of-hand, however, would have been useless without an additional precaution. If Louis had consigned the Rothschild shares directly to an English holding company, the advent of war might well have made the German-tainted property forfeit to Britain's trading-with-the-enemy act. Louis, foreseeing this even during the peacetime years of the 1930's, had first done some shunting onto Swiss and Dutch financial grounds. From these countries—which were to be neutral or Allied soil in World War II—the final transfer was effected.

Vitkovitz became a subsidiary of Alliance Insurance. But Alliance was, and is, a prominent London corporation, registered under British law, protected by His Majesty's Government, yet largely owned—and this, of course, is the point and joke of the whole matter—by the very Rothschilds who had sold it Vitkovitz.

Napoleon and Bismarck had come up in vain against The Family. Göring, though not the greatest, was certainly the clan's heaviest antagonist. *He* did not do any better. The Reichsmarschall had to retreat, not only before Jewish guile, but before an Aryan comrade. Heinrich Himmler began to muscle in.

## 5. *Heinrich Himmler Says Hello*

Early in 1939 Otto Weber, Göring's man, was arrested. Apparently the Nazis were settling an internecine conflict over Rothschild loot. Berlin shifted commands. German ransom negotiations now seemed to receive their impetus from Himmler rather than Göring. The Family, unmoved by the change of venue, stuck to their terms: all ordinary Rothschild assets in Austria to be exchanged for the safety of Louis' person, but control of Vitkovitz to be surrendered only after Louis' release—and for three million pounds.

Berlin stormed. Berlin threatened. In fact, after the rape of Czechoslovakia, German troops occupied Vitkovitz. But German lawyers knew that the British flag and international law still stood between them and legal ownership.

And so a new tone was tried. While Nazi newspapers fumed against Rothschild as the scourge of mankind, a curious event transpired in Louis' cell. The door opened. Heinrich Himmler appeared and wished the Herr Baron good morning; offered the Herr Baron a cigarette; asked whether the Herr Baron had any wishes or complaints; and, as celebrity to celebrity, tried to settle whatever trifling differences might be between them.

However the Herr Baron, a lifelong smoker, did not feel like a cigarette just then. His briefness of speech grew particularly acute. He appraised the dread face coldly. "The fellow," he said later, "had a stye in his eye and was trying to hide it." When Herr Himmler had bowed himself out, the Rothschild position on Vitkovitz had not altered by a particle.

Whereupon new blandishments spilled into Louis' bare little cubicle. One hour after the chief's departure a detail of "grenadiers" staggered in under an enormous, blowsy Louis XIV clock; returned with a vast, nonmatching, Louis XV vase; covered the prison cot with a thick orange-velvet curtain upon which they scattered multicolored cushions. Finally came a radio, around whose base a silk skirt had been sewn.

It was a Himmler attempt to make a Rothschild feel at home. It produced results. For many weeks Louis had remained stoic in the face of ugly things. Now he lost his temper. "The place looked like a Cracow bordello!" That recollection, often repeated in the years to come, carried one of Louis' rare exclamation marks.

All the garishness (with the exception of the radio, which the Baron defrocked himself) was removed at the prisoner's insistence. Quite possibly the fiasco made the SS give up. A few nights later, around eleven P.M. Louis' chief guard announced that the Rothschilds' terms had been accepted and the Baron was free to leave.

As thanks, Louis visited upon his jailers a farewell confusion. The hour was too late, the Baron said, to expect any of his friends to put him up. After all, servants were in bed by now. He would much rather leave in the morning. Since in all the Gestapo dossiers there was no precedent of an application for a night's lodging, Berlin had to be consulted by long distance. Louis' last night at headquarters was on the house.

A few days later he landed in Switzerland. And two months after that, in July, 1939, the Reich undertook to buy Vitkovitz for 2,900,000 pounds sterling.

Since the war broke out almost immediately, the contract was never consummated. But the technically English ownership of Vitkovitz remains pertinent to this day. After assuming power, the Czech Communists nationalized Vitkovitz. In 1953, however, London signed a trade agreement with Prague. One clause stated that the seized-property claims of British nationals, among which Vitkovitz figured most prominently, were to be satisfied. Prague followed through. Thereupon Parliament passed a law enabling an English corporate agent (like Alliance Insurance) to collect compensation on behalf of non-English owners (like the ex-Austrian Rothschilds, now of American citizenship).

Today The Family, still the world's greatest capitalist name, receives from a Communist government restitution that will finally amount to one million pounds.

Louis lived out the life of a storybook prince after the dragon has been slain. He settled in America. The Viennese Baron became a Yankee nob (no more subway rides); the silken bachelor, a belated but happy husband. In 1946 he married the Countess Hilda von Auersperg, one of the most attractive women of the Austrian aristocracy.

The couple visited Austria during the hungry years following the Nazi collapse. Word of the Baron's return quickly spread. A crowd formed outside his hotel, begging Rothschild for bread. With a lavish gesture Louis gave it to them: he turned over to the Austrian government all his Austrian properties. The government, accepting the condition that accompanied the gift, created a special law. It converted the Rothschild assets into a giant, state-administered pension fund. This provides for each of Louis' former domestic and business employees the same security and income as that enjoyed by retired civil servants.

Then Louis returned to his spacious farm in East Barnard, Vermont. The New England highlands evoked the Alps. The tart reserve of the Vermonters matched his own temper well. Professors of art and botany came to visit from Dartmouth. His brother, Baron Eugene (surviving today and the husband of the English stage star Jeanne Stuart), often came to visit from his Long Island estate. Baroness Hilda created a beautiful garden on the grounds, as well as something Louis had never been sure he would like: a family home. He liked it. In the last years of his life the Rothschild folks even gave open-air barn dances, and the Baron do-si-do'd with the same cool grace with which he had once waltzed on Vienna parquets. He died, in his seventies, the way a grand seigneur should—swimming in Montego Bay, under a blue and perfect Caribbean sky.

## 6. *A Dynasty Enlists*

World War II, of course, greatly affected The Family in England and France as well. When German tanks rolled into Paris in 1940, the French Rothschilds were in grave peril. The older ones, Edouard, Robert and Maurice (all grandsons of founder James), managed to escape. They ended up, by sundry paths and stops, in the United States or England.

Maurice showed himself as good a businessman as he had been an efficient scamp. On his flight to Britain he had salvaged a satchel of jewelry worth, it is said, about a million dollars. A good part of it he sold; then he began to phone his investment broker, steadily, for a few years. When he returned to France after the war, he had parlayed his satchel into a new fortune, impressive even by Rothschild standards.

The old clan members got the best of the war. The young ones, who helped wage it, saw the raw side like soldiers everywhere. Robert's sons Elie and Alain were among those manning the Maginot Line, and both became prisoners of war in Germany. Possibly because of Louis' awesome career as a hostage, no special pressure was applied to them. During the Fall of France, Edouard's son Guy was caught in the Dunkirk trap. He escaped; managed to reach New York in 1941; went to England when the Free French formed, was torpedoed while crossing the

Atlantic, swam for three hours, and was rescued by a British destroyer; executed a number of confidential missions for de Gaulle (and ever since has had close ties with the General); participated in two months of front-line fighting after D-day; and finished the war as adjutant to de Gaulle's military governor of Paris.

Not much less picturesque, but more indicative of the Family temper, were the war adventures of other Rothschilds. "We know how to run things," Baron Philippe* of Mouton Rothschild says when on the subject. "We run things all our lives, and we use unconventional short cuts—boom!—which upset the military bureaucrats."

Philippe takes his text from life. When he recovered from a severe skiing injury in 1940, Paris was swarming with Germans. He fled to Morocco, where the Vichy government arrested him at the request of the German armistice commission. In prison he began to manage things by organizing language schools and gymnastic sessions; among the fellow inmates he put through knee bends was one named Pierre Mendès-France. Brought back to France, he was released; fled to Spain by way of a forty-two-hour walking tour across the Pyrenees with smugglers (incidentally suggesting some improvements in smuggling technique); survived, and helped run several Spanish jails; sneaked into Portugal, and thence by ship into England. There he joined de Gaulle and was quartered at the Free French Officers' Club at 107 Piccadilly. This, of course, was his Grandaunt Hannah's mansion. Familiar with every nook of the place—boom!—he set about reforming the entire billeting set-up in the house. He didn't bother to inform the CO. The French brass were not pleased by such chronic enterprise. On D-day Phillippe found himself

* Philippe is a great-grandson of that English Nathaniel who moved to France. Thus his descendants are English by family tree but French by citizenship.

shunted to a dull job in the rear. The British, however, had their eye on the managerial Baron and shunted him right out again. He was put in charge of civil affairs in the critical Le Havre area during the early months of the invasion. Today he has the Croix de Guerre and is an *officier* of the Legion of Honor.

Among the English Rothschilds, Edmund (sweet Leo's grandson) and Lord Victor (Natty's grandson) were of military age. Each had inherited a handsome portion of the Family willfulness. Edmund, today head of the English bank, took part in the Italian and North African campaigns as an artillery major. The most characteristic account of a Rothschild embroiled in military hierarchy revolves around him. "Eddy," recalls a wartime pal, "made one of our keenest officers. But he never got the hang of going through channels. Anytime any of our men had an emergency—say their mother died and they needed a furlough and money—they wouldn't go about it the regular way. No, it was straight to Eddy, even if they were from a different outfit. They knew he'd pull that Rothschild checkbook out of his pocket, or he'd be on the phone—about any old hardship case—he'd be on the phone to Buckingham Palace. 'Eddy,' I used to say, 'Eddy, you can't do that. You've got to fill out a form about the bloke, and send it on with your recommendation to the CO.' 'What's the CO got to do with it?' he used to ask. The moment he did something civilian, he just couldn't understand what a superior was."

"On the command level they are superb," said another wartime observer of The Family's warriors. "Below that they can be nuisances. They are born and brought up as field marshals, you know, and it's a real problem for them to be just majors. We'd save ourselves a lot of trouble if a high enough rank would come automatically with that name."

At one point this tribe of obstinate field marshals got a dose of its own obstinacy. The scene was Robert de Rothschild's resplendent residence at 23, Avenue de Marigny in Paris, today inhabited by his elder son Alain. In contrast to all other Family palaces by the Seine, it survived the occupation virtually intact. Göring was always eager to have his boys crash the Rothschilds', and he put into the mansion the commander of the Luftwaffe in France. Surprisingly, the Kommandant left the house more or less as he had found it. Göring himself, as a rule a fond looter of Rothschild palazzos, often visited but never despoiled 23, Avenue de Marigny. It was even spared during the skirmishes accompanying the liberation.

The trouble began afterwards. A young English lieutenant-colonel moved in, bringing with him a perilous laboratory. In the immediate neighborhood of rare furniture and priceless paintings began a series of experiments with high explosives. Baron Robert had not yet returned. His servants trembled through their tasks, helpless before the flare and boom of the colonel's apparatus. The man was no idle prankster, and he was hard to dislodge. One of Britain's most successful and audacious bomb-removal experts, his work had earned him the George Medal (a very high English decoration) as well as the U.S. Bronze Star and the U.S. Legion of Merit. But what intimidated Baron Robert's retinue most was the fact that the colonel went by the name of—Victor Lord Rothschild.

The billeting authorities had thought it a charming idea to accommodate the colonel in his cousin's home; they had not considered the zeal with which Family members pursue their objectives. It took the combined efforts of the British High Command and the Monuments, Fine Arts and Archives Section of the American Army to move his Lordship's endeavors into a more suitable milieu.

## 7. *The Palace as Souvenir*

Lord Rothschild's tenancy at Avenue de Marigny was a postlude to an unprecedented situation in the art world. Like many Jews on the run after the fall of France, the Rothschilds had to leave behind most of their material possessions. Principal among these were their immense art collections, worth many millions of dollars. How could they be defended against the Nazi looters?

Actually, the defense of Family treasures had begun, with typical Rothschild far-sightedness, generations earlier. Back in 1873, after the Paris Commune, Baron Alphonse decided that his immense art properties needed fitting protection. For each painting, sculpture or *objet* a custom-tailored, specially upholstered and easily portable case was made. Since every new acquisition received its proper sheath, the private Rothschild museums vanished smoothly during World War I and during the Front Populaire crises in the 1930's.

But these early alarms were only dry runs. When the German tanks came down on Paris in the summer of 1940, a systematically rapacious enemy began to grasp at Rothschild canvases and Rothschild marble.

Occasionally he was fooled. A number of paintings were quickly spirited into foreign embassies, such as the Spanish and the Argentinian, and faithfully preserved there for the duration. A few very valuable pieces spent the war in a secret room at 23, Avenue de Marigny. The servants who knew about the room never breathed a word, and the Germans never got wind of it. Göring himself often walked right past the bookcase which stood between him and the portraits for which his agents were combing all of France.

But for the majority of Rothschild treasures, all precautions did not suffice. A whole list of important items, for example, was turned over to the Louvre, to receive protection as French national property. A useless ruse. The Family possessions were so well known, and the German dictator so art-loving, that Hitler issued a special directive bearing on "nationalized" Rothschild art. In a document later captured, the chief of the German High Command, Keitel, instructed the Nazi Military Government in Occupied France as follows:

> In supplement to the order of the Führer to search . . . the occupied territories for material valuable to Germany (and to safeguard the latter through the Gestapo), the Führer has decided:
>
> Ownership transfers to the French State or similar transfers completed after September 1, 1939, are irrelevant and invalid (. . . *for example possessions of the Palais Rothschild* *). Reservations regarding search, seizure and transportation to Germany on the basis of the above reason will not be recognized.
>
> Reichleiter Rosenberg has received clear instructions from the Führer personally governing the right of seizure; he is entitled to transport to Germany cultural goods which appear valuable to him and to safeguard them there. The Führer has reserved for himself the decision as to their use.

Alfred Rosenberg, Hitler's specially deputized pillager-in-chief, did his work well. Baron Edouard concealed most of his art works on the grounds of his stud farm at Haras de Meautry in Normandy. Baron Robert hid many treasures, particularly from his Château Laversine near Chantilly, at Marmande in the southwest of France. Rosen-

* Italics mine.

berg discovered both caches, as well as a number of others. Soon whole trains filled with precious Rothschild stuff rolled toward Germany.

After the liberation of France the Rothschild châteaux and town mansions, with the exception of Avenue de Marigny, were found to have been thoroughly emptied. The process of recuperation which began instantly and lasted years makes one long detective story.

The Sherlock Holmes of the operation was James J. Rorimer, then Fine Arts Officer attached to the American Seventh Army, now Director of the Metropolitan Museum of Art in New York. He arrived in Paris soon after the liberation and immediately interrogated a great many people on the whereabouts of looted art. From a horde of self-styled insiders, each of whom claimed to have the key to a hundred secreted Goyas, he picked out a girl named Rose Valland. A young art scholar, she had helped the Germans classify their booty. But as a member of the underground, she had also kept a sharp eye out for the destinations of the loot. It was her opinion that the Castle Neuschwanstein, near Füssen in Bavaria, was Hitler's main collection point for Aryanized masterworks.

Some nine months later Bavaria fell, and Rorimer drove in a jeep up to the castle. Neuschwanstein, built by Mad Ludwig of Bavaria in pseudo-Gothic style and perched like an evil phantasm on top of a crag, furnished a picturesque backdrop to what he was about to find. Rorimer traversed two courtyards connected by an intricate flight of steps, negotiated a spiral staircase ideal for tumbling masked conspirators. Finally he reached the room he wanted. Here was the nerve center of the entire Hitler looting project.

The Germans had lived up to their fine reputation for being methodical. Row upon row of filing cabinets filled the office. The Nazis had carefully kept, and used, the catalogues of each of the 203 private collections they had abducted. It took Rorimer, one of the great experts in the field, a whole day to take in the rough scope of what was recorded there: 8,000 negatives and individual catalogue cards for nearly 22,000 itemized major confiscations. The Rothschilds, with nearly 4,000 major items, towered far over every other name on the list.

Another crucial discovery was made in the same room. Rorimer sifted some objects out of the soot in a coal stove: the remains of a Nazi uniform, a half-consumed document with Hitler's signature, and some rubber stamps. These charred stamps proved to be the key to the world's greatest organized art theft; Rorimer noticed that they bore ciphers indicating the location of all other hiding places. A small chamber in an Alpine castle held the secret to countless and immeasurable treasures. To prevent the entry of unauthorized persons, Rorimer sealed the door with an antique Rothschild seal saying "Semper Fidelis."

Now a concerted search was on. Behind the stove of the castle kitchen Rorimer found Rubens' "Three Graces" from the Maurice de Rothschild collection and other chef-d'oeuvres. But not all Family items were so deviously concealed. In one hall at Neuschwanstein stood rows of the rarest tapestried fire screens, taken from Rothschild homes. Elsewhere Rothschild furniture, usually Louis XV and XVI, was stacked to the ceilings in specially constructed racks. There was box after box of Renaissance jewelry and eighteenth-century snuffboxes from Maurice's collection.

At other places there were other treasures. In the Carthusian monastery of Buxheim the chapel was inundated knee-deep with rugs, tapestries and textiles largely of Rothschild origin. In a salt mine near Alt Aussee in Austria investigators came upon huge accumulations kept in the name of the Führer, and containing, among others, sculptures, libraries and paintings owned by the Rothschilds.

Some of the caches, of course, had been shifted just before the collapse. Specific searches often turned into protracted, difficult or altogether futile affairs. But by and large, the great Family collections began the trek back from all corners of Germany into France. They converged on a central station for recovered art works in Paris. Here a coordinating committee of Rothschild butlers sat for weeks, identifying this Watteau as Baron Guy's, that Picasso as Baron Elie's—and was that Tiepolo Baron Philippe's or Baron Alain's?

It seems a reassuringly esthetic note on which to end the Rothschild side of World War II.

# X

# *A DYNASTY TURNS JET*

## 1. *Decline and Rise*

THINGS were getting back to normal in 1945. But what, in Family terms, was normalcy? Would it be the grandiose decay that had set in during the 1920's and 1930's? Would the Rothschilds, like the Habsburgs, begin living purely in, and on, the past?

For a while it almost looked that way. The Austrian branch had emigrated and would live, sonless, on estates in Long Island (Baron and Baroness Eugene) and Vermont (Baroness Louis). The English branch was in the throes of the austerity program. The French house, partly liquidated by the Nazi occupation, had its hands full with its own convalescence. Taxes waxed more cruel than ever. And more great Rothschild mansions succumbed.

The house at Hamilton Place, built by Leo, became one of London's most luxurious clubs (Grandees of the Expense Account now lean against the hand-carved balustrade down which Edward VII used to slide). Another Rothschild residence, in Kensington Gardens, now constitutes —*O tempora! O mores!*—the Soviet Russian Embassy. Buckinghamshire's Waddesdon Hall, inherited by colorful Jimmy de Rothschild, was rendered even more palatial by the additional French masterworks he showered on it. But when he died childless in 1957, death duties took more than twenty million dollars out of his fortune. No one inside The Family or out could provide fitting upkeep for so luscious a palazzo. Jimmy left it to the National Trust, together with 750,000 pounds (two million dollars) to defray at least part of the maintenance cost. Now sightseers aim cameras at the staircase on which Edward VII broke his leg. Mrs. Anthony de Rothschild still lives at Ascott Wing, bought by her father-in-law Leo; but this house, too, with its masses of Dutch masters and the world's greatest collection of Oriental pottery (and a parrot that announces with great majesty, "I-am-Jack-O'Rothschild!") has been made over to the National Trust.

And in France? The titanic manse at 2, rue Florentin on the Place de la Concorde has gone the way of all titanic manses. Talleyrand had lived there before Edouard de Rothschild moved in. When Edouard put it on the market, only one customer could afford the price—Uncle Sam. It became the European headquarters of the Marshall Plan and today is tenanted by the United States Mission to NATO and to European regional organizations. Henri de Rothschild's huge place at 33, rue du Faubourg St. Honoré now houses the Cercle Interallié, a fancy international diplomatic club. On the same street the United States Embassy has taken over No. 41, built by the first Baron Edmond. The Rothschild monograms still crown the great portals of both houses.

Last, not least, Ferrières, the crown jewel among Rothschild possessions: no one was rich enough to buy it, nor did the French branch want to part with such a symbol. The fifty-nine cases of rare books which the Germans had taken away came back again, as did the trainloads of looted Italian faïences and master paintings. They remained in their crates. The château was kept shut and uninhabited; it was less of a drain that way. In 1949 an American visitor walked through the dismantled palace. At first he found himself in a golden thicket of clocks. He thought he had stumbled into a clock museum until the caretaker explained that this was merely the room where the château's timepieces were stored. Next the visitor came upon a huge, glorious array of Louis XIV and XV chairs. In still another chamber there was a dazzle of tables. Finally he saw a number of objects adorably wrought out of rosewood and flowered antique Chinese porcelain. He puzzled, looked again—and understood the caretaker's smile. Here stood scores of the world's most exquisite bidets.

Year after year Ferrières signified luxury in mothballs. The existentialist era apparently did not encourage the functioning of fairytale castles. In fact, the existentialist era seemed on the point of equalizing and taxing The Family to pieces, as if it were just another collection of fustian has-beens.

But the Rothschilds did it again. Astonishingly, they became themselves once more. An old, cunning indestructibility began to reassert itself. In 1949 it became visible in traditional fashion at a traditional place: the stock exchange.

On June 30, 1949, strange things were happening on the Paris bourse. As soon as the bell signaled the start of business, Royal Dutch, the global oil company, began to fall. A great metal combine, Rio Tinto, declined steeply. There was absolutely no reason for such misbehavior; both companies were in excellent shape. Still they kept weakening. Sell orders swamped other issues as well. Le Nickel, a giant mining corporation, melted with each twitch of the ticker tape; so did the diamond trust of de Beers. Bewilderment spread, nervousness outran it, panic flooded all. Most investors joined the rush to sell. Prices reached their deepest low in months.

Few people isolated the factor common to all four slipping issues: The Family was a heavy stockholder in every one. Only other important holders of these same shares knew of Edouard de Rothschild's death that day, at the age of eighty-one. They realized that the enormous death duties would decrease the Baron's estate and thus the potential of the companies he backed. The minimization of the death levy was the call of the hour.

Next morning, of course, everyone read the Baron's obituary on the front page. Financial columns, discussing the death duties involved, stated that the tax on the dead man's stock holdings would be based on the closing price of his securities on the day of decease. And while funeral arrangements were being completed, brokers received buy orders from the same sources which twenty-four hours ago had instructed them to sell. The so-called Rothschild papers rose as punctually as they had fallen.

Suddenly there occurred without warning, though with ample precedent in Rothschild history, one of those leaps which lifted the clan off the downhill side and placed it back on the accustomed position at the top. In 1855 it had risen to crush its tormentor, the Crédit Mobilier. Some hundred years later it woke up, to turn twentieth-century with a vengeance. Almost overnight it caught on to the smallest gray practicality of our times. One day in that same year, 1949, the head of the London bank sent his butler out to buy a map of the London Underground. This plebeian item became as integral a part of Anthony de Rothschild's belongings as his checkbook. Within the city he dispensed with chauffeur and limousine, thereby avoiding the delays of midcentury traffic and contributing to subway revenues. By tube he often managed to arrive on the spot long before banking rivals who had themselves driven all the way.

It was this recrudescent ability to move in fast on the newest that got Anthony the exploitation rights to 50,000 square miles in Canada. Through a string of holding companies, New Court could now tap monumental lumber, power, mineral (particularly uranium) resources. Newfoundland's Prime Minister Smallwood called the transaction "the biggest real estate deal on this continent in this century"; and Winston Churchill, appreciative of the scale of the thing, termed it "a grand imperial concept."

After Anthony's death his two nephews, Edmund and Leopold, took over together with Anthony's son Evelyn. Under these young triumvirs the pace has increased still more; their new Canadian empire (bigger than England and Wales) is rapidly being developed. Edmund, the senior partner, struck out in still other directions. Recently he has taken a hand in the future of British pay-television. At the same time he is consolidating still further New Court's position as a key bullion broker in the English Commonwealth, as owner and operator of the Royal Mint Refinery, as gold agent to the Bank of England and as merchant banker extraordinary.

But the French Rothschilds are richer still. And they have become richer faster since Baron Guy assumed the reins at the death of his father Edouard. Guy, too, wields the accelerated energies of the present-day clan, even when it comes to his horses. He brought to an end a humiliation —and price depreciation—they had suffered for years. During the occupation the Germans had crossed Rothschild mares with the stallions of Marcel Boussac, France's textile king and Rothschild's greatest rival at Longchamps. Afterwards, Monsieur Boussac pronounced these unions unauthorized and irregular. Old Baron Edouard de Rothschild could not get his colts registered in the Stud Book, the equine Almanach de Gotha. But when Guy took over the stables, he applied a pressure so relentless that the French Stud Book did a very rare thing: it changed its mind. Today all Rothschild horses have been fully legitimized.

With similar aggressiveness Guy has fortified the position of de Rothschild Frères as the largest private bank in France. His main instrument here is the Compagnie du Nord, the railroad network which became Family property after the dynast James financed it into existence. Like all French lines, the Compagnie du Nord was nationalized in 1938. In return, Rothschild received 270,000 shares of the French State Railways and a seat on the board. But the government took over only physical assets, such as track and rolling stock. Subsidiary and affiliated firms of the Compagnie du Nord, as well as the corporate apparatus, remained in Rothschild hands. Through it The Family controlled—and, after the Nazi nightmare, controls again—great interests in metal, mining and chemical industries.

And yet it was not until Guy took over that these powerful levers began to show their full potency. Since 1950 the Paris house has performed brilliantly in the forefront of the European boom.

"He has started a new concept here," said a high aide at the bank. "Formerly Rothschild used to be the sole investor in a new enterprise, developed it alone, and *then* sold some shares of it while keeping control. Today we are a bigger bank than ever, but the funds required to start a major new company are so much bigger still that no single private outfit can finance all of it. That's why Rothschild's used to stay aloof from some new developments after the first big war. Now they are in the thick of it. Guy uses the concept of participation; he accepts other people's money from the very start; he acts as initiator and packager—and as guarantor. Apart from his share, he invests the unique moral capital of his name. And of course he keeps strictly in control."

Then there is Guy's cousin Edmond. His father Maurice, that black sheep par excellence, handed down to Edmond all his money, initiative, informality and none of his naughtiness. Edmond inherited tremendously and tremendously expanded his inheritance. Unaffiliated with the Family bank, he is faithful enough to Family discretion to keep the portals of No. 45, rue du Faubourg St. Honoré signless and anonymous. Here the young, shirt-sleeved Baron directs a staff of 150 executives and assistants, "my main business den." From this headquarters he runs the Compagnie Financière, a worldwide organization which builds villas, hotels, pipelines in Israel; throws up giant housing projects in Paris (over one thousand apartments so far); backs *Continent*, the international European news weekly; finances banks and car factories in Brazil.

It was Edmond who led The Family into fields hitherto seldom associated with its name. If Rothschild could cope with the tax-oppressed, traffic-ridden, television-happy and radioactive aspects of the midcentury, why not also deal with the new travel mania? It will be remembered that Baroness Maurice's pet project had been the development of Megève into France's most elegant Alpine resort. Her properties here included the Mont d'Arbois, a hotel of Rothschildian sumptuousness. In the 1950's her son Edmond decided to turn hobby into industry. He greatly enlarged the Family holdings on the slopes of Mont Blanc, and is now building an ultrachic new pleasure landscape complete with ski lifts, swimming pools, tennis courts and night clubs. He also underwrites and develops not merely hotels but entire new tourist regions in Martinique and Guadalupe in the French Caribbean. With Lord Rothschild as partner, he is responsible for the flowering of Israel's luxury golf resort at Caesarea.

To put it crassly, Edmond is the richest Rothschild and probably the most multiple millionaire in Europe. This amiable young carrot-top (remember his redheaded great-grandfather James?), who can choose to rusticate in either of two fairytale châteaux—one in Switzerland and one in France—and who numbers among his town residences Rubirosa's former house in Paris, is creating still another splendid roof for himself at rue Elysée.

There is more evidence that today the *mishpoche* is not selling but acquiring mansions. In the rue de Courcelles Edmond's cousin Guy has just remodeled an eighteenth-century house into a new Rothschild palace. Lord Rothschild will shortly move into a new house at Cambridge. London's N. M. Rothschild & Sons has grown too big for the big old edifice at New Court; just recently the firm has taken over a floor in a new office building to accommodate the dividend department.

And the rosewood-and-flowered-porcelain bidets of Ferrières have come into their own again. Guy has done more than reconnect the plumbing, though. After six years of renovation, he has restored this foremost tower of the clan to its full anachronistic glory. The dimensions of the demesne are as exorbitant as ever. It still covers nearly 9,000 prime suburban acres, with a farming population of 600. Twelve highly motorized gardeners supervise a horizonful of parks and pleasure lakes. Five full-time foresters patrol the shoots. The private zoo is gone because the Germans kidnaped the animals. Gone, too, is the train which brought food from the kitchen building to the château through an underground tunnel; our spoilsport century moved the chefs into the main building.

But otherwise this incredible pleasure dome is once more itself. Even the cloakroom by the entrance has recovered its frivolity: cartoons of the current *mishpoche* paper its walls. Other lampoons, mainly familial (with notable exceptions, such as a ruthlessly faithful portrait of Elsa Maxwell), decorate the adjoining silk-lined lavatory where, as a Family member put it, "they can be perused in comfort and leisure."

Inside the château itself the age of Watteau reigns unstinted. The landscaped succession of imperial salons; the chandeliers, hanging gardens made of crystal and fretted gold; the panoramic expanses of jeweled guest suite after guest suite; the profusion of precious textures: Gobelin, gold inlay, ivory, tortoise shell; the luster of the walls alternated by the idyll beyond the windows—swans rippling fountained lakes; the bathroom faucets of solid silver. . . . Did Robespierre ever live? Was the Bastille really stormed?

# *EPILOGUE 1992*

## 1. *The* Mishpoche *of the 1960's*

IN JUNE 1959, as the premier event of the summer gala week the French call "la grande semaine," Guy de Rothschild reopened his clan's principal country residence, Ferrières, with the entire Paris family in attendance. An observer would have noticed that both the château and its owner possessed the qualities of the French branch to a heightened degree. The *chef de famille* is slim, swift in his movements, and has the handsome bold-nosed profile often seen in the descendants of James. Though a bit cool, like his Viennese cousin Louis, he conveys a piquancy once enriched by a sensation.

It was, of course, a well-bred sensation. He divorced his first wife, Alix, to marry a divorcée, the Countess Marie-Hélène van Zuylen Nicolai, herself the descendant of a controversial Rothschild union a few generations earlier. In both cases the controversy centered around the Catholicism of the Rothschild's spouse. Guy had to resign the presidency of the Jewish Community in France. And Countess Nicolai needed a papal dispensation—a privilege always reserved for the most exalted mismatings—to annul the bond that stood between her and marriage to a Jew. For the first time in French Rothschild history, the head of a house married a woman outside the faith.

He and his cousins divided between them the labors and leisures of aristocracy. Guy kept up the racing tradition with his stud farm in Normandy and stables at Chantilly. As head of the French house, he was in natural rapport with the head of the state. General de Gaulle employed Georges Pompidou, Guy's right-hand man, as one of the republic's key financial advisers, and later appointed him prime minister. And there were strong personal ties between France's greatest general and her most influential banker. In Guy's photograph album, one hunt tally card records that Baron Rothschild once bagged forty-nine pheasants at Marly-le-Roi, de Gaulle's personal shoot.

"Distant times," one cannot help thinking while turning those album pages. The politicians are gone and so are their politics. The French Rothschilds and their business interests have weathered storms violent enough to uproot them—almost. Guy has survived that severe turbulence and has lived to enjoy some late triumphs. But before we move on to the present, let us review other family members active in the sixties, a decade marked by great changes. A few of these actors remain onstage to this day.

Guy's partner and cousin, Elie, is probably the fiercest, most imperious *mishpoche* member since the first Lord Rothschild. "Oh, he is a Berber!" one of the belles of his bachelor days once said admiringly. The epithet seems apt, if only because he has skillfully supervised the bank's Sahara oil ventures. On the private side, and well into the sixties, he was active in the sporting life with his almost weekly polo forays to England and Spain and his shoots in France, Austria and Africa.

His brother Alain was the family's yachtsman. A quiet, very baronial baron, Alain was at the same time the president of the Jewish Community in Paris and very "St. Germain"—a tag applied to the most muffled, conservative, impenetrable sector of French society. The combination of two such roles is uniquely Rothschild. Alain died in 1982.

The English house, being English, makes a point of being pale. While the Parisians personify the glamorous, athletic *haut monde*, the London branch seems to feel that perhaps that sort of thing would not quite do for them. Even their chromosomes appear a great deal more tradition-minded. The Parisian Rothschilds look as slender and dashing as any drawing-room-comedy marquis; the Londoners often tend to be a stoutish Savile Row–tailored, Cambridge-accented version of the German rabbi old Mayer wanted to become.

They like their sports, of course. Of the three running the London bank in the early sixties, Edmund (the senior partner) fished in the best waters of four continents. His brother Leopold sailed. Cousin Evelyn had a polo team, "The Centaurs," whose puissance was known to the teams of both Prince Philip and Cousin Elie.

But their athletics and sociabilities had a very quiet, almost introspective note. For someone of his eminence as the head of the house, Edmund listed few clubs (White's and St. James's) and was not a conspicuous member in either. He, his brother and cousin have the same right to the baronial title as the French but choose to be Mister. All the "bank" Rothschilds in England are part of a finely tuned understatement. They may know the board chairman of Britain's greatest tabloid, but they are not aware that the thing also has reporters. In brief, they take their Society without Café. The result is a prominence felt all the more because it cannot be seen or heard. And the fact remains that on Mr. Edmund's piano at Exbury there stand, among snapshots of other visitors, pictures of Elizabeth and Philip.

At the same time—and this is just as distinguished—the English branch has provided a whole dynasty's worth of eccentricity. It is from the London house that the so-called "nonbank" Rothschilds issue, with their astounding array of vocations.

The ranking member among them was Lord Rothschild (Victor), who passed away in 1990, the first of his title to forsake finance altogether. A Labor peer, a disciple of swing pianist Teddy Wilson's and last but not least an eminent biologist, he followed family tradition in matters of Jewish concern. In 1938, he composed a letter in Latin to Pope Pius XII, fiercely urging him to protest against the Nazi persecution of the Jews. He received an answer, also in Latin, as well as the satisfaction of the Pope's compliance. Later he administered, together with Dorothy (Jimmy de Rothschild's widow) and young Baron Edmond, the unpronounceable EJRMG (Edmond James Rothschild Memorial Group) Foundation. EJRMG contributed one million dollars to the Weizmann Scientific Institute in Tel Aviv, gave three million dollars toward the construction of the Knesseth and footed the bill for many of Israel's archeological expeditions. Further aspects of his career, some of which turned out to be quite controversial, will be discussed later.

His Lordship's youngest sister, the jazz baroness Kathleen Pannonica Rothschild de Koenigswarter, was thumbs-up—financially and morally—to many good musicians to whom the commercial world was thumbs-down. A resident of Weehawken, New Jersey, she was the Rothschild foundation for the needy cool. Thelonious Monk figured among her beneficiaries. He wrote "Pannonica" for her, and her name also appears in the titles of Horace Silver's "Nica's Dream" and Gigi Gryce's "Nica's Tempo." Charlie "Bird" Parker, perhaps the greatest genius of the New Sound, died in her apartment. She herself passed away in 1988.

The same year saw the passing of Philippe de Rothschild, also of the English branch, though born and domiciled in France. He owned the Mouton Rothschild wines, for which (as we shall see in detail later) he recruited Picasso, Braque and Dali to create some of the wildest bottle labels ever. But he was also a Grey Eminence. Late at night, when the servants had been sent away and weighty heads bent over old brandy, Philippe's Paris dining salon at Avenue d'Iéna became a political crossroads of the nation. It was there that a French foreign minister changed Henry Luce's mind on Algeria, there that the head of the Socialist party patched up a quarrel with a key commentator. At his Mouton château, Philippe ripened his famous wines in cousinly rivalry with Baron Elie's adjoining and equally famous Lafite Rothschild. And at Mouton he and his American wife, Pauline, created France's greatest wine museum.

Christopher Fry asked Philippe to render his plays (and therefore an enormously difficult style) into French. With typical Rothschild *chutzpah* the Baron went to work. After five years of labor, the first volume appeared in 1960, to extraordinary critical approbation. It was not the Baron's only connection with the theater. His book-length fairy tale called *Aile d'Argent* was dedicated to his daughter Philippine, a prominent young actress in the Comédie Française, who married her director in the celebration that started our story.

Baroness Philippe (d. 1976) once reflected: "Philippe always says that women and jail [during the Nazi era] taught him most. Well, I am *the* woman. But I also know that I am *the* jail. It's my job to make the cell comfortable." And Baron Elie noted that the women who married into the family often became "more Rothschild than the Rothschilds." Or, as the British biographer Derek Wilson puts it: "There is a certain irony in the fact that, while several Rothschild daughters have had to 'escape' from the family in order to do their own thing, several Rothschild wives have found their fulfillment in complete identity with the dynasty." They must have the energy needed to keep half a dozen households and to be at home in ten different fields. They assimilate the style, *le style*, as well as *le gout Rothschild* (the Rothschild taste), and frequently improve it.

The greatest task for any Rothschild wife is simply to *be* a Rothschild first and last, to be instantly responsive to every dynastic need and impulse, no matter how unexpected: In 1960, a big, heavy piece of wrapped cement arrived at the Bordeaux customs office, sent by the London bank and addressed to Baron Philippe. The customs people were puzzled by such peculiar traffic among Rothschilds. Philippe happened to be away; his secretaries could recall no correspondence with London on the subject of cement. The shipment was on the point of being returned to London, when word of it reached Baroness Pauline. And she was Rothschild enough to remember. Two months before, during one of Edmund's visits at Mouton, he had admired the many snow-white doves ornamenting the park and the air of the estate. But Pauline had complained that, for lack of the grit necessary to their gizzards, the birds pecked little holes into the manor walls. Edmund had mentioned a specially manufactured grit, and this cementlike material—a hunk big enough to serve a whole château—was exactly what the odd parcel contained. Pauline had been a clan member for less than six years: sufficiently long to know that the paramount Rothschild instinct is to preserve and defend the family substance in every way, even against tiny beaks.

### (a) *Beyond the Old World*

A concrete CARE package traveling from New Court to Mouton is not without symbolic overtones. It seems only fitting that the most sophisticated of Family châteaus should still receive incidental protection from the oldest Family bank.

Such protection, in moral form, is constantly forthcoming to the most scattered corners of the *mishpoche*. The solid, pragmatic pulse of the counting house still beats in every Rothschild, steadies his feet on the ground and, no matter what his calling, sets his shoulder to the wheel. This is the source which gives The Family a hard cutting edge, a perennial drive—rare assets among multibillionaires who could flirt their lives away on Riviera balconies and still leave their children and their children's children enough to do the same.

In the "banking" Rothschilds the drive to work can amount to obsession. Nevertheless, weekends and holidays are devoted to exquisite and exclusive divertissements. "We are bankers by trade," Baron Guy once said. "We work at our trade sixty hours a week. Some time ago I went to watch one of my horses on a Thursday. I won't do it again soon. I can't seem to enjoy it weekdays."

Most other business giants are run by hired managers on behalf of absentee owners. Here, the bosses aren't chairmen by the grace of a board, nor presidents dependent on shareholders' proxies, nor corporate servitors obliged to publish a yearly balance sheet. Their responsibility, as private partners, is just as great as their power. "If I pick up the phone now," said one of their executives, "and order Detroit to make us half a million five-wheeled Cadillacs, I may be fired. But the partners would be answerable for this stupidity—and for much less obvious ones too—with their private fortunes."

This sort of setup requires a feudal allegiance on the part of the employees. On the part of the employer it predicates a patriarchal solicitude that goes beyond maximum salaries and social benefits. There are whole families that have been on the Rothschild payroll for over a century. Just after the war a new clerk was welcomed by the staff with the question, "Who is your father?" It was naturally assumed that, as usual, the young man had been born into his job.

"The young chaps nowadays . . ." a Rothschild administrator mused. "At first they can't understand the atmosphere here. But after a few months they realize this is Rothschild's—and they catch on."

A generation ago, this spirit of the counting house was still all-pervasive. While teleprinters whirred and electric typewriters (antediluvian by today's standards) hummed, decisions were still made in the old autocratic way, in Empire leather armchairs, attended by butlers, far from the madding throng. The long-distance wires and intercoms of the London bank may have been buzzing with its newest atomic investments, but that did not keep the derby-hatted doorman in St. Swithins Lane from a perfect nineteenth-century salute. Inside the courtyard one already felt a hallowed hush. It grew in the partners' waiting room: silence here, except for the occasional swish of a butler's tailcoat, the quick tread of a messenger, the lisp of three teletypes (one for stocks, one for news, one for races) all in Edwardian casings. The next station was the Partners' Room, an institution left over from the *condottieri* days of merchant banking. Only the Messrs. Rothschild worked there—Edmund, Leopold and Evelyn. Their privacy was undiluted by secretary or assistant; the atmosphere conducive to privy consultation and secret decision. This massive Victorian parlor was the throne room of London finance, and above all a genealogical shrine. Ancestors crowded the walls. Mementos and milestones studded mantel shelves and tables: a receipt for two million pounds for paying Wellington's army; a fist-sized South African diamond next to a chunk of North American uranium ore; the founder's sample book of cotton cloth that started his English business career; some boll weevils that crept into a bullion sack and now lie, turned to gold, upon a salver.

In this venerable house everyone knew why the top echelon of executives must never go out to lunch but must take that meal in their own oak-paneled dining room. They had to be at the instant disposal of the partners who were served a floor higher amid mahogany and Russian leather. But just why did the meal have to begin at one P.M., a bit later than the usual lunchtime?

No one will be able to answer that question now—the tradition no longer exists. It is gone with the dining room and the Partners' Room, with the entire historical building at St. Swithins Lane. In 1966, it was replaced by a new one better suited to the future demands of modern banking as perceived by Evelyn, who took on Anthony's legacy (before he turned thirty) in 1961.

Change has extended far beyond architecture. In the last thirty years, the entire Rothschild enterprise in London, Paris, Geneva and elsewhere has been thoroughly restructured. The family, renowned for its ability to think and act internationally, has moved on to a global strategy. The "cousins" (as they still call each other, like true aristocrats, even when they belong to different generations) had always been able to communicate across national borders, and now they coordinated their activities in an informal holding company of their own devising.

## 2. *The Global Family*

### (a) *A Late Entrance*

In the fall of 1987, a rather unusual student was admitted to Duke University in North Carolina. He enrolled in only a few classes, drove only a modest Honda, and was occasionally—to his evident embarrassment—obliged to borrow money from his classmates. The latter were glad to help him out, believing that they would get their money back with a bonus: after all, their skinny little friend with the dark, curly hair and a slight accent was none other than Maurice de Rothschild, vagabond son of the great French banker Baron Guy de Rothschild.

Or so they thought. But after Maurice caused a stir by some particularly vulgar behavior, his Sigma Alpha Epsilon fraternity brothers decided to research his background. As it turned out, the attractive young man was a phony. His real name was Mario Cortez, and he came from no farther than El Paso, Texas.

What was interesting about this little campus farce was the aura of the *name*: even in Durham, N.C., a Rothschild was readily given credit in every sense of the term. While Americans still refer to the Rockefellers, Carnegies, Mellons or Vanderbilts when expressing the equivalent of the European exclamation "I'm no Rothschild, you know!" the banking dynasty is by no means unfamiliar to them. In Europe, the various branches of the family fast became legendary; in North America, their fame has spread in a more belated and circuitous fashion. The family's love affair with the New World came late in life.

Up to the 1850's, the Rothschilds did not grant America much importance in their strategy. It took the Civil War to open their eyes to the economic importance of the continent; it took them a little longer than some other European financiers, but they did finally lend the Union some of their gold. Together with a few other banking houses, the English branch also had the honor of providing the gold backing for the new currency of the United States.

Before that time, the Rothschilds were only indirectly represented in New York, by one August Schönberg, born in 1816, presumably in the Rhineland Palatinate. Little is known about his early years, but at the age of thirteen he started working for the Rothschilds in Frankfurt. It is said that while the family admired his financial talents, they did not approve of his manners and soon let him go. In 1837, the adventurous young man resurfaced in New York, having changed his name to August Belmont. In the city's banking circles, he soon became known as a representative of the Rothschilds, and before long he had served American economic interests so well that he was rewarded with the appointment of U.S. Consul General in Vienna. One of the reasons for this was to enable him to establish close contact with a branch of the family whose prestige he had used to enhance his own in New York. Once again, the Rothschilds did not take any particular liking to the upstart, and upon his return to America Belmont was compelled to strike out on his own—which he did, and with extraordinary success.

The Belmont episode apart, when did these otherwise so internationally minded bankers make their real entrance on the stage of American finance? "Almost too late" was the unanimous opinion of both London and Paris. By the time the economic importance of the U.S. became glaringly evident after World War I, the Rothschilds were not powerful enough to establish a new branch. Only at the beginning of the forties did the English branch decide to go for a more prominent position on Wall Street. They founded a subsidiary, "Amsterdam Incorporated," a name that almost ironically refers to the city after which New York was first named. After a few years, it was renamed "New Court Securities" in honor of its London headquarters. But it seemed that the family still was not ready to throw the full weight of its name into the American version of Fortune's scales.

### (b) *Storms in a Wineglass*

If anything symbolized the French Rothschilds' desire to revive the glory of pre–World War II days, it was the reopening of the château at Ferrières. Never mind that the surrounding world faced sobering times, never mind that the jet set did no longer strike the onlookers as "what it once was": at the balls and parties given by Guy and Marie Hélène de Rothschild, it flourished again. Everybody who still had status, money and time showed up at their fancy-dress or "Surrealist" parties or exquisite dinners. Ferrières was a dream born in the last century, an anachronism revived in the present.

That dream lasted only a decade. The Rothschilds danced through the sixties without a care in the world, showed off what they had, led the life in full view of the public. Their enjoyment of the boom years was typical of the high society of those days.

Slowly, the political map of France changed. Predictably enough, the banking classes felt the impact of that change later than most of their contemporaries. The events of the "fateful year" 1968 affected the family only peripherally, and their reactions were similar to those of their old friend and former director of the bank, de Gaulle's prime minister Georges Pompidou. While students demonstrated in the streets of Paris, Guy de Rothschild went on taking care of business and attending to his great passion, the breeding of racehorses. Then there were the wines: these loomed large in the clan's preoccupations of the still-carefree sixties.

For a better understanding of the family's internal competition in this field, we must backpedal a little. The Rothschild interest in wine came about through a coincidence: the name of the Lafite vineyard in Bordelais resembled the name of the Paris street on which James Rothschild lived, the rue Laffitte. This moved James to purchase the vineyard in 1868. Its evolution to one of the great wineries owed as much to its privileged geographical position as to its later owners' urge to perfection. Nathaniel Rothschild, who had moved from London to Paris, had already acquired the neighboring estate Brane-Mouton in 1855—not because he was particularly well-versed in viticulture, but to keep up with the Joneses, in this case the Pereire family of bankers who owned a vineyard. In the important wine register of 1855, his product —unlike Lafite and three other estates—was not ranked among the top Premiers Crus of the Médoc region.

This seems to have annoyed Nathaniel, but no matter how hard he tried, neither he nor his successors were able to advance their Mouton-Rothschild from its ranking as a "merely" second-class wine. In the 1950's, the rivalry between the wineries belonging to the French and Anglo-French branches escalated. Philippe, Nathaniel's great-grandson, demonstrated excellent marketing skills in his effort to restore the Mouton's good name. In 1924, he was the first wine grower to institute the practice of "estate bottling" ("mise en bouteilles au château"), thus taking over product control from the Bordeaux wine merchants who, until then, had received the wine in barrels and bottled it on their premises. Since then, many important wineries have adopted this practice.

That same year, Philippe came up with another innovation: he commissioned an artist to design the Mouton label. Jean Carlu's Cubist vignette graced three vintages.

After a hiatus of nine years, in 1945, the Baron revived the idea and had Philippe Jullian design the famous "V" for "Victoire." From then on, an artist has been commissioned every year, receiving his honorarium in the form of crates of Mouton-Rothschild. Labels have been designed by Jean Cocteau and Salvador Dali, Georges Braque and Marc Chagall, Andy Warhol and Saul Steinberg, and the estates of Kandinsky and Picasso have permitted posthumous reproductions. (From 1988 until the most recently released vintage, labels have been designed by Keith Haring, Francis Bacon, Setsuko, Delphus [a label banned in the U.S.] and Georg Baselitz.)

It took, however, a long time to convince the most illustrious noses and palates. Philippe's marketing ploys gained fame for him and his wine, but he was not able to break into the stronghold of the Premier Cru estates. Only after years of wars of attrition between the Bordeaux vintners (and thus also between members of the family), after petitions from Philippe to the authorities and after several summit meetings accompanied by strenuous degustations, the Mouton was finally welcomed into the circle of superior wines.

### (c) *"I've Had Enough"*

In 1973, those storms in a wineglass were superseded by other worries. The Rothschilds of Paris realized that the era of living in opulent aristocratic style in full public view was drawing to a close. They rationalized this by citing changed circumstances, general economic problems, and a lack of interest among the next generation. Indeed, such arguments, rather than financial ones, probably played a major part in Guy de Rothschild's 1975 decision to donate the château at Ferrières and part of the estate to the University of Paris.

This was a voluntary concession to the mutations of the *Zeitgeist* and not particularly onerous: the château's interior way of life was at least partially reproduced in Guy's new residence on the Ile Saint-Louis of Paris. But more serious change loomed ahead. After the family's years of peaceful coexistence with conservative governments, the winds of French politics suddenly turned against them in 1981.

In May of that year, François Mitterrand was elected president. His Socialist program included the nationalization of all private banks above a certain size. This did of course apply to the Rothschild bank, even on symbolic grounds: the Socialists had, after all, engaged in a bitter struggle with Georges Pompidou, one of that bank's former chief executives. The Banque Rothschild, a credit institution with four billion francs on deposit and a balance of almost fourteen billion, with two thousand employees and seventy thousand clients, became the "Européenne de Banque." For the termination of its one hundred and fifty years of banking history, the family was compensated—with a sum that varies depending on the source—between one hundred million and five hundred million francs (the family will no longer comment on this). In any case, the sum was regarded as far too low for the true value of the institution. Not only did the government, as Guy de Rothschild points out, gain "the position of majority stockholder in all the enterprises in which we held the majority"—and this included important industrial concerns, shipping companies and much else—but it also acquired its immaterial value, the goodwill of his house, for which no compensation was made: "If, for instance, one wanted to start IBM all over again, one would have to spend much more than IBM's stock market value in New York."

It was a hard but not entirely unexpected setback. Fourteen years before the Socialist election victory, when the enterprise had been turned into a public business bank, Guy had insisted that it would lose the right to use the name Rothschild as soon as the family was no longer in charge. Thus the name change was not merely a symbolic act—the French government had no choice in the matter. And it became apparent, soon enough, that the loss of that name also meant a loss of financial flair.

In addition, Guy and Cousin Alain had prudently arranged for their and their English cousins' participation in the Zurich branch to be considered a private affair—a fairly lucrative one at that, and out of the French government's reach. Then there was New Court Securities: relieved from his post at the French bank, Guy was now able to attend to the New York investment firm's business with renewed energy.

Nevertheless, Guy de Rothschild wanted to have the last word in his dealings with the State of France (even though it later turned out not to be a last word, after all). In the summer of 1981, the front page of *Le Monde* carried his manifesto against the new government. It was also a historical review of his family's relationship with the various regimes of the country. His topics ranged from the construction of railroads in the nineteenth century to experiences with the popular front, from traditional accusations of the Rothschilds' alleged "hypertrophy of capitalism" to citations of the services many generations of the family had rendered the common good. "The French Rothschilds," Guy wrote, "made the mistake to believe that they could evolve with their era and their country. They had reason to regret that." The article ends with these words: "A Jew under Pétain, a pariah under Mitterrand, I have had enough. To start over, from ruins, in the course of one human life—that is too much to ask. Forced to resign, I go on strike."

In the United States, a new era had begun. During his two years in office, President Reagan tirelessly warbled the praises of private enterprise and inveighed against too much government interference. To the ears of someone whose bank had just been nationalized, such words must have heralded a bright future. The media, for its part, concerned with the doings of the rich and famous, celebrated this excellent opportunity to ring in a new decade of opulence: at long last, a genuine Rothschild had arrived in Manhattan! And moved into a *pied-à-terre* that was far less modest than the term implied.

Reading the magazine articles and admiring their many pages of color pictures of those new luxurious quarters, one might have assumed that the Baron had retired to lead a pleasant life of leisure—just to annoy Mitterrand. One would have been quite mistaken. The head of the French clan used this opportunity to further business interests, emphasizing once again that the family had waited far too long: "My grandfather Alphonse visited the United States in 1848. Upon his return, he urged his relatives to establish themselves here. It is more than regrettable that his advice was not taken. Our engagement with American finance begins literally a hundred years too late."

That did not keep it from being intense. The Rothschilds undertook a collective restructuring of New Court Securities. It began with the firing of its chief executive, John P. Birkelund, who had wanted greater control over the firm. Then the name was changed. From 1982 on, the branch operated as "Rothschild Incorporated" out of offices in Rockefeller Center. With the new name came a new emphasis, shifting from venture capital finance to the emerging field of mergers and acquisitions.

Making all these decisions, Guy de Rothschild did not act alone but in concord with his English relatives, whose financial participation in the buildup of the U.S. firm amounted to fifty percent. We should now look back across the ocean—and the Channel—to consider the changes that had occurred in London since the relatively calm fifties.

## (d) *No Fifth Man*

While the French Rothschilds gained a reputation for lavish entertaining in the sixties, the cousins on the other side of the Channel continued their more subdued lifestyle. For one thing, they lacked a Ferrières: its possible counterpart, Waddesdon Manor near Aylesbury in Buckinghamshire, had been donated to the National Trust in 1957 after James Armand Edmond's demise. Even if it had remained in the family's possession, it would not have provided a backdrop for exhilarating soirees. High-level fireside conversations or the occasional polo game would have been more like it.

During the fifties and sixties, Lord Victor devoted himself with Rothschildian thoroughness to his main interest, the natural sciences. He became the vice chairman of the zoological department at Cambridge, and in the sixties he also served as the director of research at Shell Ltd. In addition to his scientific pursuits he was active on the boards of British Overseas Airlines and the British Broadcasting Corporation. In the House of Lords, he was a Labor member, but after his retirement from Shell, he accepted Conservative Prime Minister Edward Heath's invitation to preside over a governmental think tank called the Central Capability Unit. In that position, Lord Victor did not hesitate to voice strong opinions. In September 1973 he warned his countrymen that they should no longer consider Great Britain a prosperous and influential nation. His prediction of the country's industrial decline was not what Prime Minister Heath wanted to hear. Soon thereafter, Victor Rothschild resigned from the think tank, and it didn't take long before the unit itself was disbanded. "We weren't kicked out," Victor commented. "But if the prime minister does not consider the think tank worthwhile, it makes sense to close it down, better sooner than later. After all, it will always be possible to dust it off and revive it again."

But that did not happen, at least not in Lord Rothschild's lifetime. In his seventies, he decided to take an active part in the family enterprise after all. He combined his scientific interests with the possibilities provided by New Court and steered "Biotechnology Investments Ltd." in a prescient direction. This enterprise was a pioneering consulting firm in a brand-new field.

Lord Victor Rothschild was one of the most mercurial characters the family had ever produced. He could be both rude and charming, curt and gentle. His expertise ranged across an incredibly wide spectrum. Contemporaries had trouble reconciling these various aspects. "Everyone," said the London *Times* in 1970, "described him differently, as a genius or a simpleton, an academic hermit or a man of the world, a frustrated failure or a relic of the old Bloomsbury crowd, as an impassioned perfectionist, as a character from one of Francis Scott Fitzgerald's minor novels or as a genius administrator. But everyone agrees that the quadruple burden of his name, his race, his wealth and his intelligence made him into one of the most complex personalities of our time."

As quoted by Martin Filler in a *Vanity Fair* article, the painter Lucian Freud, Sigmund's grandson (whose "Man in Chair" is a portrait of Jacob Rothschild), was more outspoken: "Victor was downright proud of his horrendous behavior. . . . He was horrifyingly rude and insulting—a real Neanderthal."

Throughout his active career and into the last years of his life, Lord Victor was haunted by his early years at Trinity College in Cambridge. While no communist sympathizer himself, he had befriended some fellow students whose names less than ten years later were associated with one of the greatest spy scandals England had ever experienced: Anthony Blunt, Guy Burgess, Donald Maclean, and Kim Philby. These four had used their positions in the foreign and secret services to provide Moscow with classified information. As soon as their spy ring had been uncovered, there were persistent rumors that other, and higher-ranking, persons had been involved. Lord Victor was privy to all the details of the investigation, but as a former college associate of the spies, he was also one of the suspects.

The 1964 investigation of his past did not reveal any incriminating facts. But in 1980, after the death of Anthony Blunt and the revelation of his treasonous involvement, another search was begun for a "fifth man" from the highest level of society. Lacking concrete proof, the press floated fairly pointed innuendos. "The file is never closed," Victor Rothschild wrote in a collection of essays published in 1984. He was right about that. In December 1986, the rumors that had survived for decades were now being revived again. Victor wrote a letter to the editor of the *Daily Telegraph*, in which he challenged the head of Britain's intelligence service (MI5) to issue a public confirmation of his—Victor's—innocence. "For now," he stated in the extraordinary front-page letter, "I shall not address any other public statement to the press."

None was required: the next day, Prime Minister Thatcher issued a press release. After noting that she was making an exception to the "no comment" rule in matters of national security, she made this brief and lapidary statement on the Rothschild case: "We have no evidence that he was ever a Soviet agent."

That was not quite what Victor had expected, and the press hastened to point out that he had collaborated with Peter Wright, a former secret service agent, on a book in which the "fifth man" was identified as Sir Roger Hollis, a deceased head of a secret service branch. In any case, Victor, now seventy-six, had to be content with Mrs. Thatcher's brief response. He spent the last years of his life mainly in Cambridge and London, except for a few weeks every year at his holiday residence in Barbados. He died in London in March 1990, apparently reconciled with his eldest son, Jacob—thus bringing to a close one of the least glorious episodes of recent Rothschild history.

### (e) *A Family Feud*

In the sixties, New Court had not done as well as the Rothschild reputation would have led one to expect. After this phase in which the family bank had not yet adapted itself to the City's changing patterns, Victor's son Jacob and Jacob's nephew Evelyn became the chief executives of the London bank. In hindsight it is difficult to know whether this arrangement was doomed from the start or whether the two personalities simply grew too far apart over time. As things turned out, they became rivals instead of collaborators, and their feud ended in Jacob's defeat.

Jacob Rothschild became New Court's chairman of the

board in 1975, but Evelyn, who had inherited a forty percent share from his father (who died in 1961), was the main shareholder. For a while—especially since Evelyn busied himself with many other interests—Jacob was able to run things according to his own lights. But toward the end of the decade the atmosphere of the financial world underwent a crucial and definitive change. What until recently had constituted the charm and even prestige of N. M. Rothschild & Sons, their sedate and almost stately way of doing business was now considered antiquated and a liability. Now it was no longer a question whether one should adjust to the structural changes in the financial world—electronic transfers and new investment and leverage practices—but how quickly, how thoroughly, and to what end this should be done.

Jacob advocated expansive and aggressive change. As early as 1972, acting as the head of the Rothschild Investment Trust, he orchestrated the greatest hostile takeover in England's financial history. Guided by Jacob, Grand Metropolitan took control of the Watson Mann brewery for over half a billion pounds sterling. Looking back, Jacob is proud of having boosted the market value of the Rothschild Investment Trust from three million pounds in 1970 to eighty million in only two years: "Almost everyone who has written about our bank's renaissance dates it to 1960, which was when I started working with the family." He also includes among his personal triumphs the creation of the Zurich branch with his partner Gilbert de Botton, but without family support: "We were very much on our own."

Jacob's skillful consulting strategies earned him admiration but also a degree of fearful antipathy from London's conservative financial circles. Evelyn favored a more cautious course, a discreet and personally managed private banking operation. This disagreement led to a prolonged and embittered family feud in which Jacob's father Victor also became involved. During his 1975–76 reign at New Court, he sided not with his son but with Evelyn. Rumors of tensions between Victor and Jacob were confirmed by open hostility. The rift affected Jacob's enterprises for years. He retained control of the Rothschild Investment Trust and promptly started another firm whose name referred directly to his genealogy: Five Arrows, Ltd. But Evelyn remained the head of the bank, and Jacob had clearly lost the battle. In 1980, Jacob left the bank for good, and the two cousins parted ways in both business and private life.

### (f) *A Longing for the Insiders*

After the Spencer family moved out in the 1920's, Spencer House, an eighteenth-century town residence, one of the earliest and best examples of its neoclassical kind, was used (not too successfully) as a club and as an office building. No one was able to maintain it and make money on it—no one, it seems, except for Jacob Rothschild. He acquired a 125-year lease, hired the best experts and spent sixteen million pounds on a careful restoration of the building. The re-creation of the interior's original Carrara marble mantelpieces took years; some were tracked down and bought or borrowed back from museums and private collectors.

Combining aesthetic with practical concerns, Jacob installed offices for his holding company but turned the palatial reception rooms of Spencer House into a conference and event center. Not only NATO dignitaries and the heads of the seven leading industrial countries have convened there; wealthy Londoners have leased the festive surroundings—at a cost of up to ten thousand pounds a day.

The 1990 reopening of Spencer House was one of Jacob Rothschild's major social coups. Old nobility mingled with old money. Lady Di (née Spencer) conversed with her admirer. "Jacob was like a child under a Christmas tree," Martin Filler told the American readers of *Vanity Fair* in his London letter. The author claimed that Jacob was expressing the admiration his family had always felt for the British royal family, "the longing of perpetual outsiders for the ultimate insiders." Jacob Rothschild himself had a less romantic view of his social contact with the Princess: "It is no different than many other relationships I cultivate that do not attract so much publicity. In my opinion, there is no 'psychological element' that would cause me to feel as if I didn't quite belong and to go to any lengths to be counted among the insiders. We are simply who we are, and that's all there is to it."

Nevertheless, Jacob Rothschild's connection with Diana Spencer did provide him with satisfaction in another realm, one to which he had become increasingly drawn in recent years: the subject of modern British architecture, a point of indirect but serious contention between him and Diana's husband, Prince Charles. In 1984, the latter had launched an attack on the plan for an annex to the National Gallery. Prince Charles had called the plan to accommodate both commerce and culture in a high-tech building with a tower "a boil on the face of a beloved and elegant friend," putting an end to that particular project. It took a committee years to agree on a new plan, Robert Venturi's design for a structure that combined the tradition of Trafalgar Square with modern museum requirements. Prince Charles, however, remained skeptical. Jacob Rothschild, since 1984 chairman of the National Gallery's board of directors and a member of the committee, favored Venturi's "Sainsbury Wing." It was named after the Sainsburys, who had donated the funds for its construction—this, too, had been arranged by Jacob, who had fulfilled the board's expectation that his connections would pull the institution out of a slump caused by a lack of government support. It pleased Jacob that the building presented "no postmodern jokes" but "reflected the museum's greatness and dignity."

The wing's opening in 1991 was yet another triumph for Jacob. "Rothschild," a commentator wrote, "has worked wonders while Prince Charles still wonders how to make things work."

### (g) *The Great Deals*

In the early eighties, Sir Evelyn Rothschild spent much time in New York, enjoying Guy's hospitality and discussing joint plans for the U.S. subsidiary. "It became clear to us," Evelyn remembers, "that if we wanted to score, we would have to fight."

In their choice of a new chief executive, the Rothschilds combined business acumen with personal affinity: Robert S. Pirie had been their legal adviser and was familiar with the details of Rothschild Inc. A Midwesterner, the heir to a Chicago department store fortune, Pirie was able to attract clients from a part of the country the Rothschilds hardly knew, and the European bankers were charmed by his love of racehorses and old and rare books and his quasi-aristocratic lifestyle, which included weekends on a farm near Boston and dinners with the British royal family. All of this the Rothschilds found rather compatible.

More important, Pirie brought new energy to the

bank's flagging transactions. In the eighties, a period of daring financial maneuvers, he acquired new clients and stage-managed a few spectacular takeovers. In 1984 he helped Sir James Goldsmith gain control of Crown Zellerbach Corporation to the tune of five hundred and seventy million dollars. Rothschild Inc. worked with Hughes Aircraft, the *New York Times*, big insurance companies and a department store chain. The bank assisted the brothers Reichmann of Toronto (sons of Austrian immigrants whose firm Olympia & York is one of the giants in the real estate business) with their takeover of Santa Fe Southern Pacific Corporation. Most impressive was the tactical advice Rothschild Inc. provided the late media czar Robert Maxwell for his successful takeover of Macmillan Publishing.

As economics expert William H. Meyers has noted, today Rothschild North America Inc. has become a power player, an agile middleweight among the new "Goliaths of Wall Street." The firm makes its profits not by investing its own capital but mainly from fees for a service immensely appreciated by financiers and risk-taking capitalists: personal consultation and high-powered negotiation skills. This capacity has made it outlast the toppling fortresses of the junk bond era. Wilbur L. Ross, Jr., one of the bank's executives, specializes in the recapitalization of junk bond–damaged firms, and earns his institution an estimated million and a half dollars a month in consultation fees.

### (h) *The Return Home*

In the meantime, things had been looking up for the French Rothschilds. Despite the loss of the bank in the rue Laffitte, the family had retained a power base. Eric Alain Robert David Rothschild (b. 1940), a distant nephew of

Guy's, and his cousin David (b. 1942) had taken on the holding company of all Rothschild enterprises, the Paris-Orléans, housing it in a modest office building on avenue Matignon. This entrepreneurially minded duo did not see the "P.O." as merely a comfortable shelter from the hostile political climate, but used it to herald the return of the family's financial power.

The Paris-Orléans started out as a railroad company serving the two cities of its name. It then turned into a diversified concern with an emphasis on mineral extraction. This did not prove lucrative, and the two cousins transformed it into a modern enterprise in the financial consulting field. In five years, they had increased its capital from ten to thirty million dollars. In addition, they created an estate management firm, P.O. Gestion, with the ultimate aim of turning it into a bank, and in 1983, less than two years after Mitterrand became president, they applied for a charter.

At that time, many of the nationalized banks—showcases of the Socialist government—were running into problems. Even L'Européenne de Banque operated at a loss in the first two years of its existence. Mitterrand, on the other hand, was (still) unable to allow a policy reversal, and certainly not one in the case of the Rothschilds: after his notorious letter to *Le Monde*, Guy had gone on to write a whole book in which he accused the government of economic incompetence (*Contre bonne fortune*, 1983).

But in March 1986, on the eve of the French elections, David de Rothschild had every reason to be optimistic. "If the Conservatives win," he stated, "we won't have any trouble inscribing our family name once again above the door in rue Marignon."

True enough, the legend "Rothschild et Associés Banque" reappeared in April—but not above the doorway, since the Rothschild operation occupied only a few floors of the building. "A hot new name in French banking," read a jocular line in *Business Week*. The bank, both old and new and in fighting trim, had divested itself of the marginally productive industrial investments that had amounted to sixty-five percent of its wealth before nationalization. It was now concentrating on fewer but more lucrative holdings. The know-how in investment advising acquired in the P.O. Gestion operation was put to good use. David and Eric's bank assisted that good family client, Sir James Goldsmith, in his takeover bid for the publishing house Presses de la Cité. The new government also trusted the bank's entrepreneurial abilities and paid it more than twelve billion francs in connection with the privatization of the financial group Paribas.

The institution, later renamed Rothschild & Compagnie Banque, presently flourishes both at home and in the international arena. According to its annual reports, the majority of its stock is held by the French and English sides of the Family, but eight percent belongs to Edmond de Rothschild's Compagnie Financière. While Edmond is a descendant of the French line, he—like his father Maurice before him—represents a successful maverick strain. After inheriting his father's fortune at a young age, he has managed it wisely; he has also made headlines of a different sort.

### (i) *Life with a Perfectionist*

Even though anecdotal quotations attributed to Edmond may not always be accurate, they do reveal something about his manner of dealing with people. "That's a very beautiful diamond you're wearing," the thirty-four-year-old, married Baron Edmond Adolphe Maurice Jules Jacques de Rothschild is alleged to have said one evening in January 1960 to a twenty-seven-year-old starlet by the name of Nadine Lhopitalier. "What a shame it's a fake."

That was the unusual opening line for a relationship that has since acquired the aura of one of this century's great romances. He, a driven entrepreneur, regarded as the richest individual Rothschild even as a young man, self-assured to the point of tactlessness—as exemplified by that appraisal of a jewel's authenticity; she, a factory girl from the Parisian suburbs who had become a fashion model, bit-part movie actress and music hall dancer, conscious of her almond-eyed charm but nevertheless flustered by a stranger accosting her in a restaurant with such an odd remark. He proceeded to escort her to her car and politely took his leave after an exchange of addresses.

Three years later, the two were married—in a bedroom, because Nadine was very close to giving birth to their son Benjamin, and the obstetrician in charge was worried about possible complications. In the opinion of many of Edmond's friends, this was definitely a *mésalliance.* Nadine Talier (this was her *nom d'artiste*), now Baroness de Rothschild, had to contend with that disapproval as she learned her new role. As she has noted in ironic retrospect, she became "the manager of the hotel chain Palais et Châteaux Edmond de Rothschild." Whether in the ancestral manor Pregny near Geneva, or in the Château Armainvilliers in France, or in the Paris residence (close to both the Palais Elysée and Edmond's office at rue du Faubourg Saint-Honoré 45), or in the hunting lodge near Ischgl in the Tyrol, or wherever her husband had to attend a dinner, a conference or a party—it was her task to stand by his side as the perfect hostess. Right up to his death in 1997, she performed that task, if on a reduced scale, because the seventies, as she has observed, heralded the end of a way of life: "The inflation crisis made everything harder. Edmond worked tirelessly, did no longer go out as much; social events and receptions bored him. . . . At the end of 1979, hardly without warning, he decided to close up the château at Armainvilliers."

Thus, the Rothschilds resident in Switzerland followed their French relatives' example in withdrawing from the front lines of high-society life. There still was enough to do for Nadine, who sees a wife's main task in "pleasing her husband, and listening to him. He gives me shelter, feeds me, and clothes me; for this, I am grateful to him." Her attitude may sound rather antiquated, but it has made it possible for her to share a life with "the driven perfectionist" for more than three decades, giving the lie to her friends' prediction that it "wouldn't last twenty-four hours."

Edmond de Rothschild was also a backstage force in politics. He belonged to the steering committee of the secretive Bilderberg circle, an informal association of political and financial top brass that has sometimes been called more powerful than national governments. He met regularly with his French and British relatives "to discuss personal and business matters," and was a major benefactor of Israel. In 1972, the Baron purchased a small vineyard, Château Clarke near Listrac in the Bordeaux region, and from the 1978 vintage onward he shared some of the fame the name Rothschild has earned among wine connoisseurs.

### (j) *"Not the Greatest but the Best"*

Contrary to Baron Philippe's surmise, the Rothschilds' glory days do not seem to be over yet. In the world of banking, they are in charge of four or five active centers: the London bank, presided over by Sir Evelyn; the Paris bank, under the Barons David and Eric; Baron Edmond's

Compagnie Financière and bank in Paris and Geneva; and Lord Jacob Rothschild's London-based group of enterprises. The two first-mentioned banks see themselves as the mainstays of the "Rothschild group," but they have also founded a bank in Zurich, the Zürcher Rothschild Bank AG, and it is an important element of their collective strategy. The annual reports of all these institutions show the extent to which the "cousins" from London, Paris and Geneva are represented, and their lists of names enable "Rothschildologists" to figure out the degrees of Family involvement. The ties between Paris and London are particularly strong, and Sir Evelyn is a board member of Baron Edmond's Geneva bank.

In England, relations between Lord Jacob and Sir Evelyn are more tenuous. As recently as 1992, their comments on the schism that took place over a decade ago are still both reserved and resigned. "They have agreed to disagree," one of New Court's top managers comments on Evelyn's and Jacob's relationship. The latter confirms this with a typically British understatement issued by his office: "It is fair to say that they have gone separate ways."

Jacob still emphasizes the importance of his actions to the London bank's revival in the sixties, but is by no means content to rest on his laurels. He has said that he looks back on his work for the National Gallery with great satisfaction: "It has served the public interest, and that, I believe, is always a cause for particular pride." He has proceeded to take on the challenge of work for the National Memorial Foundation and has established J.R. Life Assurance, a company cofounded with Mark Weinberg.

Jacob Rothschild also takes an interest in post–Cold War Eastern Europe. The irony of historical events has led him to get involved with a former property of the Austrian Rothschilds, the large mining and ironworks concern

Witkowitz near Mährisch-Ostrau. In 1938, Louis Nathaniel, head of the Viennese branch, had managed to transfer this concern into British hands in the nick of time (see Chapter IX). After World War II, the enterprise was nationalized, then opened up again to privatization after the collapse of communism. Jacob Rothschild is not acting as a prospective buyer but as an adviser to the new government. He is quite unsentimental about this involvement, seeing it as part of the Rothschilds' new role. As such, privatizations are not among his major interests. He has described the difference between him and N. M. Rothschild & Sons in the following terms: "We are more concerned with investments. New Court is more interested in takeovers and privatizations."

N. M. Rothschild & Sons Ltd. see themselves as primarily merchant bankers. Until recently, that might have sounded a bit quaint, but with the change of banking tactics the term "merchant bank" has gained new luster in the City, not least thanks to the efforts of this firm which still has its headquarters in New Court, St. Swithins Lane, in immediate proximity to the Bank of England. It still functions as the Bank of England's "gold broker" and presides by tradition over the "gold fixing" in London, which still takes place twice a day in the New Court offices. However, the value of gold bars is now determined and corrected globally and round the clock: therefore, as the bank has noted, the London "fixing" represents "only a snapshot" of market events. Taking this into account, the bank has opened gold trading offices of its own in New York, Singapore and Sydney.

"We are not the greatest merchant bank in the world, but we are the best" reads a confident statement by the management of the corporate finance division. "We are more solid than the 'boutique' banks that mushroomed in the eighties to offer only specialized services. On the other hand, we are smaller than big American banks such as Goldman Sachs who have far more capital at their disposal and also function as credit institutions. We regard our advisory activities as more important than the amount of capital."

As soon as N. M. Rothschild & Sons had brought out their annual business report for 1991, it required an important correction: in late January 1992, David de Rothschild, head of the French bank and, until then, only a "non-executive director" in London, was appointed deputy chairman—a definitely executive post. Thus the ties between Paris and London are drawn tighter, and the banks' activities complement each other to a degree that made the founding of a "Rothschild Group" a logical conclusion. Its partnership council consists of Sir Evelyn, Baron Guy (David's father), Robert (Eric's brother), Bernard Esambert, and three other persons. David is the head of the management council, of which Eric is also a member, as is since 1991 Edouard (b. 1957), Baron Guy's son from his second marriage.

Edouard's name appears frequently in the society columns of French dailies and the *International Herald Tribune.* The hierarchy of Parisian society is determined by the news of who dines or dances with whom, and the Rothschilds are ubiquitous as either guests or hosts. Until her death in 1996, Marie-Hélène often threw parties at the Opéra-Comique, being one of that institution's main benefactors, and her son Edouard and his second wife Arielle ("dressed by Lacroix, as was her mother-in-law") could be seen as the inheritors of the Parisian Rothschilds' legacy of social prominence. It still remains to be seen whether Edouard will achieve similar visibility in the financial world.

The fourth center of gravity in the Family universe, namely, the late Baron Edmond's Geneva bank, deals mainly with investments and portfolio management for private and institutional clients, offering its services in branch offices in Switzerland, the rest of Europe and in far-flung locations such as Mauritius, Bermuda, Gibraltar and Jerusalem. The Baron's Compagnie Financière is a merchant bank. In 1989, it registered a net profit of seventy million francs, but the following year, due to adverse conditions, profits were down to forty million. By means of personal and organizational ties to the Geneva bank, it functions in tandem with the latter in pursuit of new business opportunities.

"The Rothschilds are returning to Frankfurt." This rumor began to circulate in the spring of 1989, becoming more sensational in the absence of any concrete evidence. In reality, the Family never contemplated a "return" but simply the opening of an office of the kind that already existed in Milan and Madrid. In the case of Frankfurt, the Family had hesitated mainly because it had observed the poor results large Swiss banks had achieved in that metropolis. Nevertheless, in the spring of 1991 a branch office of the English and French Rothschilds opened its door in Ulmenstrasse, employing a staff of eight under business manager Erich Stromeyer. The branch deals with corporate finance, financial planning, and new issue banking. After a hiatus of ninety years, a new chapter, however modest, has begun in the history of Rothschilds in Germany.

### (k) *From "Concordia" to "Continuation"*

The London and Paris banks do not limit their participation to the Frankfurt, Milan and Madrid branches. There are many other instances of concerted activities. The important part played by the Rothschilds in privatizations in Eastern Europe are ascribed to the English bank, but the latter always acts in unison with the French. Rothschild Inc. of New York has already been discussed. The banks also share offices in Australia, Bermuda, Brazil, Chile and Hong Kong, on the Isle of Man, in Japan (the good connections with the Far East date back to senior director Edmund's participation in trade missions to Tokyo in the early sixties) and Canada, on the Channel Islands (the Guernsey office for financial management adds substantially to the twenty billion dollars jointly managed by the banks), in Malaysia, Mexico, Portugal, Singapore and Zimbabwe. Sir Evelyn, Baron David, or both, sometimes in conjunction with (Edmund's brother) Leopold, often act as chairmen of these subsidiaries and branches. In a total of twenty countries, more than two thousand staff members are working for—well, for whom, exactly?

While the efficiency and know-how of these enterprises is highly visible, the underlying sources of power and knowledge are much harder to discern. As we know, the concept "Rothschild group" was created in the early eighties as an approximate description of the fact that the Family houses cooperated across national borders. Now and again, English promotional materials refer simply to "Rothschilds": "Within Europe, Rothschilds is unique in that it comprises not merely a network of offices, but a confederation of three separate banks."

According to a managing director of New Court, it is a confederation "without a formal basis." The British bank is, however, owned by a parent company, Rothschilds Continuation Ltd., registered in Zug in Switzerland. The Rothschild Concordia AG (also in Zug) is referred to as the "ultimate holding company." Even Baron Edmond's bank is part of Continuation Ltd., and the French branch is also known to be connected to the umbrella company in Zug.

Knowing that, however, one does not know a great

deal. The otherwise accommodating Rothschild Bank of Switzerland can provide only rather vague information on details of these holdings: Yes, it is possible that one of the Zug companies is a part of the other. Besides, in the fall of 1991 there was a name change, so that the former Concordia is now the Continuation. And yes, the Zug address exists primarily for the purpose of registering and managing participations. Behind the registered holdings there may be others that are not generally known.

But what sounds like a secret may well be the answer, and it is expressed in the very conscious choice of a name—*Concordia,* one of three cornerstones carried by the Rothschilds on their coat of arms for almost two hundred years. The financial and legal constructions serve only to protect what is informally understood as clearly as at the beginning of the Family's history: the communication between its branches with a view to concord and harmony.

# AFTERWORD 1998

## The Ultimate Secret?

THE FOG long shrouding Rothschild financial finesse still tantalizes historians. But there is something more important to be probed, namely the secret that keeps the Family's mystique evergreen. It is a mystique born during the musketry of Napoleon's wars and continuing today into the Internet generation. The Rothschild nimbus has outlasted and outdazzled the glamour of other money dynasties as venerable and as deep of pocket.

Why? Perhaps because "Rothschild" expresses, lustrously, a central paradox of modernity—the double-edged thing called progress.

The Rothschilds had and still have a gift for counterpointing the good and the bad of our culture. This became evident once more in two dramatic events marking the latest chapter of the chronicle. One is a personal calamity. The other flashed in shiny headlines across financial columns all over the world. Both were born of a dialectic underlying our times.

The first story began brightly enough before it ended in darkness. Amschel mayor James Rothschild, son of the late Victor Lord Rothschild, benefited from advantages accruing to the youngest sibling of a Rothschild generation. He was—initially—not expected to man the family's grander ramparts. Therefore he could enjoy an outdoor upbringing of seignorial seclusion, suiting his temperament. He became a country gentleman of near-ducal level: oversaw the family estate that spread across Suffolk hills; manufactured a select brand of apple juice; made his mark as cricketeer on many an exclusive lawn; silvered the shelves of his den with trophies from auto races; dipped on occasion into London's chic recesses, like the Club Zanzibar. It was at the Zanzibar that he noticed Anita Guinness of the banking Guinnesses, and hence a romantic object of congenial lineage. Anita stood at the club's salad bar, mixing greens. He asked for a taste. She offered a bowl. They were married not long thereafter, in 1981.

Within four years the union produced two winsome little girls as well as a handsome little boy. Because he was a Rothschild, Amschel's life seemed set on a fairy-tale course. And because he was a Rothschild, he didn't live happily ever after.

In 1987 his father, Lord Victor, asked him to enter the Family bank after all. Amschel was thirty-two. He went through a brief breaking-in period as silver trader and as assistant to New Court's head, Sir Evelyn. Then, in 1990, Evelyn put him in charge of Rothschild Assets Management. It was a rather spectacular and ultimately disastrous advancement.

But no one knew that yet, though many in the City were aware of the challenges built into Amschel's job. Rothschild Assets Management—R.A.M. for short—constituted one of eight such funds-handling companies operating under the Rothschild umbrella on various continents. There was not one world-beater among them. In fact, the London one had to make do with portfolios totaling under twenty billion, whereas the leader in the field, Boston Fidelities, husbanded four hundred.

Amschel planned to improve this un-Rothschild picture by combining the eight far-flung enterprises into a single engine of ubiquitous reach and global heft.

Even for a seasoned Rothschild of toughest vintage this would have been a thorny task. It involved long-distance strategizing, the creation of a Dutch Holding Company, the harnessing of the cousin branch in Paris with all its remote ramifications, the exploration and verification of offshore balance sheets, the integrating of sundry transoceanic executive teams, the assessing and sometimes the venturing of antipodal boardroom gambits.

Amschel poured dogged work and unstinting expense into his initiative. In 1995 it still did not pay off. R.A.M. reported a loss of nine million dollars.

A deficit of a different sort was suffered by Amschel's private sphere: No more rustic ease around the ample hearth in Suffolk. Now Amschel's schedule had to obey imperatives harsher than those of the cricket league or the breeding of exquisite apples. Chronic travel ate into what was once a close-knit family life. There was always that limousine lying in wait to dash him to the airport.

Amschel still tried to be a good father, but often he had to be good in absentia. And, of course, he turned, increasingly, into an absentee husband. After fifteen years of marriage, rumors floated through London of Amschel's rows with Anita. Friends worried over the emptiness in his eyes.

Yet toward the end of spring 1996 it appeared that Amschel's labors would find reward. By May the ink on R.A.M. ledgers turned from red to black. And in midsummer some long-missed paterfamilias joy beckoned: Amschel and his son James were to play a big cricket match on the weekend of July thirteenth.

On the Monday preceding, on July eighth, Amschel chaired a long, toilsome meeting on R.A.M. matters in the Paris family bank on avenue Matignon. Its agenda, while not sunny, was not particularly grim. When the conference ended at five P.M., none of the participants shaking hands with Amschel suspected that anything might be very much amiss.

Neither did a chambermaid at the Hotel Bristol around the corner, where Amschel lodged at $900 a night under bronze chandeliers. At 7:30 P.M. she knocked at the door of Room 402 to turn down Amschel's bed. Nobody answered. She entered with her passkey and found Amschel dead. He had hanged himself from the towel rail in the bathroom.

There was no note. No clear explanation of the suicide was ever provided. But it is fair to reason that Amschel had died of an evil all too common and too up-to-date: stress. The stress of stretching a local London-based assets-managing company into a network spanning the planet is a gold-framed mirror that reflects the pressures afflicting many of us today on a humbler scale.

From the five brothers fanning out across Europe in their coaches, to Amschel vibrating in the Concorde between London and New York, the Rothschilds have been among the principal dynamos powering the modern stress cycle. They are archdemons of our *Zeitgeist.* That is half the reason they are legend. The other half lies in their ability to transcend the very *Zeitgeist* they've been spreading. They have managed to temper universal ambition with a very specific tradition. In the teeth of their own planetary thrust they insist on family-textured closeness.

Sometimes, as in Amschel's case, they fail. Yet this recent failure focused them, even more recently, on their customary remedy.

Three months after Amschel's death, the other major event in the Rothschilds' 1990's story came to pass. Sir Evelyn, as head of N. M. Rothschild, London, made an announcement: his French cousin David, already his deputy chairman, would be director of a committee coordinating Rothschild investment banking around the world. This, reported *The New York Times,* meant "that the French and English branches had become partners again in a way not seen since the Rothschilds first invented international banking."

It was a global move by tribal means—a classic reprise of the Rothschilds myth first set in motion by old Meyer and his five boys on Jew Street.

# *BIBLIOGRAPHY*

In addition to general historical works and newspaper and magazine articles of the nineteenth and twentieth centuries, the following works have been useful to me in the writing of this book:

*The Rise of the House of Rothschild*, by Count Egon Caesar Corti, translated from the German by Brian and Beatrix Lunn (New York, Cosmopolitan Book Corp., 1928)

*The Reign of the House of Rothschild*, by Count Egon Caesar Corti, translated from the German by Brian and Beatrix Lunn (New York, Cosmopolitan Book Corp., 1928)

*The Romance of the Rothschilds*, by Ignatius Balla (New York, G. P. Putnam's Sons, 1913)

*Baron Edmond Rothschild*, by David Druck, translated by Leo M. Glassman (New York, Hebrew Monotype Press, 1928)

*Five Men of Frankfurt*, by Marcus Eli Ravage (New York, Lincoln MacVeagh—Dial Press, 1929)

*Disraeli*, by Andre Maurois, translated from the French by Hamish Miles (New York, D. Appleton and Company, 1928)

*The Magnificent Rothschilds*, by Cecil Roth (London, Robert Hale Ltd., 1939)

*A Century Between*, by Robert Henrey (New York, Longmans, Green and Co., 1937)

*The History of the Times*, 1884–1912 (New York, Macmillan, 1947)

*Trial and Error*, the autobiography of Chaim Weizmann (New York, Harper, for The East and West Library, 1949)

*Gay Monarch*, by Virginia Cowles (New York, Harper & Brothers, 1956)

*Bearsted: A Biography of Marcus Samuel*, by Robert Henriques (New York, The Viking Press, 1960)

*Letters to a Christian Friend on the Fundamental Truths of Judaism*, by Clementine von Rothschild (London, 1869)

*Lady de Rothschild and Her Daughters*, by Lucy Cohen (London, J. Murray, 1935)

*Reminiscences*, by Lady Constance de Rothschild Battersea (London, Macmillan and Co., 1923)

*Meyer Amschel Rothschild, der Gründer des Rothschildschen Bankhauses*, by Christian W. Berghoeffer (Frankfurt am Main, Englert & Schlosser, 1922)

*Survival*, by James J. Rorimer in collaboration with Gilbert Rabin (New York, Abelard Press, 1950)

*Coningsby or The New Generation*, by Benjamin Disraeli (London, Longmans, Green and Co., 1844)

*A History of the Jews*, by Solomon Grayzel (Philadelphia, The Jewish Publication Society of America, 1947)

*The Diaries of Theodor Herzl* (New York, Dial Press, 1956)

# INDEX

# The Rothschilds
# c. 1550-1985

Based on Rothschild, Victor, *Rothschild Family Tree*, 1450–1973 (Cambridge University Library) and information supplied by members of the family

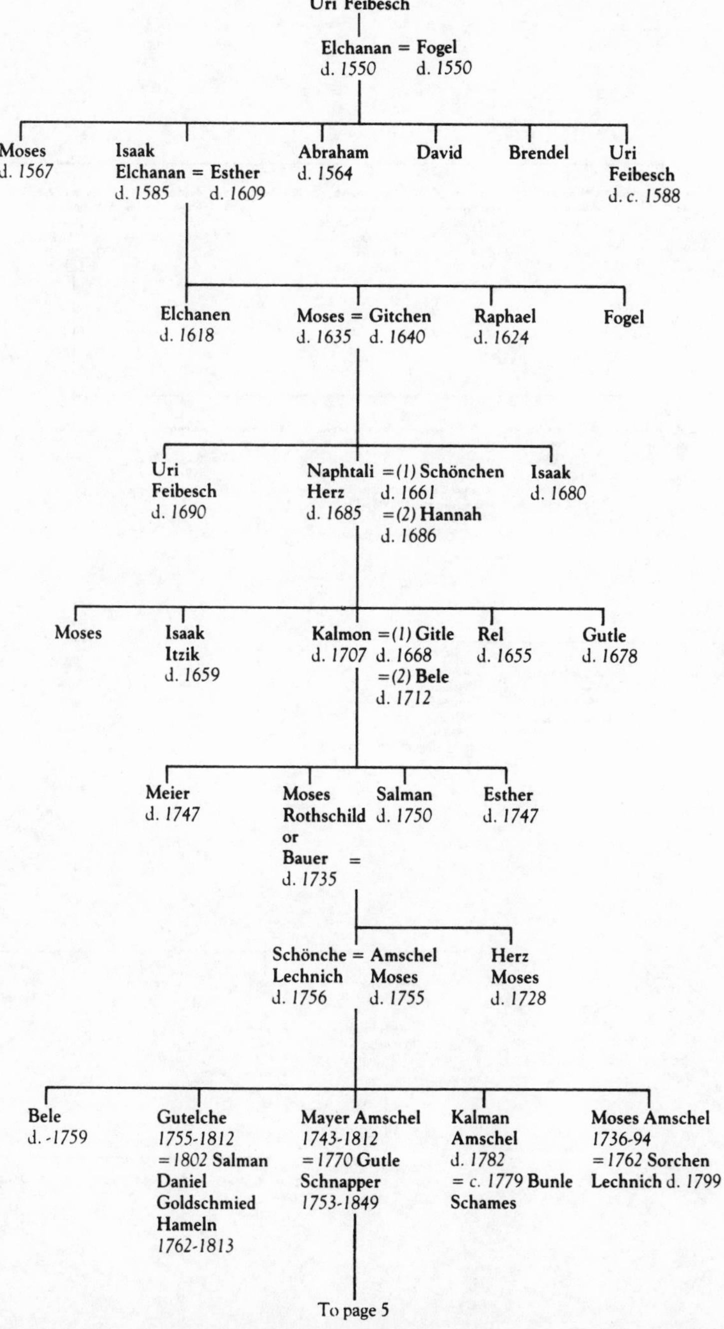

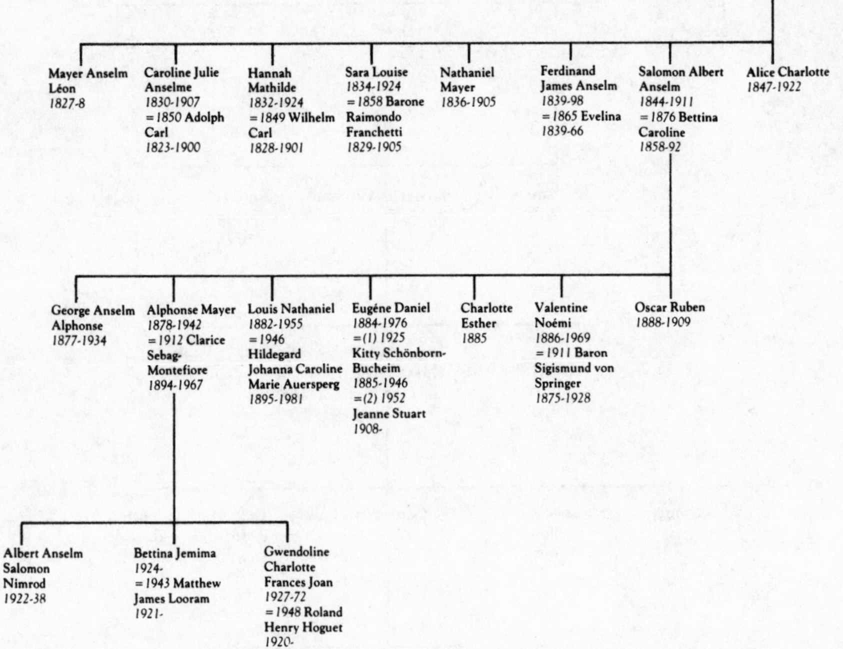
Mayer Anselm Léon 1827-8
Caroline Julie Anselme 1830-1907 = 1850 Adolph Carl 1823-1900
Hannah Mathilde 1832-1924 = 1849 Wilhelm Carl 1828-1901
Sara Louise 1834-1924 = 1858 Barone Raimondo Franchetti 1829-1905
Nathaniel Mayer 1836-1905
Ferdinand James Anselm 1839-98 = 1865 Evelina 1839-66
Salomon Albert Anselm 1844-1911 = 1876 Bettina Caroline 1858-92
Alice Charlotte 1847-1922
George Anselm Alphonse 1877-1934
Alphonse Mayer 1878-1942 = 1912 Clarice Sebag-Montefiore 1894-1967
Louis Nathaniel 1882-1955 = 1946 Hildegard Johanna Caroline Marie Auersperg 1895-1981
Eugéne Daniel 1884-1976 =(1) 1925 Kitty Schönborn-Bucheim 1885-1946 =(2) 1952 Jeanne Stuart 1908-
Charlotte Esther 1885
Valentine Noémi 1886-1969 = 1911 Baron Sigismund von Springer 1875-1928
Oscar Ruben 1888-1909
Albert Anselm Salomon Nimrod 1922-38
Bettina Jemima 1924- = 1943 Matthew James Looram 1921-
Gwendoline Charlotte Frances Joan 1927-72 = 1948 Roland Henry Hoguet 1920-

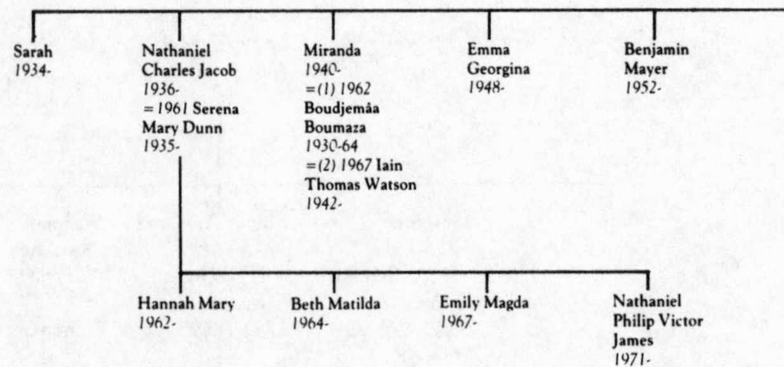
Sarah 1934-
Nathaniel Charles Jacob 1936- = 1961 Serena Mary Dunn 1935-
Miranda 1940- =(1) 1962 Boudjemâa Boumaza 1930-64 =(2) 1967 Iain Thomas Watson 1942-
Emma Georgina 1948-
Benjamin Mayer 1952-
Hannah Mary 1962-
Beth Matilda 1964-
Emily Magda 1967-
Nathaniel Philip Victor James 1971-

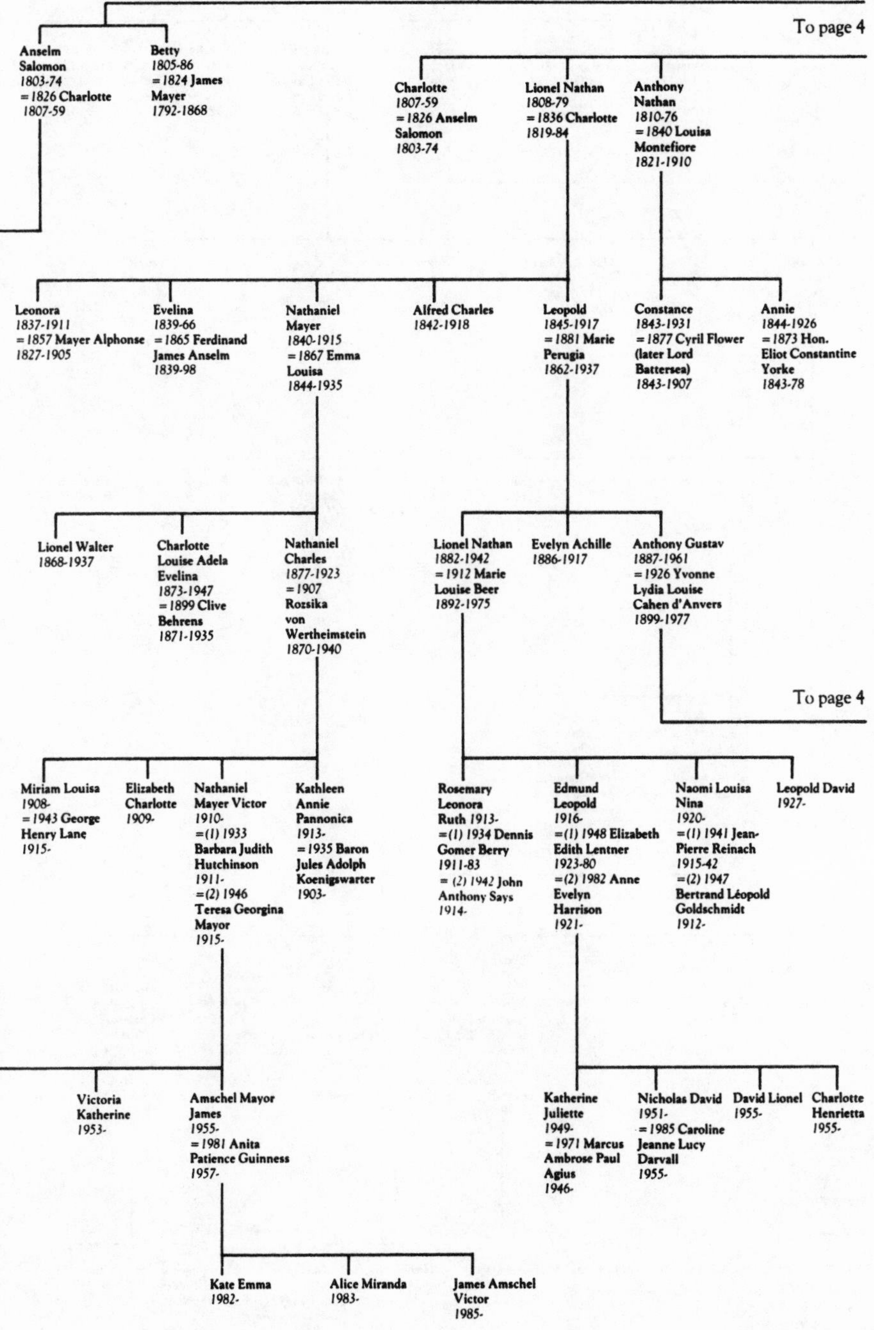

To page 4
Anselm Salomon 1803-74 = 1826 Charlotte 1807-59
Betty 1805-86 = 1824 James Mayer 1792-1868
Charlotte 1807-59 = 1826 Anselm Salomon 1803-74
Lionel Nathan 1808-79 = 1836 Charlotte 1819-84
Anthony Nathan 1810-76 = 1840 Louisa Montefiore 1821-1910
Leonora 1837-1911 = 1857 Mayer Alphonse 1827-1905
Evelina 1839-66 = 1865 Ferdinand James Anselm 1839-98
Nathaniel Mayer 1840-1915 = 1867 Emma Louisa 1844-1935
Alfred Charles 1842-1918
Leopold 1845-1917 = 1881 Marie Perugia 1862-1937
Constance 1843-1931 = 1877 Cyril Flower (later Lord Battersea) 1843-1907
Annie 1844-1926 = 1873 Hon. Eliot Constantine Yorke 1843-78
Lionel Walter 1868-1937
Charlotte Louise Adela Evelina 1873-1947 = 1899 Clive Behrens 1871-1935
Nathaniel Charles 1877-1923 = 1907 Rozsika von Wertheimstein 1870-1940
Lionel Nathan 1882-1942 = 1912 Marie Louise Beer 1892-1975
Evelyn Achille 1886-1917
Anthony Gustav 1887-1961 = 1926 Yvonne Lydia Louise Cahen d'Anvers 1899-1977
To page 4
Miriam Louisa 1908- = 1943 George Henry Lane 1915-
Elizabeth Charlotte 1909-
Nathaniel Mayer Victor 1910- =(1) 1933 Barbara Judith Hutchinson 1911- =(2) 1946 Teresa Georgina Mayor 1915-
Kathleen Annie Pannonica 1913- = 1935 Baron Jules Adolph Koenigswarter 1903-
Rosemary Leonora Ruth 1913- =(1) 1934 Dennis Gomer Berry 1911-83 = (2) 1942 John Anthony Says 1914-
Edmund Leopold 1916- =(1) 1948 Elizabeth Edith Lentner 1923-80 =(2) 1982 Anne Evelyn Harrison 1921-
Naomi Louisa Nina 1920- =(1) 1941 Jean-Pierre Reinach 1915-42 =(2) 1947 Bertrand Léopold Goldschmidt 1912-
Leopold David 1927-
Victoria Katherine 1953-
Amschel Mayor James 1955- = 1981 Anita Patience Guinness 1957-
Katherine Juliette 1949- = 1971 Marcus Ambrose Paul Agius 1946-
Nicholas David 1951- = 1985 Caroline Jeanne Lucy Darvall 1955-
David Lionel 1955-
Charlotte Henrietta 1955-
Kate Emma 1982-
Alice Miranda 1983-
James Amschel Victor 1985-

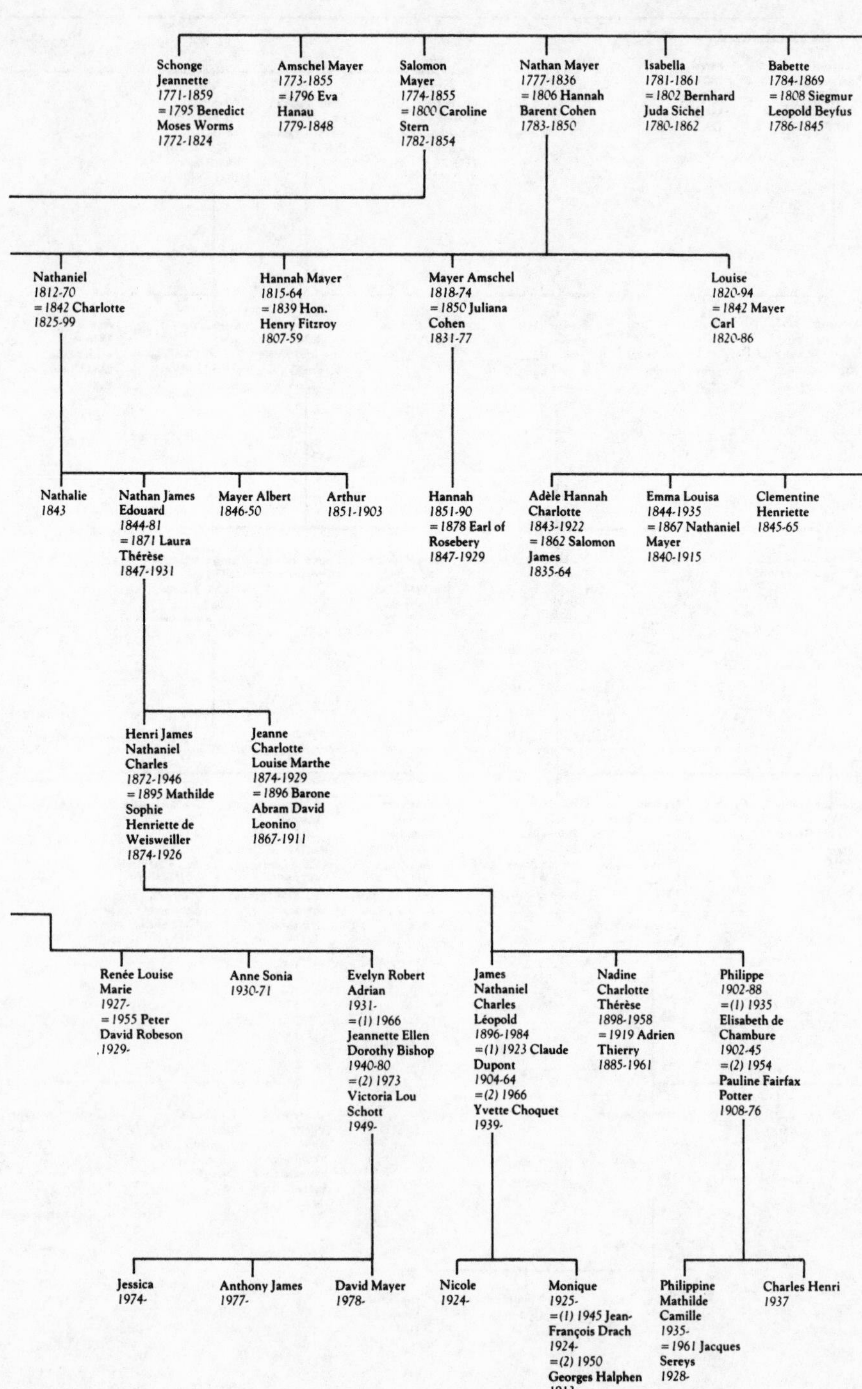

Schonge Jeannette 1771-1859 = 1795 Benedict Moses Worms 1772-1824
Amschel Mayer 1773-1855 = 1796 Eva Hanau 1779-1848
Salomon Mayer 1774-1855 = 1800 Caroline Stern 1782-1854
Nathan Mayer 1777-1836 = 1806 Hannah Barent Cohen 1783-1850
Isabella 1781-1861 = 1802 Bernhard Juda Sichel 1780-1862
Babette 1784-1869 = 1808 Siegmur Leopold Beyfus 1786-1845
Nathaniel 1812-70 = 1842 Charlotte 1825-99
Hannah Mayer 1815-64 = 1839 Hon. Henry Fitzroy 1807-59
Mayer Amschel 1818-74 = 1850 Juliana Cohen 1831-77
Louise 1820-94 = 1842 Mayer Carl 1820-86
Nathalie 1843
Nathan James Edouard 1844-81 = 1871 Laura Thérèse 1847-1931
Mayer Albert 1846-50
Arthur 1851-1903
Hannah 1851-90 = 1878 Earl of Rosebery 1847-1929
Adèle Hannah Charlotte 1843-1922 = 1862 Salomon James 1835-64
Emma Louisa 1844-1935 = 1867 Nathaniel Mayer 1840-1915
Clementine Henriette 1845-65
Henri James Nathaniel Charles 1872-1946 = 1895 Mathilde Sophie Henriette de Weisweiller 1874-1926
Jeanne Charlotte Louise Marthe 1874-1929 = 1896 Barone Abram David Leonino 1867-1911
Renée Louise Marie 1927- = 1955 Peter David Robeson 1929-
Anne Sonia 1930-71
Evelyn Robert Adrian 1931- =(1) 1966 Jeannette Ellen Dorothy Bishop 1940-80 =(2) 1973 Victoria Lou Schott 1949-
James Nathaniel Charles Léopold 1896-1984 =(1) 1923 Claude Dupont 1904-64 =(2) 1966 Yvette Choquet 1939-
Nadine Charlotte Thérèse 1898-1958 = 1919 Adrien Thierry 1885-1961
Philippe 1902-88 =(1) 1935 Elisabeth de Chambure 1902-45 =(2) 1954 Pauline Fairfax Potter 1908-76
Jessica 1974-
Anthony James 1977-
David Mayer 1978-
Nicole 1924-
Monique 1925- =(1) 1945 Jean-François Drach 1924- =(2) 1950 Georges Halphen 1913-
Philippine Mathilde Camille 1935- = 1961 Jacques Sereys 1928-
Charles Henri 1937

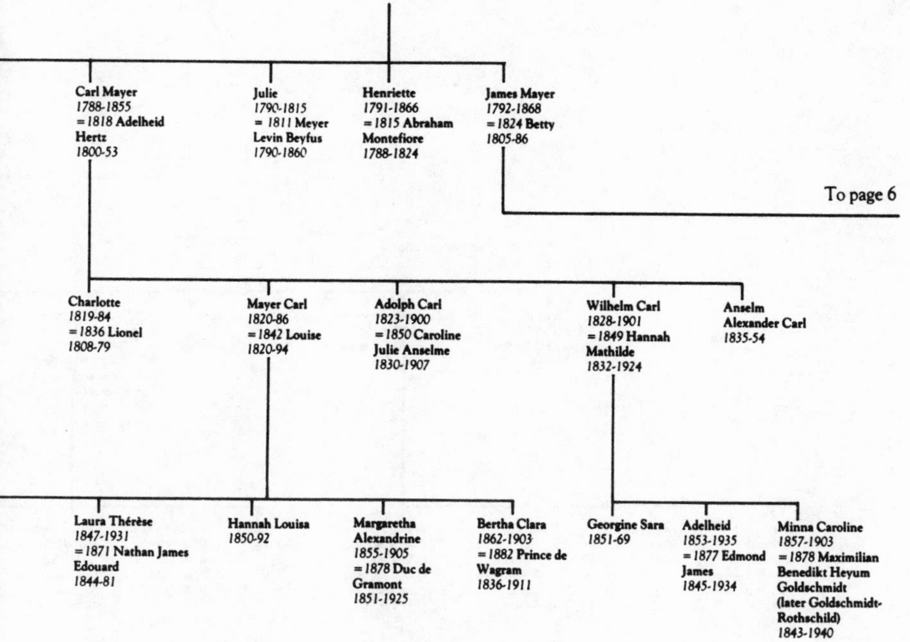

Carl Mayer 1788-1855 =1818 Adelheid Hertz 1800-53
Julie 1790-1815 = 1811 Meyer Levin Beyfus 1790-1860
Henriette 1791-1866 =1815 Abraham Montefiore 1788-1824
James Mayer 1792-1868 =1824 Betty 1805-86
To page 6
Charlotte 1819-84 =1836 Lionel 1808-79
Mayer Carl 1820-86 =1842 Louise 1820-94
Adolph Carl 1823-1900 =1850 Caroline Julie Anselme 1830-1907
Wilhelm Carl 1828-1901 =1849 Hannah Mathilde 1832-1924
Anselm Alexander Carl 1835-54
Laura Thérèse 1847-1931 =1871 Nathan James Edouard 1844-81
Hannah Louisa 1850-92
Margaretha Alexandrine 1855-1905 =1878 Duc de Gramont 1851-1925
Bertha Clara 1862-1903 =1882 Prince de Wagram 1836-1911
Georgine Sara 1851-69
Adelheid 1853-1935 =1877 Edmond James 1845-1934
Minna Caroline 1857-1903 =1878 Maximilian Benedikt Heyum Goldschmidt (later Goldschmidt-Rothschild) 1843-1940

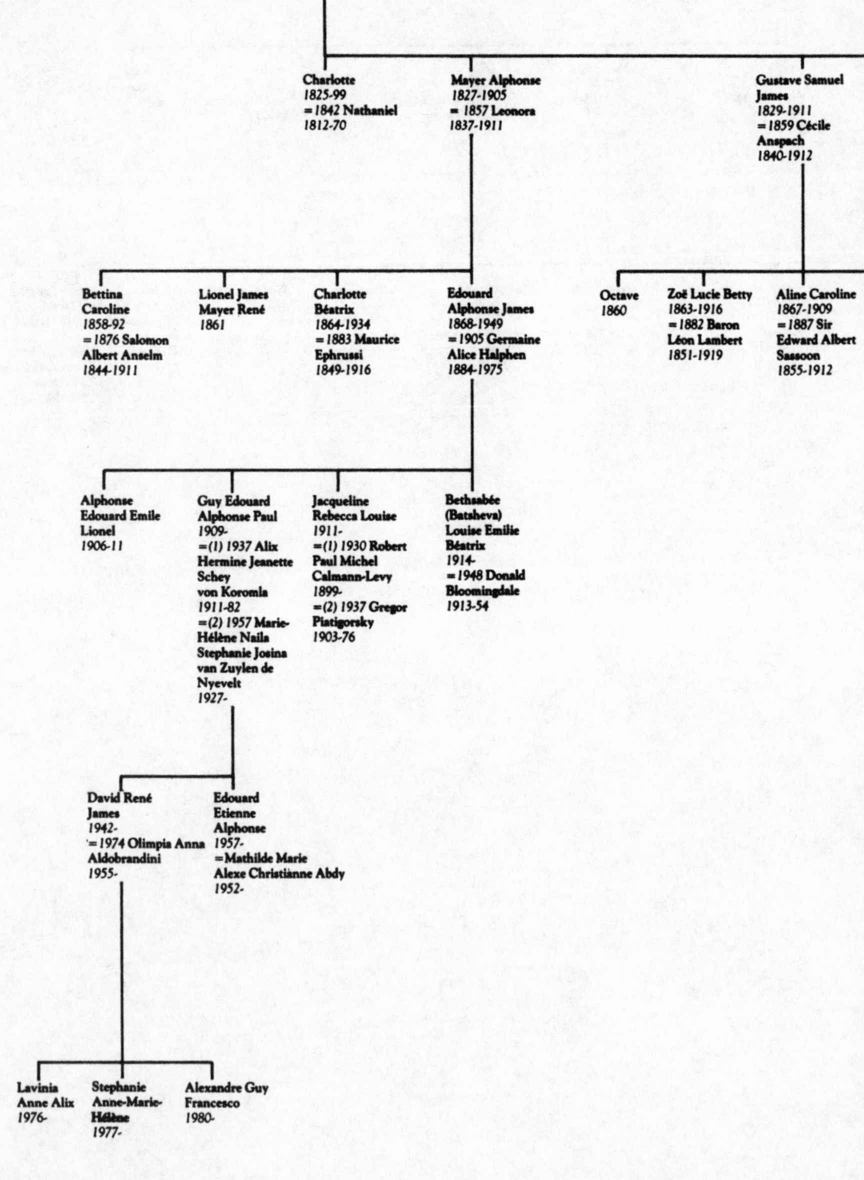

Charlotte
1825-99
= 1842 Nathaniel
1812-70
Mayer Alphonse
1827-1905
= 1857 Leonora
1837-1911
Gustave Samuel
James
1829-1911
= 1859 Cécile
Anspach
1840-1912
Bettina
Caroline
1858-92
= 1876 Salomon
Albert Anselm
1844-1911
Lionel James
Mayer René
1861
Charlotte
Béatrix
1864-1934
= 1883 Maurice
Ephrussi
1849-1916
Edouard
Alphonse James
1868-1949
= 1905 Germaine
Alice Halphen
1884-1975
Octave
1860
Zoë Lucie Betty
1863-1916
= 1882 Baron
Léon Lambert
1851-1919
Aline Caroline
1867-1909
= 1887 Sir
Edward Albert
Sassoon
1855-1912
Alphonse
Edouard Emile
Lionel
1906-11
Guy Edouard
Alphonse Paul
1909-
=(1) 1937 Alix
Hermine Jeanette
Schey
von Koromla
1911-82
=(2) 1957 Marie-
Hélène Naila
Stephanie Josina
van Zuylen de
Nyevelt
1927-
Jacqueline
Rebecca Louise
1911-
=(1) 1930 Robert
Paul Michel
Calmann-Levy
1899-
=(2) 1937 Gregor
Piatigorsky
1903-76
Bethsabée
(Batsheva)
Louise Emilie
Béatrix
1914-
= 1948 Donald
Bloomingdale
1913-54
David René
James
1942-
= 1974 Olimpia Anna
Aldobrandini
1955-
Edouard
Etienne
Alphonse
1957-
=Mathilde Marie
Alexe Christianne Abdy
1952-
Lavinia
Anne Alix
1976-
Stephanie
Anne-Marie-
Hélène
1977-
Alexandre Guy
Francesco
1980-

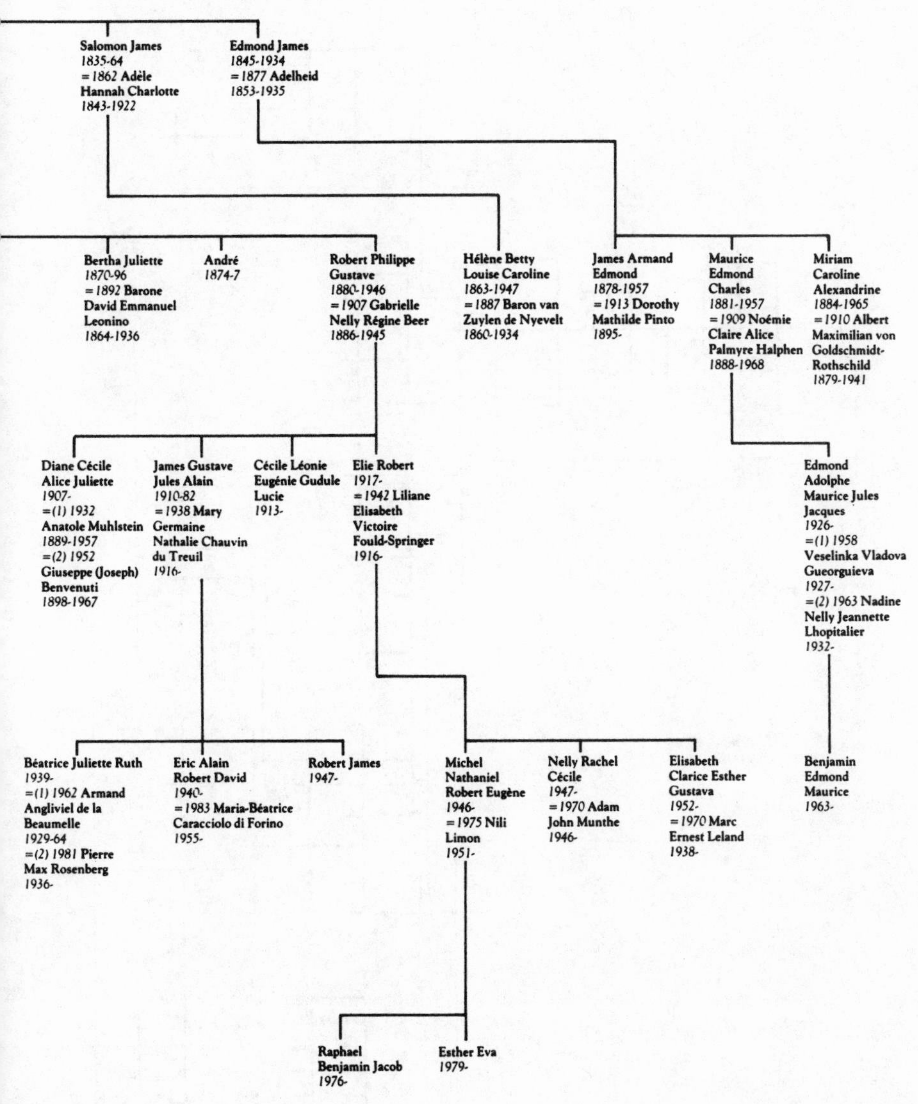

Salomon James
1835-64
= 1862 Adèle
Hannah Charlotte
1843-1922
Edmond James
1845-1934
= 1877 Adelheid
1853-1935
Bertha Juliette
1870-96
= 1892 Barone
David Emmanuel
Leonino
1864-1936
André
1874-7
Robert Philippe
Gustave
1880-1946
= 1907 Gabrielle
Nelly Régine Beer
1886-1945
Hélène Betty
Louise Caroline
1863-1947
= 1887 Baron van
Zuylen de Nyevelt
1860-1934
James Armand
Edmond
1878-1957
= 1913 Dorothy
Mathilde Pinto
1895-
Maurice
Edmond
Charles
1881-1957
= 1909 Noémie
Claire Alice
Palmyre Halphen
1888-1968
Miriam
Caroline
Alexandrine
1884-1965
= 1910 Albert
Maximilian von
Goldschmidt-
Rothschild
1879-1941
Diane Cécile
Alice Juliette
1907-
=(1) 1932
Anatole Muhlstein
1889-1957
=(2) 1952
Giuseppe (Joseph)
Benvenuti
1898-1967
James Gustave
Jules Alain
1910-82
= 1938 Mary
Germaine
Nathalie Chauvin
du Treuil
1916-
Cécile Léonie
Eugénie Gudule
Lucie
1913-
Elie Robert
1917-
= 1942 Liliane
Elisabeth
Victoire
Fould-Springer
1916-
Edmond
Adolphe
Maurice Jules
Jacques
1926-
=(1) 1958
Veselinka Vladova
Gueorguieva
1927-
=(2) 1963 Nadine
Nelly Jeannette
Lhopitalier
1932-
Béatrice Juliette Ruth
1939-
=(1) 1962 Armand
Angliviel de la
Beaumelle
1929-64
=(2) 1981 Pierre
Max Rosenberg
1936-
Eric Alain
Robert David
1940-
= 1983 Maria-Béatrice
Caracciolo di Forino
1955-
Robert James
1947-
Michel
Nathaniel
Robert Eugène
1946-
= 1975 Nili
Limon
1951-
Nelly Rachel
Cécile
1947-
= 1970 Adam
John Munthe
1946-
Elisabeth
Clarice Esther
Gustava
1952-
= 1970 Marc
Ernest Leland
1938-
Benjamin
Edmond
Maurice
1963-
Raphael
Benjamin Jacob
1976-
Esther Eva
1979-

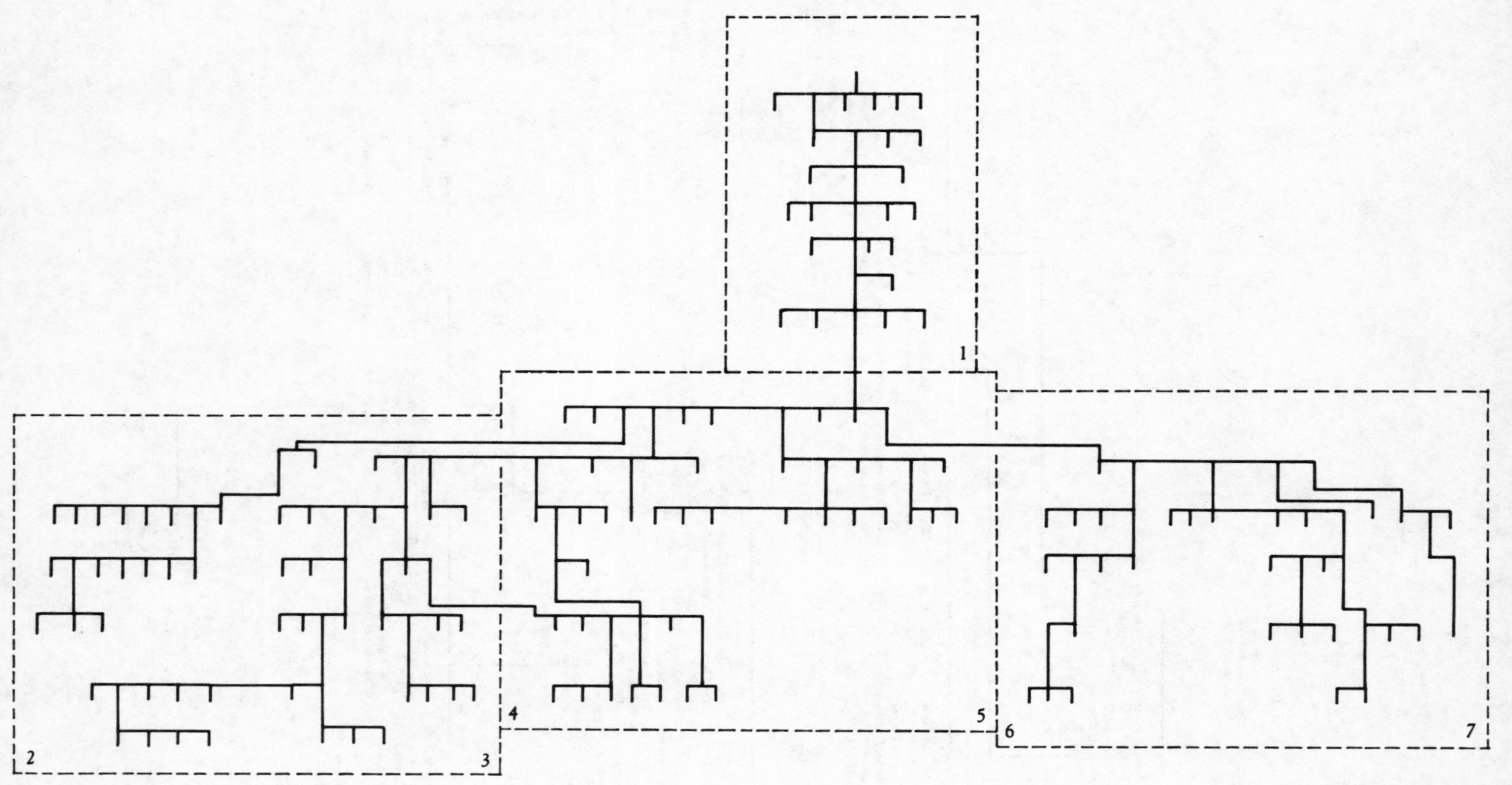

1
2
3
4
5
6
7

FREDERIC MORTON was born in Vienna. In addition to *The Rothschilds*, which became a Broadway musical, Mr. Morton has written several novels and other works of nonfiction. His short fiction has appeared in *Esquire, The Atlantic, Playboy* and *Hudson Review* as well as in Martha Foley's *Best American Short Stories* and other anthologies. His most recent work is *A Nervous Splendor: Vienna 1888-1889*. Mr. Morton lives in New York City.